# TEN THINGS I WISH
# JESUS NEVER SAID

# TEN
## THINGS I WISH
# JESUS
## NEVER SAID

## VICTOR KULIGIN

CROSSWAY BOOKS

A PUBLISHING MINISTRY OF
GOOD NEWS PUBLISHERS
WHEATON, ILLINOIS

**Library of Congress Cataloging-in-Publication Data**
Kuligin, Victor, 1964–
  Ten things I wish Jesus never said / Victor Kuligin.
   p. cm.
  Includes bibliographical references and index.
  ISBN 13: 978-1-58134-775-3
  ISBN 10: 1-58134-775-8 (tpb)
  1. Jesus Christ—Teachings. 2. Christian life—Biblical teaching.
3. Bible. N.T. Gospels—Criticism, interpretation, etc. I. Title.
BS2417.C5K85  2006
232.9'54—dc22           2005035777

| VP | | 16 | 15 | 14 | 13 | 12 | 11 | 10 | 09 | 08 | 07 | 06 |
|----|----|----|----|----|----|----|----|----|----|----|----|----|
| 15 | 14 | 13 | 12 | 11 | 10 | 9 | 8 | 7 | 6 | 5 | 4 | 3 | 2 |

I dedicate this book to my mother,
who taught me to fear God and shun evil.

# CONTENTS

Acknowledgments     **9**

Preface     **11**

**1** The Art of Spiritual Poverty     **15**
*"Blessed are the poor in spirit, for theirs is the kingdom of heaven."*

**2** The Art of Spiritual Self-Mutilation     **43**
*"If your right eye causes you to sin, gouge it out and throw it away."*

**3** The Art of Spiritual Commitment     **61**
*"No one who puts his hand to the plow and looks back is fit for service in the kingdom of God."*

**4** The Art of Spiritual Self-Crucifixion     **85**
*"If anyone would come after me, he must deny himself and take up his cross daily and follow me."*

**5** The Art of Spiritual Martyrdom     **109**
*"Blessed are you when people insult you, persecute you and falsely say all kinds of evil against you because of me."*

**6** The Art of Spiritual Love     **135**
*"You have heard that it was said, 'Love your neighbor and hate your enemy.' But I tell you: Love your enemies and pray for those who persecute you, that you may be sons of your Father in heaven."*

**7** The Art of Spiritual Forgiveness     **159**
*"If you do not forgive men their sins, your Father will not forgive your sins."*

**8** The Art of Spiritual Self-Loathing     **185**
*"If anyone comes to me and does not hate his father and mother, his wife and children, his brothers and sisters— yes, even his own life—he cannot be my disciple."*

**9** The Art of Spiritual Discernment 219
*"Judge not, or you too will be judged."*

**10** The Art of Spiritual Self-Assessment 245
*"Not everyone who says to me, 'Lord, Lord,' will enter
the kingdom of heaven."*

**11** The Art of Spiritual Surrender 273
*"Come to me, all you who are weary and burdened, and
I will give you rest. Take my yoke upon you and learn
from me, for I am gentle and humble in heart, and you
will find rest for your souls. For my yoke is easy and my
burden is light."*

Notes 285

Author Index 295

# ACKNOWLEDGMENTS

I must thank my wife, as many husbands who have become authors do, simply because she allowed me the free time to complete this project. Without her willingness to grant me the freedom to express my thoughts and emotions on paper, I could never have completed this book.

My children often wondered why Dad had to spend so much time in his office while I was working on this task. My hope is that one day they will read this book for themselves and understand a little better why it took so much time.

My good friend of almost twenty years, Wayne Harbuziuk, read many of the chapters as I produced them, giving me thoughtful and helpful advice each step of the way. (Let me thank God for e-mail while I am at it!) Wayne provided me with a good perspective and insight, from larger concepts to nitty-gritty details of syntax and structure.

Lastly, I thank Crossway Books for helping me with this project and for their willingness to publish this, my first book. I know it is a risk to publish the work of an unknown. Hopefully, they will be happy to have done so. I especially appreciate the help from Jill Carter and editors Julie-Allyson Ieron and Lila Bishop.

# PREFACE

*Now the most free and full and gracious words of the gospel were the greatest torment to me; yea, nothing so afflicted me as the thoughts of Jesus Christ, the remembrance of a Saviour.*

JOHN BUNYAN (1628-1688),
GRACE ABOUNDING TO THE CHIEF OF SINNERS

**M**y working title for this book was *Ten Things I Hate About Jesus*. The title was meant to be provocative, much like the teaching of Jesus. There was a certain shock value to his teaching that we have unfortunately lost in our teaching today. We have become so comfortable with Jesus after two thousand years of dissecting his instruction and parsing his words that often the shock value is entirely muted. Crossway Books opted, perhaps wisely so, for a less offensive title, but one that still attempts to maintain a certain provocative value.

"Unless you eat my flesh and drink my blood" and "If your right eye causes you to sin, pluck it out" were shocking statements. You could not hear such things and not be at least mildly intrigued, if not outright offended. Or how about this one, "Unless you hate your father and mother, you cannot be my disciple." Jesus used the word *hate* to grab his listeners' attention. I wanted to use it in much the same way with the working title of this book.

With the rise of the health-and-wealth gospel and prosperity preaching, we have become accustomed to a comfortable, "What a Friend We Have in Jesus" Messiah. It is a picture of Jesus I call "Jesus-lite." Great taste, less demanding. Jesus is just interested in my happiness and nothing more. He wants me to be financially comfortable, physically fit, mentally and emotionally stable. He never demands of me anything that would cause these basic goals to be missed, if only I have the faith to believe. Difficulties, trials, and hardships in my life are only there because of a lack of faith on my part to believe that Jesus truly wants me to be happy.

There is an irony in popular evangelical and Pentecostal Christianity today. We often find ourselves fixating on the end times, and it is no wonder that many best-selling books of the past years have been on this topic. So much so that many Christians have become preoccupied with eschatology at the expense of solid Christology. The book of Revelation should play a prominent role in our Christian psyche; yet many believers today virtually ignore its picture of Jesus as the terrible Judge. More movements today portray him not as the Lord of glory, but rather the promoter of happiness.

Thirty years ago Dorothy Sayers had this to say about the growing picture of Jesus in her day, and her words are no less appropriate for us today: "We have very efficiently pared the claws of the Lion of Judah, certified Him 'meek and mild,' and recommended Him as a fitting household pet for pale curates and pious old ladies."[1] We love the Lamb of God, but we have discarded the Lion of Judah.

There have been several works on the "hard sayings" of Jesus, but those works have concentrated on the difficulty in understanding parts of his teaching. They were more of an academic exercise, a study in biblical interpretation. This work is also along the line of hard sayings, not because of the difficulty of understanding them, but rather because of the difficulty in applying them. Mine is more concerned with a practical need to rightly practice these teachings, as opposed to an academic need to rightly understand them.

The teaching of Jesus was often harsh. He was not a preacher of convenience, but hardship; not a preacher of comfort, but suffering. Whereas today we fixate on the happiness of believers, Jesus was much more concerned with their holiness. Often a pursuit of the latter does not produce any inkling—especially in a worldly sense—of the former. Even a cursory reading of the teaching of Jesus shows us that he expected his disciples to be people accustomed to suffering and trials. His was a call not to prosperity and comfort, but to hardship and holiness. As the Beatitudes show us, his was a call to poorness in spirit, meekness, and mourning.

Perhaps the best way to summarize the intention of this book is to ask the question, "Is following Jesus Christ easy?" The answer this book gives is a resounding "No!" And it was never meant to be. We will look at ten teachings of Jesus that appear impossible to follow.

This book comes from my own struggle. I am aware of my shortcomings and failings. My struggle with sin is ongoing, and it is from this perspective that I often find the teachings of Jesus to be shocking, almost vulgar, certainly repulsive. They go so against the grain of selfishness and self-centeredness in my life that part of me would prefer they not exist, that I be left alone to wallow in my own selfish pursuits and pride, than to be told to conform to teaching so alien to my being.

Perhaps this perspective will resonate with some of my readers. However, if your Christian walk is characterized by constant victory, then I fear much of what I am going to say in this book will make little sense to you. You may be tempted to think I am making the Christian life more difficult than it was intended to be. I envy you. I do not find taking up my cross easy, or loving my enemies particularly palatable, nor do I enjoy plucking out my right eye or cutting off my right hand because, frankly, I often enjoy the sinful things I gaze upon or handle. How is this yoke easy and this burden light? Lord, help me.

The following ten items, then, are things I find extremely taxing in the Christian walk. Sinfully speaking, I would not mind seeing all of them excised from the requirements for the disciples of Jesus. The remaining discipleship training of a believer would certainly be much easier. From the spiritual perspective, of course, it would also be less profitable and fruitful.

Lastly, if misery loves company, then my studies through church history of the great men and women who committed their lives to Christ may reasonably be expected to uncover similar feelings. I have pored through the writings of such notable believers as Martin Luther,

## TEN THINGS I WISH JESUS NEVER SAID

John Wesley, Saint Bernard of Clairvaux, Albertus Magnus, Saint Augustine, John Bunyan, and many others, with an eye for similar feelings as mine—feelings of frustration, inadequacy, anxiety, and failure—and I have not been disappointed. All speak as if with one voice that the life of a disciple of Jesus Christ is wrought with difficulty, frequent bouts of depression, and bitter disappointment. Yet in all things God's grace overcomes—if only we trust in his ways.

# 1

# THE ART OF
# SPIRITUAL POVERTY

*Blessed are the poor in spirit, for theirs is the kingdom of heaven.*

JESUS CHRIST, MATTHEW 5:3

*I bewail that my apprehensions are so dull, my thoughts so mean, my affections so stupid, and my expressions so low and unbecoming such a glory.*

RICHARD BAXTER (1615-1691),

*THE SAINTS' EVERLASTING REST*

*To comfort a sorrowful conscience is much better than to possess many kingdoms.*

MARTIN LUTHER (1483-1546), *TABLE TALK*

When I was growing up, one of my mother's favorite adages was, "Nobody likes a party pooper." She insisted that we always remain upbeat and positive, something I admire about her to this day.

She also taught us to be self-confident. I can recall her telling me many times that it is not the people who are talented who succeed as much as it is the self-confident. My mother endeavored to instill in her children a healthy self-image.

As I became an adult and began to study God's Word and particularly the teaching of Jesus, I began to question how right my mother was. There is next to nothing in all the Scriptures about having a healthy self-ego, or thinking highly of yourself, or striving for self-confidence or self-esteem. In fact, whenever we find Scripture investigating the nature of man, it is almost always negative.

Thus I had these two contrary pictures to balance, the one of my mother's that taught me to grow in self-confidence and the biblical picture that taught me to think lowly of myself. Which one was correct? If I were to consult the manuals on living produced by the world, clearly my mother had it right. A casual survey of the books sold in a typical bookstore will uncover all the *self* books: self-esteem, self-help, self-actualization, self-confidence, self-awareness. Our culture is obsessed with self. We do more navel watching than a rear admiral. We are expected to be in love with ourselves, and if we are not, the world tells us something is drastically wrong with us.

Enter Jesus Christ. He opens his most famous sermon, The Sermon on the Mount, with these words: "Blessed are the poor in spirit," the first of the so-called Beatitudes. Does Jesus mean, "Blessed are the party poopers"? There is a paradox at play here if one understands *blessed* as *happy*. In other words, what Jesus is saying is, "happy are the unhappy."[1] Jesus uses language that causes us to ponder his words. It was difficult to hear Jesus speak and not walk away scratching your head.[2] People truly committed to following him were forced to think. Those not committed errantly thought his teachings at best mildly odd, at the worst offensive and heretical.

I have to admit that I prefer the world's view to that of Christ. I do not like party poopers either. I prefer spending my time with light-hearted and jocular types, not depressing, sober, serious ones. It is the first thing I find unbearable about Jesus. Must his disciples really be poor in spirit? And what, precisely, does that mean?

## JUST A CLOSER WALK WITH THEE

The more you walk with Christ, the more you should become aware of your fallenness, with an ever-increasing awareness of your sins. This is the universal experience of the great saints of Christendom. They do not find themselves at the end of their lives touting their own sanctification, patting themselves on the back, and proclaiming how holy they are.

Rather, they are broken, contrite people who have wept bitterly over their fallen state and continue to do so. Those who are poor in spirit mourn over their sinfulness.

The closer you are to the perfect Son of God, the more you come to realize how far short you fall of that perfection. The nearer you approach the Light, the more your imperfections are exposed. Consider a porcelain vase. From a distance it appears smooth and blemishless, but the closer you come to inspect it, the more the imperfections appear.

> A good man always finds enough over which to mourn and weep . . .
> the closer he examines himself the more he grieves.
>
> Thomas à Kempis (1380-1471), *The Imitation of Christ.*

King David asked God not only to keep him from willful sins, but also to expose his hidden faults (Ps. 19:12). Only the self-righteous believe themselves to be spiritually healthy. Show me a genuine believer who has walked with Christ for fifty years, and I'll show you a person deeply aware of his spiritual poverty and his need for constant grace.

A holy realization of our sinfulness is the prerequisite for a healthy relationship with God, but it does not simply exist at our moment of conversion and end there. This holy realization continually grows. The farther we walk down the path with Christ, the more aware we become of how short we fall. That process made Martin Luther consistently refer to himself as "a stinking sinner." This was his cry to his dying day, so much so that many people thought he was demon-possessed, because he mourned so often over his sinfulness.

## BLESSED ARE THE CRYING?

Following the first Beatitude is the second, which echoes this sentiment: "Blessed are those who mourn, for they will be comforted" (Matt. 5:4). The question rightly may be asked, "Does God want me to be happy?" Yes, but for the right reasons. If you believe you will find happiness in a bigger home and a fancier car, you are sorely mistaken. In fact, is this not the point Jesus intends to make later in the Sermon on the Mount when he commands his disciples to "seek first his kingdom and his righteousness" (Matt. 6:33)? Is it not the pagans who make earthly matters their primary concern?

This second Beatitude is as shocking as the first. Normally when we see people mourn, we feel sorry for them and hope that their situation will change or improve. But Jesus tells us the state of mourning is actually the state of blessedness, and we can understand that those who do not mourn are those who are not blessed. The standards of the world are turned on their heads.

Thirteenth-century German theologian and scientist Albertus Magnus (1193-1280), whose most famous pupil was Thomas Aquinas, beautifully stated this picture of mourning in his work *On Cleaving to God*:

> We should not desire any pleasure of this present, mortal and physical life but rather to mourn, bewail and lament our offences, faults and sins without ceasing, and to perfectly despise and annihilate ourselves, and from day to day to be considered more and more abject by others, while in all our insignificance we become worthless even in our own eyes, so that we can be pleasing to God alone, love him alone, and cleave to him alone.

Attempting to preach such a message today would be looked upon with great suspicion in many of our churches, but this is precisely what Jesus means when he claims that those who mourn are those who are blessed. There can be no true godly joy without mourning over our sinfulness. There can be no true godly contentment without a realization of our unworthiness. There can be no true godly prosperity without hardship. Unfortunately, many in our churches today want joy, contentment, and prosperity in every *material* sense of those words.

## IT'S ALL GREEK TO ME

Most Christians think studying the original Greek of the New Testament is only for eggheads and academics. That is an unfortunate impression, because looking into the Greek can be enlightening. Often looking at the original Greek can provide us with valuable insight into the reason the author or speaker chose a specific word to convey his meaning. This is particularly true with the command of Jesus to be poor in spirit.

The Greek word translated *poor* is *ptōchos*. Literally, it means "one who crouches and cowers," but it can also have a metaphorical sense, which is the case in our present passage.[3] Pictured is a poor beggar low to the ground looking for a handout—in this instance a spiritual handout.

Paul uses the same Greek word when he is speaking of the theology of the Judaizers in his Epistle to the Galatians. There Paul is unhappy with Galatian believers who are falling for the lie of the Judaizers that converts must first conform to the Old Testament law before they can become genuine Christians. Paul refers to their teaching as "weak and miserable" (Gal. 4:9), the same Greek word *ptōchos*. The teaching of the Judaizers is low and beggarly and cannot stand on its own.

The glorified Christ uses the word in a metaphorical sense when he speaks to the church in Laodicea. "You say, 'I am rich; I have acquired wealth and do not need a thing.' But you do not realize that you are wretched, pitiful, poor, blind and naked" (Rev. 3:17). The chastisement the Lord has for the Laodicean believers should sober this present generation, especially those who believe blessedness from God is embodied in material and physical comforts. Of course, any blessings may rightly be said to come from God, but it is when we believe that material blessing forms the heart of God's approval that we quickly fall from grace. Often we cite the approval of God as a guise under which we seek material blessing.

"Happy are those who are unhappy." That is the paradox embodied in the first two Beatitudes. Jesus proclaims a truth alien to our present world: Poverty is blessedness. We should not be surprised that such a proclamation is received with looks of doubt and suspicion. The world would prefer an adage like "blessed are the strong," or "blessed are the rich." This also has been the case throughout the church's history.

## LESSONS FROM HISTORY

This call to spiritual poverty was shocking to many in the Middle Ages, and seemingly only the very pious committed themselves to it. When Saint Francis of Assisi (1181-1228) founded his monastic movement of poverty known as the Franciscans, many within Catholicism—particularly those in the higher echelons of church leadership—thought he was fanatical. The notion that spiritual and physical poverty must be combined was anathema to many elite Christians of his day.

Sixteenth-century Catholic humanist Erasmus of Rotterdam (1469-1536) told the story of the apostle Peter trying to get into heaven. Unfortunately for him, the pope would not allow him in because Peter was too poor. Satirically, Erasmus noted how far the popes had traveled from the founding pope. According to them, true Christianity was to be found in wealth and privilege, false Christianity in meagerness and poverty. As Erasmus said in his famous treatise, *In Praise of Folly*, "You'll meet with some so preposterously religious that they will sooner endure the broadest scoffs even against Christ himself than hear the Pope or a prince be touched in the least, especially if it be anything that concerns their profit."[4]

Today we face a similar ethos with the rise of health-and-wealth Christianity throughout the world. These adherents tell us God wants us to be happy. As it is self-evident that happiness is directly tied to our physical and material well-being, they claim God must desire for us health and financial security. They conclude that if our personal experience falls short of such ideals, we are to blame for our lack of faith and trust in God.

Often this view results in what I call "spiritual blackmail." Young Christians are told that if they do not bring money to the church, normally understood as a tithe but often referred to as "seed money," they will not be financially blessed by God. Conversely, if they do lay their tithe before the altar, God will give multifold blessings.

## The Art of Spiritual Poverty

While working as a missionary in Namibia, southwestern Africa, I serve as a pastor of a small church in the capital city of Windhoek. After several years of meeting in a high school auditorium, we began to build a church on the outskirts of the city. For two years we raised enough money to complete the building up to the roof.

On an Easter Sunday we decided we would begin to worship in our new building even though the roof was not complete. We hoped that sitting in a church without a roof would spur our members to give enough to complete it quickly. Two Easters later, we still did not have a completed roof. Mercifully, God never allowed it to rain on a Sunday morning or during any other church meetings. A gift bequeathed to us by a faithful member who died provided us with enough funds to finish the roof shortly thereafter. It was over four years from the time we broke ground until the time we had a church building with a roof. Of course, there were still plastering, flooring, painting, and other matters to do, which we are still completing.

During this time, another church purchased a plot of prime real estate in downtown Windhoek, on the main street running through the capital. In less than a year they constructed a church building five times the size of our church, a magnificent structure that could seat nearly 1,000 people. This church came to Namibia roughly around the same time our church started.

Which church is blessed by God? If you were told nothing other than these details, which church would you say God favored?

Our small church believes the Bible to be God's inerrant Word and a sure authority for our lives. We preach the gospel in its fullness, the need for repentance and faith in the atoning work of Jesus, and the salvific work of Christ as the only Mediator and Savior. The other church teaches its members that God wants them to be happy and healthy, financially comfortable and physically whole. They believe a glass of water blessed each morning by their pastor and drunk by the parishioners will protect them throughout the day, and that God demands their faith be expressed in the bringing of their tithes each week. Much like a slot machine, the proper number of coins placed on the altar will ensure them a healthy return from God.

I hope the church I attend is honoring God, but I am fairly certain that the other church is not. However, someone outside the faith would conclude that our church was not blessed by God in comparison to the other, and I would venture to say a fair number of Christians would think similarly.

Many people did not think the apostle Paul to be blessed by God either. Listen to how he described what he had endured, and consider whether this is the experience of someone we normally consider to be blessed by God:

> *I have worked much harder, been in prison more frequently, been flogged more severely, and been exposed to death again and again. Five times I received from the Jews the forty lashes minus one. Three times I was beaten with rods, once I was stoned, three times I was shipwrecked, I spent a night and day in the open sea, I have been constantly on the move. I have been in danger from rivers, in danger from bandits, in danger from my own countrymen, in danger from Gentiles; in danger in the city, in danger in the country, in danger at sea; and in danger from false brothers. I have labored and toiled and have often gone without sleep; I have known hunger and thirst and have often gone without food; I have been cold and naked. (2 Cor. 11:23b-27)*

I wonder how many Christians today would consider such an experience as God's blessing. We have a tendency to attribute all the bad, nasty things that happen to us to Satan, while all the good things come from God. The latter is not all wrong, of course, but the former is not all right either. Certainly, Satan's attacks are real, but so are the trials and tribulations sent our way by God. All we need do is consider the lives of Job and Jesus to recognize this.

The simple truth is, once we lose any idea of physical poverty in Christ, we begin to lose the concept of spiritual poverty as well. This truth was told in the straightforward teaching of Jesus concerning a rich man. "It is easier for a camel to go through the eye of a needle than for a rich man to enter the kingdom of God" (Matt. 19:24). There is good reason why all three synoptic authors recorded this teaching, just as there is good reason why Jesus spoke so often about issues of money in general. The temptation toward material comfort is shockingly strong, and the presence of excess in this area can be a quick stumbling block for one's faith. As the apostle Paul wrote, "The love of money is a root of all kinds of evil" (1 Tim. 6:10).

I think the monks had it right, at least to a certain extent. There is a bond between the body and the soul, the physical and the spiritual. Man is made of two primary components, the material and the immaterial. It is impossible to separate the two, and in attempting to do so, you are left not with a human being but a disembodied soul or a soulless body. It was the heresy of Gnosticism that treated the body as a commodity separate from the soul, and it is the common failing of similar belief systems today to mistreat the disease of sin, when they find it only in one component of man. The monks recognized a connection between body and soul, and considered discipline of one necessarily to affect the discipline of the other.

To be sure, we need not go to the extremes of rabid asceticism often found in the movement of the monks (with self-flagellations, forced fasting, and deprivations of comforts even as extreme as loss of sleep and water). I do not think spiritual poverty is necessarily hindered by a comfortable bed and nice-fitting clothes. The monks did what sinful man often does by taking a good thing and in their excesses making it evil.

However, just because the monks erred in their excesses does not mean they did not hit the mark in regard to original intent. I would like to consider the spiritual discipline of fasting as an example, and in so doing, we will begin to see how a person can become poor in spirit.

## WHAT'S FOOD GOT TO DO WITH IT?

When was the last time you heard a sermon about fasting? Now compare that to how often you have heard lessons on prayer or received encouragements to read your Bible daily. Fasting is a spiritual discipline that is all but lost in churches today. Certainly, there are some people who practice it, but most Christians look at it as something strange and foreign.

In Jesus's day, the opposite was true. Fasting was so common that the Pharisee in the temple could speak of doing it twice a week (Luke 18:12). When Jesus gave commands about it in the Sermon on the Mount, he did not state "if you fast," but "*when* you fast" (Matt. 6:16). It was a familiar spiritual discipline during his day, and he expected his disciples to practice it.

Not so today in our society of satisfaction and plenty. The notion that we should give up something as basic as food is bizarre and strikes us as outlandish. There seems no good reason to do so.

In the Sermon on the Mount, Jesus's commands concerning fasting come with instructions concerning two other spiritual disciplines, prayer and almsgiving. The latter two we are familiar with and admonish our churchgoers to do. So why have we avoided the other one?

A simple study of the Bible on this topic uncovers an amazing list of people who practiced fasting. In the Bible we have at least fifty references to fasting. Moses, David, Elijah, Daniel, Jesus, and the disciples fasted. From church history we have such notable leaders as Martin Luther, John Calvin, and John Wesley regularly fasting. Just from the biblical and historical data alone, we would not be wise to ignore this topic, but unfortunately we do.[5]

One reason could be that some people are theologically unclear on the reason for fasting. One pastor I know preached a series to his church from the Sermon on the Mount and decided to skip the passage on fasting. His reason was that he was not certain himself whether or not we should fast; so he did not feel comfortable speaking to his congregation about it. But did this pastor not communicate to his church that fasting is unimportant by skipping the passage?

Another reason could be because through the centuries of church history, fasting moved from something voluntary to something obligatory. The Jews moved from one mandatory fast each year as prescribed in the Torah, during the Day of Atonement, to the time of Jesus when fasting several times a week was practiced. Similarly, the early church moved from fasting as a voluntary practice to one that was mandatory. Believers were forced to observe weekly fasts, and those who did not fast were viewed as immature, if not sinful.[6]

The Protestant churches reacted against this religious coercion, and rightly so. But they may have reacted too negatively, to the point where today we rarely speak of fasting at all and have lost sight of the importance of this spiritual discipline.

My task now is not to provide a full exposition on the topic of fasting, but rather to use it as an example of how physical poverty can influence spiritual poverty.[7] In addressing this issue, we should be mindful of the two common errors concerning fasting. One is to move to a rigid asceticism with forced times and dates to fast. This approach entirely loses the spirit of the discipline. The second error is to ignore fasting altogether.

Fasting is a spiritual discipline, much like Bible reading. We encourage people to read the Bible every day, but nowhere in the Bible is it actually commanded. Still, we recognize that daily Bible reading is a profitable spiritual exercise; so we encourage people to do so. Of course, if someone misses a day here or there, they lose out, but they have not particularly sinned.

However, if they decide *never* to read the Bible, they are sinning. The same may be said about fasting. It is a wise spiritual tool that has been used by countless saints throughout biblical times and the history of the church to draw closer to God. If we do not avail ourselves of this spiritual tool, we are going to lose out on a spiritual blessing.

## REASONS TO FAST

There are several reasons people fast, from its humbling, sacrificial nature to the desire to seek the will of God in a particular circumstance, but for our purposes we will look at only one reason: to learn self-discipline and self-control.

Self-control is a fruit of the Holy Spirit (Gal. 5:22-23). Christians consistently are commanded in Scripture to be self-disciplined and self-controlled. Paul, for example, wrote that he beat his body until it became his slave (1 Cor. 9:25-27). There is a distinct difference between an animal that can only mechanically act upon its bodily desires and a human being who has the ability to control them.

"Fasting has the power to detach one's mind from the world of sense and to sharpen one's sensibility to the world of spirit."[8] If you can abstain from the strongest of human desires, the body's need for food, then you can control yourself completely. Often Christians fall into sin simply because they do not possess the self-control necessary to resist temptation. As we are told that no believer is tempted beyond what he can endure (1 Cor. 10:13), the simple conclusion is that all willful sin is the result of a lack of self-control and self-discipline on the part of the believer. This seems to be the point of James in his epistle when he speaks of people being "dragged away and enticed" by "[their] own evil desire" (1:13-14).

Fasting is a spiritual discipline that helps a believer learn self-control. If we can train ourselves to forego basic bodily needs such as food and water, will we not also then have the ability to resist other carnal things that tempt our bodies? Clearly, here the monks, ascetics, and mystics had it right. Denying ourselves certain physical or material pleasures can help us discipline ourselves in denying sinful pleasures as well. Of course, we must guard against the mistake of rigid or forced asceticism, but we also must not miss the usefulness of this spiritual discipline by ignoring it.

The comparison between the first Adam and second Adam is striking in this regard. The first Adam in the Garden of Eden could not resist the temptation to eat from the forbidden tree while in the midst of numerous trees from which he could eat. The second Adam, Jesus Christ, after fasting forty days in the wilderness, was able to resist the temptation of Satan to make bread out of stones with no other food available. Jesus had learned to control his physical cravings and desires, and from that discipline came the ability to resist spiritual temptation as well.

From lack of self-control and self-discipline flow all sorts of sins, but when a believer possesses self-control, he is able to withstand much temptation. Fasting helps a believer develop this self-control.

## HOW DOES ONE BECOME POOR IN SPIRIT?

At this point the reader may be asking, "Why all this talk about physical poverty and fasting? I thought this chapter had to do with spiritual poverty?"

As we noted earlier, the Greek word translated "poor" is used metaphorically to refer to those people who are "low and beggarly" in spirit. This is not a demeanor that comes naturally for most people; nor is it an attitude that is easily adopted. Believers throughout history have recognized the need to inculcate this attitude into their mind-sets. One way to do this was to submit the body to "physical poverty." In this way, they began to train themselves to develop a poverty of spirit as well. Because a person is made both of material and immaterial components, it was rightly believed that one naturally affects the other. Just as surely as a lack of spiritual discipline can result in physical missteps, so too a presence of physical discipline can work to produce spiritual discipline.

The above discussion concerning fasting, then, addresses the question, "How do I become poor in spirit?" One way is to discipline one's physical appetites and desires.

Another way to develop a spirit of poverty is to make a radical change from the past. Because being poor in spirit recognizes that as sinners we bring nothing to God and that he must create a new creation from us, anything short of a complete break from our past will simply not do.

In his complaints concerning the church and its designs on "cheap grace," twentieth-century German theologian Dietrich Bonhoeffer recognized the drastic nature of the call of Jesus on those who would deign to become his disciples. "Costly grace" involves a completely new work, a dramatic break with the past and a move into new life. Peter was not simply allowed to continue tending his nets; nor was Matthew able to maintain the tax-collecting table. Both had to leave the past straightaway. Anything short of this radical break is "cheap grace" according to Bonhoeffer.[9]

The apostle Paul has a similar mind-set when he speaks about his life before his conversion to Christ as "rubbish" (Phil. 3:8). Literally, the Greek *skubalon* means "refuse" or "dung," denoting something to be entirely discarded and thrown away.[10] Only someone with poverty of spirit can recognize that his pre-conversion life was worthless. This is why Paul can say, "If anyone is in Christ, he is a new creation; the old has gone, the new has come!" (2 Cor. 5:17). A "new creation" signifies a completely new work, not the reshaping or reworking of existing material.

For Paul, the act of conversion is an act of creation. Earlier in the epistle he uses creation language to signify this change: "For God, who said, 'Let light shine out of darkness,' made his light shine in our hearts to give us the light of the knowledge of the glory of God in the face of Christ" (2 Cor. 4:6). Just as God had created "in the beginning," so again does he re-create us. Just as in Genesis we see God taking an earth that was "formless and void," so too does he take our formless and void lives and remake us. Just as in the beginning he spoke, "Let there be light," so too he makes light shine in our hearts.

The term "new creation" echoes the words of Jesus when he said, "You must be born again" and, "Flesh produces flesh, but spirit produces spirit" (John 3:7, 6). It is not the taking of old material and just reshaping it. It is the re-creation of something entirely new. Rebirth. Renewal. New creation.

When God pardons, therefore, he does not say he understands our weakness or makes allowances for our errors; rather he disposes of, he finishes with, the whole of our dead life and raises us up with a new one.[11]

People who lack a spirit of poverty approach God with a certain arrogance about them: "God got someone pretty good when he got me." They do not recognize their complete spiritual destitution and rather think of themselves higher than they ought. Only genuine conversions are accompanied by genuine poverty of spirit. If we cling to this or that part of our past life in our confession of Christ, we are only fooling ourselves. Those are the kinds of disciples Jesus is not interested in.

## ABANDONING THE WORLD'S STANDARDS

Another way to develop a spirit of poverty is to work consciously to abandon the world's standards. Nowhere does Scripture call believers to be "successful." Nowhere in the New Testament are the disciples of Jesus promised material blessing. In fact, the opposite is true. Believers are promised persecution, tribulation, and opposition.

What we *are* promised is God's constant presence and love. He will never leave us nor forsake us. Nothing can separate us from his love. But in this world, that may very well mean persecution, imprisonment, loss of every material possession we have, and the gravest moments of discouragement and doubt.

I was recently given a book by a friend who asked me to read it and tell her what I thought. The book is written by the pastor of one of the largest churches in America. In virtually every way measurable, this church is a success story. Early in his book the pastor tells about a tour he and his wife took through a newly constructed home. He tells us the home was magnificent and much better than the old, little home they lived in at the time. After leaving the new home, his wife boldly proclaimed that one day they too would live in such a house. The pastor admits he did not have the faith to believe it, despite being a man of God. Later, though, he began to believe it as well, and in subsequent years it came to pass.

This we are told is an example of godly faith, the kind God expects from us. But instead of being godly faith, this attitude is simply worldly desire. "God wants me to have a magnificent home" is an arrogant, selfish statement, not a statement of faith. Unfortunately, this anecdote sets the tone for the book and its message, which serves as an example of the hedonism and narcissism that has quietly crept into evangelical Christianity. There is no sense of sacrifice in such an attitude.

Those who seek and expect material blessing from God have it wrong on two fronts. First, they believe material blessing is a sure sign of God's favor. Certainly, material blessing *can* be a sign of God's favor, but it does not automatically signify it. There are many rich, ungodly people in the world today, just as there are many poor, godly people.

This was the mistake made by Bildad, Eliphaz, and Zophar, the friends of Job. They worked backward, determining that Job's loss of material blessing must point to some moral failing on his part. They were ultimately chastised by God for this unwise counsel. Of course, Jesus stands as the quintessential example of someone who had the complete favor of God upon him, but who gained little material blessing from it.

The second mistake made by those who expect material blessing from God is that eventually it makes material desires the sole aim. Sermons become great motivational endeavors meant to make the listeners feel good about themselves, all in the hope of creating a positive self-image. The argument follows that this "faith" will produce blessings from God. What is lost is any spiritual poverty, replaced by a secular understanding of self-esteem.[12]

However, this is a wrongheaded view of self-esteem. Healthy self-esteem is not comprised of feeling good about oneself. Rather, it is an honest recognition of one's fallenness and the constant need for mercy and grace. It is the fair, reasonable esteem of oneself that takes into account the understanding that we are spiritually bankrupt.

Prosperity preaching esteems man more highly than we ought, thereby yielding an unhealthy self-esteem. Again, this is where the world's standards and those of Christ come into conflict. The world cannot imagine a healthy self-esteem that is not comprised of feeling good about oneself; conversely, it cannot recognize a healthy self-awareness in one's recognition of fallenness and spiritual bankruptcy. Talk of sin appears self-defeating to the world, but it is precisely one's recognition of sin that sets a person free. Lying to oneself can never be healthy.

The world says, "Show me a person with high self-esteem, and I'll show you someone who will accomplish great things for the world."

God says, "Show me a person who does not esteem himself at all, and I'll show you someone who will do great things for me."

Those who preach the gospel of prosperity have forgotten that this is not our home. Believers are "aliens and strangers in the world" (1 Pet. 2:11). Unfortunately, many Christians look to make this temporary life on earth their permanent residence. They have lost sight of the spiritual goal and have replaced it with material ones. Their desire for temporal satisfaction and success has choked out eternal vision. They will gladly trade a mansion in heaven for one in Beverly Hills or Malibu.

> It is all too possible to want gifts from the Lord, but not the Lord himself—which seems to imply that the gift is preferable to the Giver.[13]
>
> Saint Augustine (354-430), *Confessions*

I must admit, I am incredibly attracted by such things. I desire to be successful in every worldly sense of the word. I want fame. I want wealth. I want all the comforts this world can afford me. The notion that I may not attain such lofty heights depresses me, and I find myself resenting God for it.

When I became a missionary, my father told me it was a bad career move, and he was right. At the time I possessed a degree in engineering and an MBA and was working at a good-paying job with a company car and expense account. When I decided to go to the mission field, I took a 75-percent pay cut. I left the blandishments of a comfortable suburb of Chicago to go to the Dark Continent. Many people thought I was just stupid; and I must admit, that thought often crossed my mind as well. Today I am in my forties, and I do not own any property or home. From the world's point of view, I am a failure. And if material blessings and comforts are any measure of God's favor on my life, I am a failure in the eyes of many Christians as well.

The pull to measure my success based on material considerations is a powerful one. That gravity at times is overwhelming; it tests my faith to the core. But I can say without qualification that if I had five times as much money as I do now, owned a large home and brought in a hefty salary, such things would be immaterial to determining my spiritual success and the favor of God upon my life. The fact is, material blessing and the favor of God are often inversely proportional. Put another way, you simply cannot look at a person's wealth and possessions and automatically conclude that such a person is favored by God.

The great English evangelist John Wesley said that if he died with more than five pounds in his pocket, he would be ashamed to face God. I admit that the more money I have in my pocket, the more secure I feel. If I were living at the time of the Israelite wanderings in the desert, I wonder how long it would have taken me to learn not to collect more manna than one day's worth.

A subtle inference exists that so long as we have material blessings, we are successful in the eyes of God, but if we are plagued by difficulties and adversity, we are not blessed by him. This worldly point of view, however, is turned upside down by Jesus, and we would do well to recognize it. There are many ungodly, successful people in the world today, and many godly men and women who are complete failures according to the world's standards. We must be mindful to not discard God's standards and replace them with those of the world. That is what the serpent did in the Garden, and he continues to do it today.

Put another way, what normally characterizes a person who is *not* poor in spirit? He is driven by worldly ideals. His heart is filled with ungodly desires. His thoughts are dominated by material concerns. Jesus tells us this is how pagans behave, not how his disciples will conduct themselves (Matt. 6:32).

Material blessing could never be our aim. As Jesus clearly tells us elsewhere in the Sermon on the Mount, we must store up treasures in heaven. Earthly treasures are subject to decay (Matt. 6:19). As wonderful as material blessings are, they do not last. Only heavenly treasures last for an eternity.[14]

## BUT DOESN'T GOD WANT ME TO BE HAPPY?

"God's people should be the happiest people on earth." This is often said by the prosperity preachers, and there is some truth in it, but not for the reasons they usually give. Referring to the book mentioned earlier, nowhere does it speak about God's forgiveness. Nowhere do we see why believers should be joyous—because they have been reconciled to God. Rather, this happiness is thought to come from the fact that "God has big plans for your life" and the hope that you can own a big home and get a better job.

We are told to "envision your success" and to "program your mind for success." We must abandon the "weak worm-of-the-dust mentality" and the "poverty mentality" and replace them with a "prosperous mind-set." Our goal is "the best this life has to offer." Readers are advised to develop an image of victory, success, health, abundance, joy, peace, and happiness, and then nothing on earth will be able to hold those things from them.

The author is correct when he calls his readers to a change of thinking, and on the surface this reflects Paul's admonishment in Romans 12:2: "Do not conform any longer to the pattern of this world, but be transformed by the renewing of your mind." But whereas Paul's command to renew our minds is coupled with the command not to conform to the standards of the world, this prosperity preacher's encouragements point us exactly in that direction.

Two opposing depictions of the relationship between man and God compete in our churches today. The one views God as holy and righteous, a Judge who will deal heavily with sin. He does so by sending his own Son to pay the penalty, fulfill the righteous requirements of the Law, and bear the punishment we rightly deserve for our sins. As believers, we are "reconciled enemies" of God.

Our duty, therefore, is to serve God completely and always to walk in the knowledge of the grace that has saved us. Certainly we are called his children, having been adopted into his family, but we are also called his servants, enlisted to a life of sacrifice and commitment. The disciple of Jesus does not find the world a comfortable home, but he looks forward to his eternal place of residence.

The other picture is that of God wanting to bless us if only we have enough faith. The emphasis is moved from spiritual matters of sin and salvation to material issues of blessing and prosperity. The problem is not sin but low self-esteem and negative thinking. The goal is not salvation but success. If only we can think more highly of ourselves and fill our minds with positive thoughts, we can shape a more prosperous future that will be blessed by God. The disciple of Jesus should feel comfortable in the world and expect material blessing from God. In fact, in some ways, he should demand it.

The prosperity gospel does not go so far as liberal Christianity with its rejection of the traditional tenets of the faith, but it still packs the same empty punch. God becomes a sort of cosmic Santa Claus who is there to bless us, if only we believe it to be so. Things of eternal significance are discarded for temporal considerations of happiness.

One of the great classics of Christian literature was penned by the German monk Thomas à Kempis (1380-1471), *The Imitation of Christ*. Next to the Bible, this book is thought to be the most-read book throughout the Middle Ages. It reflects an attitude sorely needed in today's Christendom. Kempis recognized the need for a poverty of spirit that is often lost in the church. "Lighthearted and heedless of our defects, we do not feel the real sorrows of our souls, but often indulge in empty laughter when we have good reason to weep." [15]

## DEVELOPING AN ETERNAL PERSPECTIVE WITH EARTHLY SIGNIFICANCE

Let me attempt an analogy to show the faultiness of those who concentrate on material blessings. Consider a beggar who sits on the side of the road begging for food. If I give him food for one day, I have certainly helped him, but come tomorrow, he will be hungry again. If I could give him food for the rest of his life, I have done him a much better service. Should I not help him for the one day? I certainly should, but help for the rest of his life would be preferable.

Similarly, when we focus our attention on temporal, material blessings to the exclusion of eternal, spiritual matters, we are only feeding the beggar for one day and not his whole lifetime. We have only addressed the temporary needs of the day, not the eternally significant ones.

I have always been amazed by those Christians who concentrate on healing, for example, to the exclusion of more spiritual matters. Certainly, it is great if a blind man is granted his sight, but there will come a day when that blind man will die. Then who cares if he could see during his lifetime if in his death he is separated from Christ? "What good will it be for a man if he gains the whole world, yet forfeits his soul?" (Matt. 16:26).

In the mission organization in which I work, we once had a similar dilemma. Fellow missionaries ran a soup kitchen that helped hundreds of street children with one nutritious meal each day. What a great blessing for those needy children. But as we continued to evaluate the ministry, we found that the gospel was not being presented to these children. We were told that the gospel was "silently" being shared, but the fact is, all that was shared was a hot meal. To be sure, helping these children was important, but if that is all that was shared, at the end of the day all we did was feed children and nothing more.

Conversely, James deals with believers in his time who made the exact opposite mistake. They would see a person in need and tell him, "God loves you," but they would never actually help the person. "Suppose a brother or sister is without clothes and daily food. If one of you says to him, 'Go, I wish you well; keep warm and well fed,' but does nothing about his physical needs, what good is it?" (James 2:15-16). James goes on to tell us that such a faith is dead (vv. 17, 26).

Perhaps you have heard the saying, "He is so heavenly minded that he is of no earthly good." As disciples of Christ, we must treat both the physical and the spiritual needs of people. If we concentrate on the physical needs to the exclusion of the spiritual, we have only provided a temporary balm. If we concentrate on the spiritual to the exclusion of the physical, we have shown no earthly compassion. Both approaches are signs of dead faith.

The latter half of the aforementioned book has many wonderful teachings that appear to reflect some of the teachings of Jesus found in the Sermon on the Mount. There are biblical directives concerning compassion, giving, mercy, and integrity. Unfortunately, though, it seems that these are taught with a selfish intention. I would paraphrase the basic message as, *Do these good things so you can receive God's blessing in your life*. There is no inkling that we should be giving people, for example, and expect nothing in return because giving is simply our duty as believers. Rather, there is always some payoff for giving, some material return we can expect if all we do is give. As the old adage goes, "Nothing is free," and apparently, that includes charitable Christian giving and acts of compassion and mercy, according to this teaching.

The attitude, "What can I get out of this?" seems to permeate the gospel of prosperity. I think Jesus would be horrified to see such a mindset. In the classic 1970s song by Keith Green, "Asleep in the Light," he chastised the church for its self-centeredness: "'Bless me, Lord, bless me, Lord,' You know, it's all I ever hear." Green then reprimands Christians who have received all the benefits of Christ and yet simply lie back and soak them in without ever working for his kingdom.

There is something appealing about the prosperity gospel being preached today. The desire for comfort and the drive for success is endemic to the human condition. I doubt there are many people who from their earliest years desire to be poor and destitute. It is human nature to desire success, to yearn for popularity and prestige, to seek comfortable surroundings. It is in this environment of the universal human desire for success that Jesus tells us, "Blessed are the poor in spirit."

Jesus has taken the world's standard for blessedness and turned it on its head. We would expect the world to object to such a ridiculous turnaround of ideals; but unfortunately many in the church also object to it. A powerful delusion is currently taking place in churches throughout the world, one that has rejected this command of Jesus wholesale. Church members and attendees are being sold a rotten basket of fruit, replacing poverty of spirit with the richness of pride. Like malnourished children, their bellies appear full, but they are starving to death.

As surely as the serpent contradicted the command of God in the Garden by replacing "the day you eat of that fruit you will surely die" with "the day you eat that fruit you will be like God," preachers of prosperity and the power of positive thinking replace poverty of spirit with a giddy optimism.

> *To happier life, knowledge of Good and Evil;*
> *Of good, how just? of evil, if what is evil*
> *Be real, why not known, since easier shunned?*
> *God therefore cannot hurt ye, and be just;*
> *Not just, not God; not feared then, nor obeyed:*
> *Your fear itself of death removes the fear.*
> *Why then was this forbid? Why but to awe,*
> *Why but to keep ye low and ignorant,*
> *His worshippers; he knows that in the day*
> *Ye eat thereof, your eyes that seem so clear,*
> *Yet are but dim, shall perfectly be then*
> *Opened and cleared, and ye shall be as Gods,*
> *Knowing both Good and Evil, as they know.*
> John Milton (1608-1674), *Paradise Lost*

In replacing God's will for our lives with our own will, we have bought the serpent's lie. Just as the serpent took a promise of God and twisted it into a lie, the health/wealth/prosperity preachers get it wrong. They take something that is true (God will care for Christians) and twist it into something that is expedient for them and others (God will give me everything I want here on earth to make me happy and comfortable).

If I were to say to myself, "God wants the best for my life," I would be right. But if I coupled that with, "Therefore, my wife will live as long as I do," then I have filled the promise with my own wishes and desires. God's best for my life may well be poverty, persecution, and pain. Was that not the case for our Master, Jesus Christ? "No servant is greater than his master" (John 15:20) has been forgotten by many Christians today.

Prosperity preachers rarely speak of sin. One televangelist who has a worldwide audience of millions of viewers each week proudly claims that he never speaks about sin in his church. The topic is too depressing and will drive people away, so he says. Talk of sin can ruin a person's self-esteem, and we never want to do that. Now compare that to how often Jesus spoke about sin, and you will see how far some Christians have fallen from the true gospel message. It is impossible to speak about salvation when you refuse to speak about that from which you have been saved. The simple fact is, the prosperity gospel is no gospel at all.

Our problem is not low self-esteem. Our problem is that we esteem ourselves too highly.[16]

Whenever I hear someone say all God wants is for us to be happy and prosperous, I cannot help but think, *Tell that to the martyrs.* Consider the people throughout the history of the church who lost all they possessed because of their faith. They lost family. They put their health in jeopardy. The prosperity gospel is easier to sell in America than in places like Sudan, Iran, or China. As the author of Hebrews catalogues concerning the great saints of the Old Testament era:

> *Others were tortured and refused to be released, so that they might gain a better resurrection. Some faced jeers and flogging, while still others were chained and put in prison. They were stoned; they were sawed in two; they were put to death by the sword. They went about in sheepskins and goatskins, destitute, persecuted and mistreated— the world was not worthy of them. They wandered in deserts and mountains, and in caves and holes in the ground. (Heb. 11:35b-38)*

The reason we shun poverty of spirit is because we implicitly understand the consequences of such an attitude. "For your sake we face death all day long; we are considered as sheep to be slaughtered" (Rom. 8:36). Simply put, we are not willing to make that kind of sacrifice to please God because we do not possess a proper eternal perspective. The natural tendency of sinful man is to concentrate on the material or physical to the exclusion of the immaterial or spiritual. We are so tied to this world of sense and taste and smell that we often lose sight of the eternal goal.

## WHAT POVERTY OF SPIRIT DOES NOT MEAN

We should briefly note what poverty of spirit is not. It does not mean all people who lack self-esteem and behave like lickspittles are necessarily poor in spirit. Nor does it mean that all Christians must be party poopers who do not know how to have fun. The opposite is true.

I have a missionary friend who always ends his correspondence by saying, "choose stubborn joy." Only a poverty of spirit can produce genuine, godly joy. When we seek the pleasures of the world, that is all we get. Those pleasures "last for but a season" (Heb. 11:25, KJV). Anyone who is honest knows such pleasures do not last and must be constantly replaced by more pleasure-seeking. This is the wisdom Solomon taught in the book of Ecclesiastes.

Christians should possess real joy and contentment because the eternal matters of life have been addressed in their faith. Nothing should rob us of that joy, not because we have optimism in the material blessings of God, but because we have eternal assurance of our salvation. Certainly, we wrestle with the difficulties of life like anyone else, and at times they can bring us despair and depression. But we should possess a security and peace that only come through God's Spirit, a peace the world cannot know.

I am not disagreeing with those who say Christians should be the happiest people on the planet. Christians who think a dour expression and an absence of a sense of humor is what Christ expects from us simply do not understand what poverty of spirit entails. But whereas some believe happiness should come from material comforts, I believe it comes from something much more eternal. If we walk around angry and short-tempered all the time, we should not mistake that for poverty of spirit. The Christian is called to a life of tension that balances a mourning over his sinfulness with a celebrative demeanor that recognizes his eternal state of redemption. "Happy are those who are unhappy."

# TEN THINGS I WISH JESUS NEVER SAID
## THE ART OF SPIRITUAL POVERTY

My mother was right. If I want to be a success in the world, I need to exude confidence and self-esteem. Unfortunately, though, Jesus is not interested in whether I am a success according to the world's standards. He expects me to exude a poorness of spirit.

To be "poor in spirit" is such a foreign-sounding phrase to our ears today, but without it we cannot be pleasing to God. We have seen four ways to instill poverty of spirit in our lives.

- By disciplining the physical cravings and desires we have.
- By making a radical change with the past.
- By abandoning the world's standards.
- By developing an eternal perspective.

God intends to create in us a wonderful masterpiece of his grace, but a recognition and ongoing realization of our spiritual poverty is the prerequisite for such an activity. There is no forgiveness without repentance. There is no purging of all that is bad in us until we admit that it exists. The constant attitude that marks the genuine disciple of Christ is one of spiritual poverty and mourning.

Jesus tells us that only those who are poor in spirit will enter the kingdom of heaven. This should serve as a warning to all those who claim to be followers of Jesus and yet do not continually mourn over their sinful state. The true disciple of Christ "has a deep sense of the loathsome leprosy of sin which he brought with him from his mother's womb, which overspreads his whole soul, and totally corrupts every power and faculty thereof."[17]

If left to my own sinful inclinations, I must admit that I dislike this teaching of Jesus. I would much prefer a more upbeat, positive message. However, if that is truly what I desire, I need only turn to the world and its ideals. Jesus has spoken the truth, and instead of being distressed by it, I must embrace him. I am a "stinking sinner" in need of great, great mercy and grace. Nothing short of this admission on my part will allow me entrance into fellowship with God.

> Jesus has always many who love His heavenly kingdom, but few who bear His cross. He has many who desire consolation, but few who

care for trial. He finds many to share His table, but few to take part in His fasting. All desire to be happy with Him; few wish to suffer anything for Him. Many follow Him to the breaking of bread, but few to the drinking of the chalice of His passion. Many revere His miracles; few approach the shame of the Cross. Many love Him as long as they encounter no hardship; many praise and bless Him as long as they receive some comfort from Him.

Thomas à Kempis (1380-1471),
*The Imitation of Christ*

# 2

# THE ART OF
# SPIRITUAL SELF-MUTILATION

*If your right eye causes you to sin, gouge it out and throw it away.*
JESUS CHRIST, MATTHEW 5:29A

*I could even have wished to be deaf, blind, and dumb, that nothing might divert me from my love of God.*
AUTOBIOGRAPHY OF MADAME GUYON (1647-1717)

*Forbid it, Lord, that I should boast,*
*Save in the death of Christ, my God;*
*All the vain things that charm me most,*
*I sacrifice them to His blood.*
ISAAC WATTS,
"WHEN I SURVEY THE WONDROUS CROSS," 1707

have a confession to make: I like sin. As surely as Eve saw the forbidden fruit and found it "pleasing to the eye," I too find a certain pleasure in sin. At times I wonder what it would be like to be unable to sin, to be in that heavenly state where I not only no longer want to sin, but could not do so. I admit, a state such as that seems strange to me. I'm not entirely sure I want it.

What a horrible confession to make, but what I am admitting is my comfort with sin. Certainly, all sin at its foundational level is active rebellion against God, but I do not always sin because I am angry with God and want to shake my fist at him. Fact is, I have rarely sinned in

**43**

that way. Rather, I do sinful things because I like them. They are pleasurable. They are enjoyable. They seem natural to me.

If I were asked here and now to choose between an existence where I could no longer sin and my present existence, I know the correct spiritual answer. But deep down inside, in the inner recesses of my soul, I know that giving up sinful pleasures would be against my desire.

If sin were only like sticking a fork in an electrical outlet, I would have no problem. But sin comes in pleasurable, delectable forms that appeal to my basest lusts. The reason it woos me is because I want to be wooed by it. No one is enticed by a lover he does not want to love. Sin courts me, and its silky-smooth sounds resonate in my sinful ears.

Every member of my body joins in the beguilement. My eyes love to gaze upon that which I should not study; my ears long to listen to that which I should not heed; my hands enjoy caressing that which I should not touch; my tongue lisps things I dare not utter; my feet are swift to take me to desire's destination.

"If your right eye causes you to sin, pluck it out." Does Jesus truly expect me to dissect myself? If I did this, not only would I be without two eyes, but two hands, two feet, two ears, and virtually every other part of my body. Like a child being asked to give up his lollypop, I stubbornly resist this command of Jesus, and at times it engenders hatred in me.

## DID JESUS FIND IT EASY NOT TO SIN?

The Gospels record in detail the last three and a half years of Jesus's life, in sparse detail the first two years, and virtually nothing at all in between. The writers purposefully intended to concentrate on the latter years of Jesus, especially his crucifixion and resurrection. Yet the *whole* life of Jesus was important if he was to become a vicarious atonement for sinners.[1]

If Jesus had sinned just once, a small indiscretion or a slip of the tongue with one careless word, his bloody death on the cross would have been meaningless. Entirely meaningless. Jesus had to be a spotless, blemishless sacrifice to take the wrath of the Father upon him and endure it. Nothing less would have been sufficient.

That means Jesus had to live a perfectly sinless life. From the moment he emerged from Mary's womb to the time just before they laid him in the tomb, Jesus had to obey God the Father 100 percent of the time. Had he maintained a purity, say, of Ivory soap's level (99.44%), it would not have been good enough. Only by being perfect could he earn the perfect righteousness that he gives to all sinners who by faith receive it.

I recall once telling this to a Sunday school class of senior citizens. After repeating part of the Apostles' Creed to them ("He was born, crucified, and buried"), I noted that we have missed an important segment of the ministry of Christ. Not his "official" ministry, mind you, which began with his baptism by John. Rather, the ministry of his entire life, from birth to death, a ministry devoted totally and completely to the Father's will. In essence, the Creed skips thirty-plus years.

One elderly gentleman piped up and asked me how I suggested we correct the Apostles' Creed. He was being sarcastic, and he got his punch in. But I am serious. The Apostles' Creed is insufficient in this respect, but I do not plan to suggest changes to it. I do recognize, though, that we have a tendency to concentrate on the miraculous events in the life of Jesus while forgetting the long, hard haul of thirty-three years of sinlessness.

Each time Jesus was tempted to sin, he chose not to. Whenever he was faced with the prospect of going against the will of his Father, he always chose to obey it.

This is not because he was God in the flesh. We cannot lay the sinless perfection of Jesus at the feet of his deity alone. If we do, we rob his temptations of their power, as well as his example for us. So could Jesus have really sinned? Though a minority opinion among evangelical theologians, my answer is yes, an answer that helps me make sense of Jesus' true humanity.[2]

Jesus knew precisely what it meant to fight sin tenaciously, without giving up. The author of Hebrews makes it clear: "Because he himself suffered when he was tempted, he is able to help those who are being tempted" (2:18). Jesus knows *exactly* what we are going through.

Later we learn, "For we do not have a high priest who is unable to sympathize with our weaknesses, but we have one who has been tempted in every way, just as we are—yet was without sin" (4:15). None of this would make sense if Jesus really could not sin; nor would it bring comfort to us. Jesus can only serve as our example in fighting sin if he is tempted to the same degree as we are tempted.[3] That is why the author of Hebrews says Jesus "shared in [our] humanity" (2:14). He did what Adam was unable and unwilling to do in the Garden, and he did what we are also unable and unwilling to do. Jesus possessed the perfect human nature that Adam had before his Fall; but unlike Adam, Jesus never failed in his representation of the human race.

The beauty of all this is that Jesus never asks us to do anything that he himself was not willing to do first. As such, when Jesus talks about sin, we can be sure he knows exactly what he is talking about. His knowledge of sin and temptation was fashioned by sweat and blood experience. When he commands us to withstand temptation, this directive only comes from someone who himself resisted it. So when Jesus tells us to deal with sin drastically, we should take heed. His are not idle words or mild suggestions. This is a life-and-death imperative.

> Lord, give me weak eyes for things that are of no account, but clear eyes for all Thy truth.
>
> Søren Kierkegaard (1813-1855), *Preparation for a Christian Life*

## THE PATTERN OF TEMPTATION

Part of understanding this radical command by Jesus concerning sin is found in a passage in John's first epistle. There we find something of the mechanism of sin: "For everything in the world—the cravings of sinful man, the lust of his eyes and the boasting of what he has and does—comes not from the Father but from the world" (1 John 2:16).

Here we find three principles concerning sin and the means by which it operates; sinful cravings, lust of the eyes, and what the King James Version calls the "pride of life." I see a parallel between John's description and two other important events in the biblical history of humanity concerning sin: Adam and Eve in the Garden of Eden and Jesus in the wilderness temptation.

In the Garden the serpent played word games with Eve while Adam stood by and watched. In Genesis 3:1-5 the tactic of the serpent involved: 1) warping the words of God by misquoting the command not to eat the forbidden fruit—*"Did God really say, 'You must not eat from any tree in the garden?'"*; 2) outright lying about the command and intention of God in that command—*"You will not surely die"*; and 3) substituting the command of God with a false promise—*"You will be like God."*

Verse 6 says Eve, wooed by the sweet-sounding words of the serpent, perceived three things about the fruit, which we see paralleled in John's passage: 1) the fruit was good for food—*John: cravings of sinful man;* 2) the fruit was pleasing to the eye—*John: lust of the eyes;* 3) the fruit was desirable for gaining wisdom—*John: pride of life.*

If we move to the wilderness temptation of Jesus (Matthew 4), we again see this threefold pattern. As in the Garden, Satan purposefully mishandled the Word of God, but Jesus was not fooled. In all three instances, Jesus adeptly reproved Satan with a proper understanding of God's commands. Note the parallels between the temptation of Jesus, the temptation of Eve, and John's threefold description of the mechanism of sin: 1) Satan first tempted Jesus to turn stones into bread, and this after Jesus had fasted for forty days—*John: cravings of sinful man;* 2) next he tempted Jesus to throw himself down from the highest point of the temple where Jesus would be miraculously preserved by the angels—*John: pride of life;* 3) last, Satan offered Jesus all the kingdoms of the world if only he would bow down and worship him—*John: lust of the eyes.*

There is an unmistakable pattern when it comes to Satan and his temptations. In one instance with Jesus, Satan actually quoted the Word of God. This is incredible if you think about who Satan was speaking to. Whereas the first man and woman were duped by the serpent's peddling of false promises, the Son of Man stood his ground. Whereas our first parents botched their representation of humanity, our Mediator and Redeemer did not fail us.

# TEN THINGS I WISH JESUS NEVER SAID

I once told a small group Bible study that you must be perfect if you want to be in heaven. Almost all of them immediately objected. I later told the same thing to a group of seminarians, many of whom also objected. Their main complaint was that if perfection were the requirement, none of us would go to heaven. Of course, that was precisely my point. None of us deserves to go to heaven because the requirement is sinless perfection. Jesus came to do for us what we could not do for ourselves, earn that perfect righteousness, the white robe that is standard attire in heavenly mansions.

He refused to succumb to cravings, the lust of the eyes, and the pride of life that form the tactics of the Evil One. Were those temptations real? You bet they were. He even needed angels to come and strengthen him afterward. It is no coincidence that this testing of Jesus's mettle came at the beginning of his ministry, but let us not make the mistake of assuming it ended there. If he were truly tempted like we are in all ways, he endured such testing throughout his earthly life.

On the opposite end of the spectrum, we will take a look at a biblical character who did not fare so well when it came to dealing with the sinful cravings, the lust of the eyes, and the pride of life.

## THE FALL OF ABRAHAM'S NEPHEW

Moses was an excellent storyteller, and like all good authors, he often conveyed his message through literary form rather than through bald statement of fact. For example, he used contrast several times in the early chapters of Genesis to expose the differences between those who follow God's plan and those who oppose it.[4]

One such instance involves the lives of Abraham[5] and Lot.[6] We are introduced to Lot at the end of chapter 11, and we soon learn that he loses his father and grandfather. The patriarch Abraham takes Lot under his wing as he moves from Ur to Haran and then to Canaan. Lot actually plays a prominent role in the next eight chapters of Moses's account, but his significance is often swallowed up by the sweeping story of Abraham.

Childless Abraham must have cared deeply for his nephew. We see this love in chapter 13, where we learn Abraham and Lot have become so blessed by the Lord that the land can no longer support both of them. Abraham proposes they part ways, but the senior gives his junior first choice. "Lot looked up and saw that the whole plain of the Jordan was well watered, like the garden of the LORD" (13:10a), and he soon pitched his tents near Sodom (v. 12).

In chapter 14 Moses reports that Lot is now living in Sodom (v. 12) in an almost offhanded manner, a classic literary device. Here Lot finds himself in trouble, and again Abraham displays his care for his nephew by taking all the men of his household and waging war against Lot's captors. The rescue of Lot is the last we see of the young man until the account of Sodom and Gomorrah in chapter 19, but we must not lose sight of the fact that Abraham's pleading with the Lord over the destruction of those cities has Lot's well-being in mind (19:29).

In the opening verses of chapter 19, we learn that Lot is sitting in the gateway of the city, a position of prominence in those days. Despite the warnings of the angels to flee from the city, Lot stubbornly resists to the point that the angels must forcibly drag him out of the city. In the ensuing judgment of sulfur and brimstone, Lot loses his wife along the way.

The last scene involving Lot is a pathetic one. Living in a cave with his two daughters, while in a drunken stupor he is raped by each of them. The offspring of these unholy acts become the Ammonites (known for their worship of the god Molech) and the Moabites (who seduced the Jews at the suggestion of Balaam, for which God sent a plague and killed 24,000 Israelites in Numbers 25).

Moses covers the life of Lot in the span of nine chapters. In Lot we find a man who went from being blessed with flocks and herds so great that he needed to find larger pastures, to living in a cave and being raped by his two desperate daughters. His posterity was corrupt to the core, and evidently Lot lost everything he had.

Why have I chosen the life of Lot when by all accounts he seems to be a rather evil man who got what was coming to him? Because Peter, in his second epistle, gives us inspired insight into Lot's life that we do not have in Genesis. Peter's perspective is shocking given what we know about Lot from Moses's account. In speaking about God's judgment, Peter uses three examples to show that God's judgment is real and imminent. The first two involve fallen angels and the victims of the Great Flood. The third comes from Lot's life.

*If he condemned the cities of Sodom and Gomorrah by burning them to ashes, and made them an example of what is going to happen to the ungodly; and if he rescued Lot, a righteous man, who was distressed by the filthy lives of lawless men (for that righteous man, living among them day after day, was tormented in his righteous soul by the lawless deeds he saw and heard). (2 Pet. 2:6-8)*

I must admit that my first impression—and many subsequent ones as well—of Peter's take on the life and character of Lot was, well, to be shocked. A righteous man? Is Peter serious? What we have here is a New Testament author giving us greater insight into the life of an Old Testament character. This is nothing new and should not shock us, but often it does.[7] The same Spirit who inspired Peter also inspired Moses.

When I consider the account of Lot from the perspective of Lot being a righteous man, I read it with new eyes. Lot was not the morally degenerate person I assumed he was, given the Genesis account. Rather, he was a righteous man who was overcome by sin.

Lot had enjoyed the blessing of the Lord that flowed from his association with his uncle. He must have known about the promises God gave to Abraham, for he spent many years with him. Then came a fateful choice when Lot and Abraham separated, and Lot threw his lot into the lush, promising land of Sodom. Although he knew the cities were evil, Lot was willing to bear it for some reason. There was obviously something more that he wanted, and he was willing to tolerate the most heinous evil around him in order to have it.

Precisely what it was that Lot craved we do not know, but we do know that whatever it was, he was unwilling to forego it. The angels had to force him to leave the cities, and evidently his wife was likeminded, ultimately losing her life because she longed more for Sodom than for safety.

Paul tells us these Old Testament situations "happened to them as examples and were written down as warnings for us, on whom the fulfillment of the ages has come. So, if you think you are standing firm, be careful that you don't fall!" (1 Cor. 10:11-12).

Lot was a man who lived by sight and not by faith. He was driven by material desire. When given the chance to part with Abraham, he chose the best for himself, even if it meant putting himself in the neighborhood of evil. The lust of his eyes was too much for him to withstand. As we noted in the previous chapter, much of the prosperity gospel is motivated by a similar ethos of sight and not faith.

At some point Lot allowed sin to so dominate him that he lost the ability to choose better. Sin was creeping at Lot's door, and he opened it wide to let the monster in. His example is a warning to all of us who take sin lightly.

So many believers today are like Lot, enticed by sin's sleek suggestions. In many instances it is nearly impossible to tell the difference between Christians and people of the world. We have the same hopes, the same desires, the same motivations. We squander our money on the same frivolous things. We enter and exit marriages at the same imprudent rate. We waste our time on the same mindless entertainment that absorbs the world. We fill our minds with the same cinematic trash and silver screen garbage. If not for the grace of God, many of us would have found ourselves in exactly Lot's predicament—destitute and pathetic, with only ourselves to blame.

Jesus wants to protect us from going the way of Lot. Rather than flirting with sin, we need to flee it. Instead of cavorting with it, we need to combat it. There is no room for complacency in the Christian life when it comes to sin. That is why we must not hesitate to pluck out our offending eye.

> Behold, thou wretched little man, how in the liking of fleshly lust the cruelty of endless damnation sleeps.
>
> Richard Rolle, fourteenth-century English mystic,
> *The Fire of Love and the Mending of Life*

## LESSONS FROM HISTORY

Some have argued in the past that this verse (Matt. 5:29) is too dangerous and that ignorant people might mistakenly take it literally. For example, shortly after William Tyndale (1490-1536) published his English translation of the Bible, those opposed to vernacular translations fought to limit its circulation. One argument they used was that the whole realm of England might become filled with men with no eyes or hands, "to the great decay of the nation and the manifest loss of the King's grace." Those who supported Tyndale's translation countered by saying that even the simple can tell the difference between literal and figurative language.[8]

The early church father Origen (185-254) is one who took seriously the commands of Jesus in this regard. Known to be a rigid ascetic who slept little, fasted frequently, and walked around barefoot, Origen took literally the words of Jesus in Matthew 19:12 and castrated himself to remove any potential of scandal as he taught young women in his school in Alexandria. Today we might be tempted to attribute a "martyr complex" to Origen who, as tradition records, was saved from martyrdom in his teen years by his mother. As the story goes, Origen's father was being taken away to be executed for his faith, and the young man wanted to go die along with his father, but his mother hid his clothing so Origen could not go out in public.[9] For Origen, martyrdom was the ultimate way to prove one's faith in Christ. That being the case, it is no wonder that he believed physical self-mutilation to also be acceptable.

Church history is filled with examples of godly men and women who took seriously the mandate to slay sin in their lives. Some may have taken things a bit too far, as in the case of Origen, but they stand nonetheless in stark contrast to believers today who are so characterized by a worldly Christianity.

In Augustine's famous autobiography, *Confessions*, he gives details concerning his pre-Christian days, ones filled with lust and promiscuity. So powerful was the pull of lust in his life that once he became a believer, he took dramatic measures to guard himself from it. He covenanted to never be alone with a woman, even when it came to his sister. We might find such a plan fanatical, but then perhaps that is only because we do not understand sin—and ourselves—to the degree that Augustine understood both. We have a tendency to lie to ourselves about ourselves.

John Calvin (1509-1564) recognized this universal human characteristic: "For since blind self-love is innate in all mortals, they are most freely persuaded that nothing inheres in themselves that deserves to be considered hateful."[10]

What Jesus, Augustine, and Calvin knew about man we too often ignore today. In our love affair with self-esteem and positive self-image, we eschew any notion of personal destitution and corruption. But if we are going to adequately deal with sin in our lives, we need to stop lying to ourselves. Twentieth-century French theologian and Calvinist scholar Pannier noted that when we recognize our "moral impotence, we are led to seek power and deliverance from God."[11]

## HOW TO DEAL WITH THE BEAST

By using the graphic language of self-mutilation, what is Jesus trying to teach us about sin and about ourselves?

1) *Sin wants to consume us.* Moses used an incredibly vivid metaphor concerning sin when he recounted the story of Cain and Abel. Cain had just found his stingy fruit and vegetable sacrifice to God unacceptable, and as a result he became angry. God's advice to Cain was simple: "If you do what is right, will you not be accepted?" (Gen. 4:7a). But then he gave Cain a warning, one we must take to heart: "But if you do not do what is right, sin is crouching at your door; it desires to have you, but you must master it" (v. 7b).

Sin is creeping at our door and wants to master us. Its sole aim is our ruin and nothing less. Whenever we take it lightly, we underestimate the beast. Jesus wants us to take it seriously. Jesus knows how dangerous it is, and he is concerned lest we be devoured by it.

## TEN THINGS I WISH JESUS NEVER SAID

*Christian, dost thou see them on the holy ground,*
*How the pow'rs of darkness rage thy steps around?*
*Christian, dost thou feel them, how they work within,*
*Striving, tempting, luring, goading into sin?*
John Mason Neale,
"Christian, Dost Thou See Them?" 1862

I recall a time when I had come home from college for the holidays, and I was watching a television program with my father and sister. My mother was working in the kitchen, and occasionally she popped her head into the family room. At one point in the show, lewd humor occurred, and all three of us got a good laugh. My mother became furious.

It is twenty years later, but her words still stick clearly in my mind. "That's exactly how Satan works," she said. "He first gets you to laugh at the sin, and before you know it, you find yourself approving it and maybe even practicing it." Godly words of wisdom from my mother.

2) *We must deal ruthlessly with sin.* Our sinless Savior, one who knew temptation and knew the heart of man, did not take sin lightly. He knew how insidious it is, and he was familiar with all its tricks. He knew that if we coddle sin, if we decide to play its game and allow it the least bit of space, we will lose the battle. Jesus is telling us to draw the line at the beginning. Anything short of this, and we will surely fail.

Unfortunately, though, we tend to do the opposite. Our mentality is to see how close we can get to the fire before we singe our fingertips. This attitude is a recipe for failure, as I have experienced time and time again.

Consider this analogy. How many of us would willingly put our outstretched hand in front of a rabid, foaming dog? If we were to encounter such a beast, is it not more natural to keep our hands—and our whole body for that matter—as far away from the animal as possible? Yet sin, which can inflict far more damage than any creature, is the same sort of ravenous fiend. Why do we flirt so often with it? Most likely because, instead of seeing sin for what it is, like Adam and Eve we view it as tasty and sweet.

Christ employs an exaggerated form of speech to show that whatever hinders us from yielding that obedience to God, which he requires in his law, ought to be cut off. And he does so expressly because men allow themselves too much liberty in that respect.

John Calvin (1509-1564), *Commentary on Matthew*

James speaks of the small spark that begins a raging forest fire (3:5b). How many lives have been needlessly set on the path of ruin because of one initial indiscretion? The slide often begins with a small, seemingly insignificant decision and can ultimately yield complete destruction.

Gouging out our eyes is what some might call "radical spiritual surgery,"[12] but it is necessary. In his *Conferences*, John Cassian (360-435) called this concept the "entire mortification of dangerous pleasures." We must root out all of it, lest it grow like a cancer from within. As surely as a doctor is willing to cut off a gangrenous leg to save the rest of the body, so too must we brutally deal with sin.

There is a flesh-and-spirit battle raging in our bodies, as the apostle Paul intensely portrays in Romans 7. Elsewhere he tells us plainly, "For the sinful nature desires what is contrary to the Spirit, and the Spirit what is contrary to the sinful nature. They are in conflict with each other, so that you do not do what you want" (Gal. 5:17). Rather than ignoring our spiritual poverty or allowing ourselves to occasionally indulge it, we must endeavor to destroy it for fear that we become like Lot.

Dr. Erwin Lutzer, senior pastor of Moody Church in Chicago, recently said on Moody radio that if we envision what it means to truly pluck out an eye, we will note that it is painful and irreversible. Plucking out an eye or cutting off an arm is always painful and bloody. This provides some idea of what is involved with spiritual self-mutilation. If our problem is the lust of the eyes, we have to be vigilant about what we view. Movies with lewd scenes or television shows with suggestive situations must be avoided. Too frequently Christians flirt with these seemingly harmless activities, but they can easily lead to grosser sins.

Spiritual self-mutilation will often involve ridding ourselves of things that by themselves are harmless (like watching television shows), but can smuggle in harmful content. For example, our favorite drama on television may occasionally contain questionable content. That being the case, instead of putting up with the bad content because, well, most of it is pretty good, we may have to excise all of it.

How many times have you heard Christians say, "That movie was pretty good, except for that one sex scene," or, "That drama was excellent, except for the foul language"? Is it really so vital to us that we watch that movie or television show, while in the process willingly putting up with the trash that comes with it?

In the previous chapter, we looked at ways at curbing the cravings of our sinful nature. This involved developing our self-control, and I used fasting as an example of the principle that physical poverty is often intimately associated with spiritual poverty. I will provide more concrete suggestions in the next chapter about self-control in specific areas of commitment. We will also look at ways of addressing this matter as it concerns the pride of life in chapters 4 and 8.

3) *Not only must we be concerned with our own sin, but we must also be careful to avoid causing others to stumble into sin.* In two similar passages elsewhere in the Gospels (Matt. 18:8-9 and Mark 9:43-47), Jesus couples the idea of spiritual self-mutilation with his concern that we do not cause others to stumble into sin. Jesus is not calling us to produce an individualistic, egotistical viewpoint of sin where we are only concerned with ourselves. Rather, his is a corporate vision, a mutual spiritual accountability.

As believers, we form the body of Christ. Just as all parts of a human body work to fight off a virus, so too must we work together to fight sin. I am not advocating an overly judgmental approach whereby we become hypercritical of each other. That would create a negative atmosphere where each of us would play the part of spiritual police, constantly pointing out the sins of others. Such churches tend to be small, critical, and unwelcoming.

Rather, we need a more positive approach where we exhibit concern and care for each other. We should place our own needs, and particularly our own freedom, after the needs of others. Paul speaks of this attitude in Romans 14, and he envisions a church where believers look out for the spiritual well-being of their brothers and sisters in Christ. Those who might exhibit a weaker faith should be protected and cared for, not criticized and condemned.

Jesus has harsh words for those who cause others to fall into sin. As surely as we should be concerned with our own sin, we should equally be concerned with causing others to falter. A number of times I have been in the presence of fellow believers who flaunted their freedom to drink alcohol in front of other believers who thought it was wrong. Both Jesus and Paul condemn such arrogant behavior.

We tend to go to one of two extremes in our churches: Either we do not regard sin as critically as we should, or we are so critical that we cease to be a loving, welcoming community. Striking the proper balance is difficult, but we must endeavor to inculcate an attitude in our churches where we love each other so much that we would never place stumbling blocks before fellow believers.

4) *When we fall, it is our own fault.* God is fair to us. Despite our active rebellion against him, we are told that God does not allow us to be tempted beyond what we can endure (1 Cor. 10:13). So, each time we yield to temptation, it is our own fault.

When we flirt with sin, when we decide to give it a foothold, we are acting like spiritual fools. How many people have become alcoholics because they decided to take that first drink? How many men have admitted to being addicted to pornography because they allowed themselves to take that first "harmless" look?

James gives us a good picture of the slyness of sin: "Each one is tempted when, by his own evil desire, he is dragged away and enticed. Then, after desire has conceived, it gives birth to sin; and sin, when it is full-grown, gives birth to death" (1:14-15).

Still more foolish are the people who have had a problem with a certain sin in the past and yet continue to place themselves in situations where they can easily fall into it again. Thus the alcoholic frequently finds himself entertaining clients in the pub, overestimating his ability to resist "just one drink." The man struggling with pornography lingers on the Internet just a little too long, thinking he will not surrender again to the familiar cravings of lust. Yet building walls against known areas of weakness in our lives is prudent behavior for believers. God does not allow us to be tempted beyond what we can endure, but so often we willingly march ourselves into territory we know we are unfit to withstand.

As Jesus tells us, the trick to defeating sin in our lives is to act harshly against it. If we allow an iota of space for it to work, it can grow into something we can no longer handle or control. My grandmother used to say, "Nip it in the bud," and she was right. As the author of Hebrews writes, sin so easily entangles us (Heb. 12:1), and he tells us to discard everything that hinders our running the race of faith. Can you imagine an Olympic sprinter appearing on the track wearing a tuxedo? That is the imagery we find in this Hebrews passage. If the sprinter truly wants to run the best race possible, he will throw off everything that could hinder his movement.

Lot fell for it. He allowed sin to enter his life subtly, and in time he lost all ability to stop its growth. In the end, it produced the bitter fruit of a ruined life.

## A GREATER JOY THAN SIN

Lastly, Jesus reminds us that we need an eternal perspective. There is a greater pleasure than sin. Sin's joy lasts but a season (Heb. 11:25), but godliness lasts an eternity. It will do us no good if we keep our sinful eyes, hands, and feet intact, but end up in hell. Jesus was tempted in all ways as we are and yet did not sin because he knew the joy set before him.

Instead of hating Jesus's command to drastically deal with the sinful pleasures in my life that I so much enjoy, instead of picturing him as a killjoy, I should recognize that this command is motivated entirely by love. He loves me so much that he is willing to talk straight to me, what some today call "tough love." Rather than fight and struggle against Christ, I should embrace him with my entire being—my hands, my eyes, my heart, my mind, my strength, my will. Jesus wants me to be free, but I stubbornly clutch those things destined to fade away. May God grant me the grace and mercy I need to withstand temptation, and after I have accomplished everything, to stand.

> In examining ourselves, the search which divine truth enjoins, and the knowledge which it demands, are such as may indispose us to every thing like confidence in our own powers, leave us devoid of all means of boasting, and so incline us to submission.
>
> John Calvin (1509-1564), *Institutes*, 2.1.2

# 3

# THE ART OF
# SPIRITUAL COMMITMENT

*No one who puts his hand to the plow and looks back is fit
for service in the kingdom of God.*
JESUS CHRIST, LUKE 9:62

*He must have all our heart, or none.*
J. C. RYLE (1816-1900), ANGLICAN MINISTER, *LUKE*

*We can please God in no state or employment of life, but by
intending and devoting it all to His honour and glory.*
WILLIAM LAW (1686-1761),
*A SERIOUS CALL TO A DEVOUT AND HOLY LIFE*

The 2005 Tour de France ended with American Lance Armstrong winning an unprecedented seventh consecutive title. Armstrong was a man entirely devoted to his craft. Despite the naysayers, and despite the fact that he was approaching his mid-thirties, Armstrong handily won the race. Few athletes can boast the dominance in their sport that this Texan can.

Last year I heard an interview with Armstrong, who had then just broken the consecutive winning streak record by claiming his sixth title in a row. When asked about his secret to success, instead of talking about his rigorously controlled diet or the six-hour training sessions he has virtually every day, Armstrong said something that stood out in my mind. He said, "I live for the Tour. Everything I do throughout the year has the Tour in mind. My sole ambition every year is to win it."

The words were almost evangelistic, and if one were to replace the word *Tour* with *Lord*, I can well imagine the apostle Paul saying something similar. Lance Armstrong stands out as a man of absolute, unwavering commitment and devotion to his profession. Of course, I can think what a waste for him to be committed so much to something that will eternally amount to so little, but I admire the man nonetheless.

After being so consumed by something for so many years, though, what does a man do afterward? Will anything satisfy him? Will he be able to find something into which he can equally throw his full vim and vigor? What if he were to throw these energies into a relationship with Christ? Can you imagine Lance Armstrong as a missionary or evangelist? Consider what would happen if he took that determination he had for winning the Tour and used that energy for winning converts to Christ.

Here I sit, looking at Lance Armstrong as somewhat of an anomaly. Few people have his level of commitment. When I think of myself, I am not sure I have ever had such commitment to *anything*. Yet, as I read the words of Jesus, I find that this is precisely the type of commitment he expects of his disciples. There is no room for halfheartedness if one is to follow Christ.

Reflecting on my Christian journey, I realize how terribly short I fall of this ideal. How many times have I placed my hand on the plow of holiness, only to turn back to sin? If this type of commitment is what Jesus requires of me, am I honestly able to attain it? And if I cannot attain it, how fair is it that Jesus would expect this of me? As I weigh my commitment in the scales, I find myself wanting, and this only engenders bitterness in me toward Jesus.

My approach in this chapter will be simple. I will begin by briefly examining the commitment Christ had to the Father and then will discuss what it means for his disciples to be fully committed.

## A MODEL OF SINLESS COMMITMENT

In Jesus Christ we have the standard of commitment by which all others will be measured. As we have discovered, Jesus does not ask us to do anything he was not willing to do himself. When he tells us he demands a commitment that is wholehearted and forward-looking, we know he possessed that same devotion.

Of course, as the sinless Lord of glory, Jesus's level of commitment will always be greater than our own. In using him as an example, then, some of us might become discouraged, thinking, "I can never attain that level of commitment; so why even try?" Much like his command to "be perfect, as your heavenly Father is perfect" (Matt. 5:48), this example of perfect commitment might seem unattainable.

However, what alternative is there to obedience? Can you imagine God saying to us, "Go ahead and sin but not too much"? The only ideal our holy Lord can set before us is perfection. If he were to prescribe anything less, we would never attain the quality of Christian life we are called to attain, and he could not be considered holy in his judgments.

What can we learn, then, from Christ's absolute commitment to obedience? Let me briefly outline five observations:[1]

1) *In Christ this obedience was a life principle.* It encompassed everything he did: every intention, every thought, every deed. Jesus said, "For I have come down from heaven not to do my will but to do the will of him who sent me" (John 6:38).

2) *In Christ this obedience was a joy.* Jesus delighted to do the will of the Father. He even likened it to something as life-sustaining as food: "My food . . . is to do the will of him who sent me and to finish his work" (John 4:34). This absolute commitment of Jesus produced joy, not drudgery (Heb. 12:2).

3) *In Christ this obedience led to a waiting on God's will.* This is evident particularly in the Garden of Gethsemane where we see the clearest evidence of Christ's struggle in drinking the cup of the Father's wrath. Yet he was willing to subject his will to that of the Father, something he had proved time and time again leading up to his crucifixion (John 14:10).

4) *In Christ this obedience was unto death.* Not even the greatest phobia of man was able to deter him from obeying the Father (Phil. 2:8).

5) *In Christ this obedience was of faith—in entire dependence upon God's strength.* Jesus said, "By myself I can do nothing " (John

5:30). "Rather it is the Father, living in me, who is doing his work" (John 14:10).

The unqualified obedience Jesus had for the Father was based on an intimate relationship of trust and commitment. This communion with the Father informed every choice Jesus made, and as his disciples, we are called to a similar relationship with God.

> Defective obedience is always the result of a defective life. To rouse and spur on that defective life by arguments and motives has its use, but their chief blessing must be that they make us feel the need of a different life, a life so entirely under the power of God that obedience will be its natural outcome. The defective life, the life of broken and irregular fellowship with God, must be healed, and make way for a full and healthy life; then full obedience will become possible. The secret of a true obedience is *the return to close and continual fellowship with God.*
>
> Andrew Murray (1828-1917),
> *The School of Obedience*, (emphasis in original)

## LESSONS FROM HISTORY

The sixteenth-century Protestant Reformation was filled with people who devoted themselves fully to the cause of Christ. Their dedication and zeal for the Lord stand as a testament to us today who often lack the same commitment. I will cite three such people, and I have purposefully chosen ones with whom many of us might be unfamiliar.[2]

Jerome of Prague (1365?-1416) stood out as a man of sharp mind and tough spirit who had a lasting impact on the Reformation in his homeland of Bohemia. Jan Hus is clearly the better known of the Czech reformers, but Jerome's life displayed much the same determination for Christ and the gospel as that of Hus. Opposing many errors in the church at that time, both men were condemned by the Council of Constance for heresy and were martyred for their faith.

Poggio Bracciolini, the papal representative at the Council of Constance, who was no friend of Jerome, witnessed Jerome's execution. Here is what he recorded:

He stood before his judges undaunted and intrepid. Not only not fearing, but even seeking death . . . he was indeed a man worthy of eternal memory in men's minds. With joyful brow, cheerful countenance, and elated face he went to his doom. He feared not the flames, not the torments, not death. When he had reached the spot where he was to die, he divested himself of his garments, and knelt down in prayer. Logs of wood were then piled about his body, which they covered up to the breast. When they were lighted, he began to sing a hymn, which was interrupted by the smoke and the flames. This, however, is the greatest proof of the constancy of his mind, that when the official wished to light the stake behind his back, that he might not see it, he said, "Come here and light the stake before my eyes, for if I had feared it I should never have come to this spot, as it was in my power to fly."[3]

Thus perished a man eminent beyond belief.

My second example comes from the Polish Reformation. John Laski (1499-1560), also known as Johannes Alasco, was born to riches and royalty. Groomed to take the primateship of Poland, Laski instead rebelled against the abuses of the Catholic church. In many respects he was a Polish Moses, looking for the liberation of his people from oppression when he could have chosen to sit comfortably with those in power. He stands as an example of a man who had earthly glory and wealth and yet gave it all up to follow Christ.

Laski took the hard path. Several times he had to flee his homeland because of his commitment to the gospel and God's Word. He spent considerable time in the Netherlands and England, and he helped produce the first Polish translation of the Bible. Possessing a keen intellect, he developed a creed for the Protestant churches in Poland that later influenced the Heidelberg Catechism. Through the years, Laski had personal contact or correspondence with other prominent men of his era such as Zwingli, Menno Simons, Bucer, Calvin, Bullinger, Melanchthon, Erasmus, and Cranmer.

Laski stands out in another way, this time in comparison to many other Protestant reformers. He was evangelical and looked for unity among the differing Protestant groups. When most Protestant sects were concentrating on their differences, Laski attempted to forge reconciliation and harmony. Despite his zeal, Laski was only able to influence his homeland during the latter years of his life. How much easier his life would have been had he simply taken the easy way of wealth and privilege.

We next consider Spain, a country that enjoyed little Protestant exposure in the sixteenth century due to its position at the heart of the Holy Roman Empire and as home to the emperor. Francisco de Enzinas (1520?-1550) was a young man moved by God's Spirit to see the Bible translated into the language of his fellow Spaniards. This was no simple desire, though, as the feared Spanish Inquisition made it nearly impossible to produce a Bible translation without being detected.

De Enzinas left the country to work on the project, and at the age of twenty-three produced the first New Testament translation into Spanish. Instead of attempting to sneak the Bible back into his homeland, he had a conference with the emperor and appealed to him for its adoption. However, the emperor consulted the bishop concerning the matter, who promptly had de Enzinas imprisoned. For fourteen months de Enzinas languished there until he escaped and fled to Germany, where he died at barely thirty years of age. "He probably did more than any other individual in Spain to enlighten the people with the gospel."[4]

All three of these men could have easily chosen the safe road. Unlike Martin Luther, who at times had virtually an entire nation behind him, men like de Enzinas were able to trust few of their own countrymen. All three faced opposition to varying degrees, but they all possessed boldness and commitment to Christ that leave a lasting impression. Their lives remind us that Christ expects nothing less from us today.

*Come, all Christians, be committed, To the service of the Lord.*
*Make your lives for Him more fitted, Tune your hearts with one accord.*
*Come into His courts with gladness, Each his sacred vows renew.*
*Turn away from sin and sadness, Be transformed with life anew.*

## The Art of Spiritual Commitment

*Of your time and talents give ye, They are gifts from God above,*
*To be used by Christians freely, To proclaim His wondrous love.*
*Come again to serve the Savior, Tithes and off'rings with you bring.*
*In your work with Him find favor, And with joy His praises sing.*

Eva B. Lloyd,
"Come, All Christians, Be Committed," 1966[5]

## WHAT IT MEANS TO BE ABSOLUTELY COMMITTED

In one chapter I cannot exhaust the possibilities of such a topic as the title of this present section. The following, therefore, will provide a brief sketch of some of the ways we can strive for a holy commitment to Christ and his kingdom. I will first investigate five areas where we can concentrate on commitment in our lives and then address reasons why we often fail in this endeavor. In each area of commitment, I will suggest brief, practical ways we can improve our commitment level.

### Commitment of Money

Martin Luther once said that the last thing of a man to be converted is his wallet. Show me how a person handles money, and I will have great insight into that person's relationship with God. I have seen polls, such as ones from the Barna Group, that show that American Christians tithe around 1 to 2 percent of their income. Imagine how different world missions might be if we gave more generously.

Jesus spoke frequently about money. In fact, few topics appear more often in his teaching; some scholars estimate that one-third of everything he said involved it. He often used money in his examples, simply because it is so important to us. In his parables alone we see it often employed (e.g., parables of the hidden treasure, workers in the vineyard, rich fool, ten minas, rich man and Lazarus, and the lost coin).

Perhaps one of the most difficult parables to interpret, the parable of the shrewd manager (Luke 16:1-8), gives us valuable insight into Jesus's view of money and how to use it properly. This complicated parable has a dishonest manager seemingly commended by Jesus because of how astutely he deals with finances, all in a desperate bid to keep himself from the unemployment line. Of course, the point is not that we should act like dishonest money managers, as the parable seems to teach on the surface. As with virtually all the teaching of Jesus, one needs to dig deeper to find the true meaning. The enigmatic moral of the story is found in verse 9: "I tell you, use worldly wealth to gain friends for yourselves, so that when it is gone, you will be welcomed into eternal dwellings."

Jesus wants to teach us that if the people of the world are shrewd enough to use their earthly possessions to acquire a better future, should the people of the light not act in a superior fashion? Put another way, should we not be concerned with using the possessions we have for something far greater, such as for the kingdom of heaven? Worldly people use their possessions to obtain a better future for just this life. Citizens of the kingdom of heaven have a far greater future to look forward to, and we should use our earthly possessions with that future in mind.

Jesus said in the Sermon on the Mount that we cannot serve both God and money (Matt. 6:24). This comment comes right after his discussion about treasures on earth versus treasures in heaven. So many of us are only focused on earthly things. We pay little mind to eternal matters, and in this way the church has lost her saltiness and the glow of a light on a hilltop. We claim to serve God, but all the while we are serving the almighty dollar, or rand, or pound, or pula. Some people have sarcastically noted that on American money we have the phrase, "In God we trust." Certainly, many people overseas think that American money is precisely the god in which Americans do trust.

Luke's Gospel follows the parable of the shrewd manager with a similar comment about serving God or money. Jesus tells us that if we cannot be trusted with earthly riches, we will not be trusted with the true riches of God's kingdom (16:10-12). Then Luke records the parable of the rich man and Lazarus. Jesus warns of a great reversal to come. Those who were found trusting in their money in this life will have nothing to show for it in the next. How believers handle their money is perhaps the single best litmus test for measuring spiritual maturity.

*Use of money:* For the next month, keep track of how you spend every dollar that you make, with particular attention to how you use your disposable income. Are you wasting too much money on frivolous items, when it could be better spent on the Lord's work?

## Commitment of Time

In the opening verses of his Epistle to Titus, Paul speaks of a "faith and knowledge resting on the hope of eternal life" (v. 2). No matter how much we may rightly emphasize the importance of good Christian living—as Paul will do time and time again in this letter—believers should have their eyes set on something greater: eternal life and eternal matters.

When was the last time you thought about eternity? The furthest most of us think into the future is retirement. Consider this. In about twenty-five years, I will have reached retirement age. If I am fortunate, I will only be on this planet for a total of thirty or forty years from now. What comes after that? Eternity. As the hymn "Amazing Grace" says,

*When we've been there ten thousand years, Bright shining as the sun;*
*We've no less days to sing God's praise, Than when we first begun.*

In other words, after ten thousand years in heaven, we will still have an eternity left. And here I am worrying about a piddling thirty or forty years.

We need to develop an eternal perspective. Often we are caught up in the world's ideals—what can we own, how much money can we make—while our Christian faith and knowledge truly rest on the hope of eternal life. What are we doing for God that will have eternal significance? What are we doing for ourselves that will only last a short time?

The hope of eternal life should drive the Christian to worry more about godly things and less about worldly ones. In this way, we will begin to use our time properly. Wouldn't it be wonderful if we could look back on our lives and know that we drained and squeezed out every moment for its greatest significance?

# TEN THINGS I WISH JESUS NEVER SAID

On January 12, 1723, I made a solemn dedication of myself to God, and wrote it down; giving up myself, and all that I had to God; to be for the future, in no respect, my own; to act as one that had no right to be himself, in any respect. And solemnly vowed to take God for my whole portion and felicity; looking on nothing else, as any part of my happiness, nor acting as if it were; and his law for the constant rule of my obedience: engaging to fight against the world, the flesh and the devil, to the end of my life.

Jonathan Edwards (1703-1758), American theologian and philosopher

When I was younger, deathbed conversions always struck me as the easy way out. I reasoned that when someone was facing death and had no other recourse, professing Christ was undemanding. How mistaken I was.

Deathbed conversions are among the most difficult. Obviously a person cannot fool God with an empty confession; so assuming a deathbed conversion is genuine, that person must admit that his entire life—every single moment, all his activities and plans and designs—was a complete and utter waste. He must acknowledge that he spent his life working for things that were temporal and finite. He has nothing of eternal significance to show for all his labors, and like the apostle Paul, he must confess that before his conversion, all was dung.

What a horrible conclusion to make about your life, especially when you are lying on your deathbed and can do nothing to change it. All opportunities to do anything of eternal significance with your life have slipped away. The regret must be incredibly bitter.

Perhaps the only thing worse would be the case of a believer who has been a Christian for most of his life and still has next to nothing to show for it. Time may be the most precious commodity God has given us, and we need to use it to the fullest for his glory. As J. C. Ryle says, "Let us be willing to do anything, and suffer anything, and give up everything for Christ's sake. It may cost us something for a few years, but great will be the reward in eternity."[6]

*Use of time:* For the next two weeks, keep details of how you spend every minute of the day, from eating and sleeping, to work, church, watching television, prayer, etc. How can you use your time to be more eternally minded? In what ways are you wasting time on temporal concerns, and how can you use that time more efficiently for God's kingdom?

## Commitment of Employment

The father of the modern missionary movement, William Carey (1761-1834), became increasingly appalled by the churches in his homeland of England whose people seemed to care little for the lost of the world. In his seminal work, *Enquiry into the Obligation of Christians to Use Means for the Conversion of the Heathens* (1792), he chastised fellow believers who seemed more concerned with the ways of the world than the ways of God. Driven by a desire to see the gospel spread throughout the globe, he tackled the typical arguments used against foreign missions.

The five main objections usually voiced against missions to foreign soils were: the distance, the barbarism of the people there, the dangers involved, the difficulty of raising support, and the language barriers. Carey effectively argued that if people were motivated by making money, all these barriers would be readily circumvented. "It only requires that we should have as much love to the souls of our fellow-creatures, and fellow sinners, as they [merchants] have for the profits arising from a few otter skins, and all these difficulties could be easily surmounted."[7]

So many of us work ourselves to death so we can make a name for ourselves or buy a bigger home or a fancier automobile, but we hardly lift a finger for the Lord's work. There are people in the world—ungodly, selfish people—who by their work ethic put to shame many evangelical Christians. They will work their fingers to the bone to make more money; yet we who know eternal truths and the eternal God can be among the laziest people in the world. As Christian singer Keith Green sarcastically sang in "Asleep in the Light":

> *Jesus rose from the dead,*
> *And you, you can't even get out of bed.*

We sometimes see this contrast best when it comes to members of cults. In the several years that I lived in a suburb of Chicago, I had religious proselytizers visit my home on five different occasions. In all five instances, they represented cults, such as the Mormons or the Jehovah's Witnesses. Not once did I have someone from a typical, evangelical community come to share the gospel with me.

We must not work for work's sake. Even with our employment, we must look to use it in the best way possible for God's kingdom and his glory.

I am reminded of a missionary who was sent to work on the Muslim-dominated islands of the Comoros in the Indian Ocean. There you are not allowed to outwardly evangelize and witness to people; yet through lifestyle and in private conversation you can share your faith. This missionary had been clearly informed of this, but instead of following the rules, he set out immediately to walk the streets, clearly evangelizing. It was only a few months before he was deported.

I am certain he must have thought he was doing a godly work, but I have doubts about its effectiveness. Had he played by the rules of the country, he might have served many years in the Comoros Islands as salt and light.

I am not advocating that we spend all of our time at work doing things for our church or witnessing to people while we should be preparing reports. We must strike the proper balance between obligation to our employer and obligation to God. But often we are so consumed by work that we do not pause to think about how we can better use it for God's glory.

If we spend all of our time witnessing to people at the water cooler, without doing the work we are being paid to do, we will not make the gospel attractive. As believers, we should be known as the hardest-working, most dependable and honest employees in our company. In this way we can silently share our faith. But I also propose that we look for more overt means. We should not shirk our responsibilities to our employer and busy ourselves with "God's work." That is certainly a recipe for embarrassment. But we can investigate how to use our position at our employment more effectively to attract people to the gospel.

During my years after college, I worked for a metallurgy company as a sales engineer. I called on purchasing agents, plant managers, design engineers—you name it. Had I determined that in every instance I would make sharing the gospel my number one priority to the exclusion of my actual work responsibilities, my employer would have received many complaints, and I would have lost my job. However, in the course of my work, I had many opportunities to share my faith. In some cases, it was with the person I sat next to while on a flight. Or it was the taxi driver who took me from the airport to my hotel. I often took clients out to lunch, and because I did not drink alcohol, I was sometimes asked why. Although my abstaining was not only for religious reasons, it provided an opportunity to speak about my faith nonetheless.

In the normal course of the chitchat that often ensues in sales, I would be asked personal questions about hobbies or free-time activities. This was another opportunity to speak about my faith in inoffensive, unassuming ways. To be honest, I was not always proactive, and I often was lazy and silent in this respect. But never once did anybody complain about it when I did share my faith in these ways. I was able to discern between those who were genuinely interested, and those who, if pushed, would be offended.

Sharing the gospel is not an accidental activity. We must be proactive with it. For many of us, we spend at least forty hours a week—one-third to one-half of our waking hours—employed in the secular world. God has placed us there, not simply to make money or to earn a living but for something far greater. Once we ask God why he has placed us at this job at this specific moment in our lives, we will begin to think of better ways to use that opportunity.

> [The Christian] should look upon every part of his life as a matter of holiness, because it is to be offered unto God.
>
> William Law (1686-1761), *A Serious Call to a Devout and Holy Life*

*Use of employment:* Consider during the next six months how you can use your position at work more strategically for God's kingdom, while always being mindful to strike the proper balance between obligation to your employer and obligation to your Creator.

*Commitment of Talents*

When we truly begin to understand that everything we have is given to us by God, we will become motivated to use all that we have for his glory. So often we act selfishly, as if we exist only for ourselves. My mother used to tell me during my arrogant teen years, "The world doesn't revolve around you, Victor!" I sometimes perceive God still telling me that.

There is perhaps no greater satisfaction than to be complimented for our talents. Some are gifted athletes, others talented musicians, still others endowed with great creative skills. Unfortunately, many of us use these endowments only for our own benefit and praise, while God has given them to us for a greater purpose.

Quite possibly the best-known teaching from Jesus on this subject comes in the parable of the talents (Matt. 25:14-30). Three servants were given talents, a form of money, before the master left for a long journey. Upon his return, only two of the servants had used the talents for greater gain. The last servant simply buried his in the ground. To this servant the master delivered a harsh reprimand, reckoning him as "wicked," "lazy," and "worthless," and the servant was thrown out into the darkness. If this teaching by Jesus does not motivate us to better use of our God-given abilities, nothing will.

On a related matter, we should also work to discover what spiritual gifts we have. Paul tells us God has given each believer certain spiritual gifts, by fact of the indwelling presence of the Holy Spirit (1 Cor. 12:7). I believe discovering those gifts should be a top priority. In my early twenties, taking spiritual gifts tests was instrumental in my recognizing where God wanted me to serve.

Let me use an analogy. So many times Christians struggle with determining what God's will is for their lives. Now consider a spoon and a shovel. You wouldn't take the spoon out to the backyard and start digging a ditch with it, any more than you would take the shovel into the kitchen and use it to stir your coffee. Both the spoon and shovel are designed for specific purposes. So often Christians who are designed to be spoons attempt to perform the work of shovels.

If you want to know God's plan and purpose for your life, look to see how he has designed you. What gifts has he equipped you with for service in his kingdom? There are so many believers in our churches who do not use their spiritual gifts because they do not even know they have them. Even worse, there are some Christians who know they have them but are too lazy or preoccupied with other things to use them. God expects us to do the work he has designed us to do. Our task is to discern that design.

*Use of talents:* Are you using all your abilities in some way to benefit God's kingdom, or only yourself? Take a spiritual gifts inventory to determine how God has gifted you for service in his kingdom and in the body of Christ.

## Commitment of Mind

> The demons, therefore, if they see all Christians . . . labouring cheerfully and advancing, first make an attack by temptation and place hindrances to hamper our way, to wit, evil thoughts.
>
> Athanasius (296-377), *Life of Antony*

How often do we spend time working to increase our career opportunities by furthering our education but do little to advance our understanding of Christian doctrine and piety? In the passage we saw earlier from Titus, Paul speaks of "faith and knowledge," but often evangelical believers begin with the former and never move to the latter.

Paul speaks elsewhere of "renewing your minds" (Rom. 12:2) and concentrating our thinking on noble and godly things (Phil. 4:8). So much of Western Christianity, though, is based on emotion and fluff. We spend time in praise and worship with outstretched arms and open hands but rarely crack open a book during the rest of the week. How many believers today claim to be relying on the Spirit but cannot even name all sixty-six books of the Bible? For all our talk about commitment to the Holy Spirit, we often display little commitment to the Spirit's Word.

Some of the best-selling Christian books today entertain but do not challenge, and in so doing, they discourage Christian maturity rather than encourage it. We are still infants, tossed back and forth by clever heresies and deceitful schemes (Eph. 4:14). Instead of renewing our minds, our minds have become sated by mushy believism.

But the pattern of biblical faith is always proper thinking coupled with proper living, what we call orthodoxy and orthopraxy. The two go side by side. For example, Paul spends the first eleven chapters of Romans speaking about right thinking and proper doctrine (orthodoxy), before he begins to speak about how to live an appropriate Christian life (orthopraxy). He uses the same pattern in Ephesians.

Our actions are determined by our thoughts. What we think will ultimately determine what we do. How we believe will dictate how we live. The notion of a good Christian who lives a life pleasing to God but who knows next to nothing about Christian doctrine and faith is a foreign concept to biblical Christianity.

> First, a mere thought comes to mind, then strong imagination, followed by pleasure, evil delight, and consent.
>
> Thomas à Kempis (1380-1471), *The Imitation of Christ*

Consider what we saw in the previous chapter: When Jesus was tempted by Satan, he used the Word of God in his defense. Conversely, when Eve was tempted by the serpent, she misused the word of the Lord, misquoting what God had said in the commandment (Gen. 3:3). In her mishandling of God's word, coupled with the serpent's warping of it, Eve was deceived and fell into sin.

Too many Christians today are ignorant of God's Word and so fall into deception and sin. They are not adequately prepared to use the "sword of the Spirit" (Eph. 6:17) because they have not studied it or committed it to memory. Can you imagine if Jesus, upon the misuse of Scripture by Satan, had to excuse himself for a moment in a frantic search for his holy book? "I know it's around here somewhere, Satan.

Just wait a minute while I find it. I'm sure my Bible says something about that, I just can't recall off the top of my head." A most pathetic scene it would have been.

The psalmist says, "I have hidden your word in my heart that I might not sin against you" (Ps. 119:11). Instead of viewing Bible study as droll and tiresome, we should recognize it for what it is—life giving and life preserving.

When Paul speaks of "faith and knowledge," we note several things. First, growing in Christian knowledge is important for every believer—not just for pastors and seminary professors. Every Christian must make it a point to grow in knowledge of the truth. This can involve making Bible reading a regular part of the day or week; going to classes that help one grow in understanding of Christian doctrine and beliefs; reading and studying learned books on Christian living, practice, and theology; or regularly attending small-group Bible studies. People do not become knowledgeable Christians by accident. It involves work and commitment.

Second, we learn that faith and knowledge go together. Many Christians today believe they do not need knowledge or understanding. The Holy Spirit will do all the work for them. They do not need to do the hard work of studying; all they need to do is rely on the Spirit. This creates a false dichotomy between faith and knowledge. It encourages believers to act as if the Christian life only involves the heart and not the mind.

Would you prefer that your pastor spent several hours this past week preparing for his sermon so that it makes sense and shows study of God's Word? Or would you rather he sat around and watched television all week, assuming that come Sunday morning, the Spirit would tell him what to say? Have you ever sat through a sermon that was not well prepared? Few things in this world are worse than wasting thirty or forty minutes listening to someone who does not know what he is talking about.

The third thing we learn from Paul's comment about faith and knowledge is that it rests on the hope of eternal life, something we have already discussed. How we use our mind can have eternal consequences.

In the Philippians 4:8 passage, Paul says we should concentrate our thinking on true, noble, right, pure, lovely, admirable, excellent, and praiseworthy things. Stop and think about the opposites of these adjectives and then think about what has been filling your mind. What types of movies do you watch? What television programs do you most enjoy? What jokes do you like to hear? In what types of conversations do you frequently engage?

Do you realize how much filth we allow into our minds? Some Christians frequently rent videos filled with violence, cursing, and sex; yet we wonder why we are not more godly people. Whatever we feed into our minds will ultimately come out in our life and actions. We are what we do, and we do what we allow our minds to dwell upon.

We all know that if all we eat every day is junk food, our bodies will go to waste. The same applies to our minds. If we feed our minds junk food, we can expect our minds to produce junk. Lance Armstrong knows that unless he maintains a strict diet, he cannot compete in the Tour de France. As Christians, we must train ourselves to filter out the junk and filth that surround us every day, or we will not be able to effectively run the race of faith.

In committing our minds fully to God, then, we need to excise those things harmful to our faith and piety and build up those things that help us to grow in knowledge and wisdom.

*Use of the mind:* In what concrete ways can you increase your knowledge of the Christian faith? Do you voluntarily feed your mind with junk food? In the next year find opportunities for joining a small-group Bible study or taking a course at a nearby Christian college or via distance learning, or read several books on select topics. If you normally read five books of Christian fiction per year, exchange two of those slots for meatier reading on Christian doctrine or Christian living.

*So whether you eat or drink or whatever you do, do it all for the glory of God.*

The apostle Paul, 1 Corinthians 10:31

Even something as seemingly mundane as eating or drinking can be done to the glory of God. Let us look to better use our money, time, employment, talents, and minds for God's kingdom and his glory. In this way, we will be placing our hands on the plow and moving forward.

## WHY CHRISTIANS OFTEN LACK THE COMMITMENT OF TRUE DISCIPLES

Luke provides three examples in the context of the plow passage (9:57-62). There he recounts three men who each make a certain level of commitment to following Christ but who do not take it to the level necessary to please Jesus.

The first man approaches Jesus with an offer to follow him. Jesus reminds him that such a commitment will not be easy. "Foxes have holes and birds of the air have nests, but the Son of Man has no place to lay his head." In other words, becoming a disciple of Christ will not involve the perks one might expect to accompany such a calling. Even the Son of Man does not have a regular place to rest, let alone other luxuries that we anticipate in life. Only those truly serious should apply for the post.

The second man is invited by Jesus to follow him. In this case, though, the man first asks to go and bury his father. The seemingly cold-hearted reply by Jesus must be understood in the context of first-century Judaism, which will only make it appear even more coldhearted. "The duty of burial took precedence over the study of the law, the Temple service, the killing of the Passover sacrifice, the observance of circumcision and the reading of the Megillah."[8] In this case, the man is told that even the most stringent need of his culture is not enough reason to excuse himself from the duty of following Christ. Everything else must become secondary.

The third man makes an offer similar to that of the first but with a caveat. It is in Jesus's reply to this man that we have the statement that forms the subject of this chapter. In all three cases, the men show themselves to be unfit for service as Christ's disciples. This attitude is also seen in the well-known "bread of life" passage of John 6, where we are told that after some hard teachings from Jesus, "many of his disciples turned back and no longer followed him" (v. 66).[9]

Why do we so often find people who initially are willing to commit themselves to Christ but who later turn from the plow? For the remainder of our time, let me briefly suggest three reasons many believers do not possess the commitment required to be a disciple of Jesus.

### Sunday-morning Christians

A synonym for *commitment* is the word *devotion,* and in studying these two words, we gain valuable insight into the error many Christians make in envisioning devotion. Normally, we speak of "devotions" as either the time of corporate worship, such as Sunday morning at church, or our personal quiet times when we read God's Word and pray. With this approach, we have produced a bifurcation between "sacred" and "secular" time.

The first day of the week we sing hymns of praise to God and give him all the glory, while the other six days of the week we give him nary a thought or care. Sunday we proclaim, "Glory to God," and Monday through Saturday it is, "Glory to me." It is almost as if we are saying, "God, here is the time during the week that I allot to you. The rest of the time is *my* time, and I plan to do anything I want with it."

It reminds me of the anecdote about the church that would collect the tithes and offerings and deliver them to the front of the sanctuary. An elder would take the offering plate and throw the money up into the air, with it tumbling back down all around him. A visitor one day asked the pastor after the service why they did that with the money, to which the pastor replied, "Oh, you see, we throw it up into the air, and everything God catches he can keep."

Our entire lives should be devotional. When Paul speaks of offering our bodies as "living sacrifices," he concludes by calling this life commitment a "spiritual act of worship" (Rom. 12:1). "Devotion" is a twenty-four-hour activity, not just something we do several hours on Sundays or Wednesday evenings.

Our commitment to Christ is so paltry at times. I must confess that my time during the week is frequently absent of concentration on God as I am consumed by other pressing matters. Come Sunday morning, I feel the need for recommitment, and I sense the Spirit urging me onward. But come Monday morning, I fall back into my lackadaisical attitude. Often my commitment is only stoked from Sunday to Sunday, as if the Sabbath were the only day granted for God.

## Are We Self-Deceived?

The risen Lord said to the church at Laodicea, "I know your deeds, that you are neither cold nor hot. I wish you were either one or the other! So, because you are lukewarm—neither hot nor cold—I am about to spit you out of my mouth" (Rev. 3:15-16). This statement by our Lord confused me the first several times I read it. I can understand why he would want us to be hot instead of lukewarm, but why cold? Wouldn't that be worse? The answer is found in what it means to be hot, cold, and lukewarm.

Someone who is hot is obviously on fire for Christ and his kingdom. This is the type of disciple the Lord desires. Someone who is cold is far away from his kingdom and the life of faith God requires. The problem rests with someone who is lukewarm. This is the type of person who thinks he is quite okay but in actuality is not. With the cold person, there is a genuine hope that such a person will recognize his spiritual poverty and repent. But a lukewarm person who is self-deceived does not recognize his spiritual destitution. Instead of understanding his need, as the cold person can do, he actually thinks he is hot.

Is this not the position in which the believers in Laodicea are found? The Lord says to them, "You say, 'I am rich; I have acquired wealth and do not need a thing.' But you do not realize that you are wretched, pitiful, poor, blind and naked" (Rev. 3:17). What a horrible position to be in, to think yourself safe and secure, while you are in dire danger.[10]

In the Sermon on the Mount, Jesus speaks of salt that has lost its saltiness (Matt. 5:13), an image similar to that of being lukewarm. So many believers are self-deceived. Like the Christians at Laodicea, they claim to be committed to God, but they are wretched and pitiful. Thinking themselves hot, they are really tepid, and as such, their lives lack the commitment required of the disciples of Christ.

## Double-minded Disciples

In the last chapter, Abraham's nephew Lot served as an excellent example of someone who lived by sight and not by faith. In this chapter, it is his wife who serves as a ready example of double-mindedness. Lot's wife was not turned into salt just because God felt like creating a nifty judgment with spices. Rather, as the sulfur and brimstone came falling from the sky upon Sodom and Gomorrah, Lot's wife turned back to the cities. We should not make the mistake of thinking this was a simple glance. Rather, it was a full movement backward, a returning to the cities.

Moses makes it clear in the account that not only were the cities destroyed, but everything in the general vicinity as well. In turning back and attempting to return to Sodom, Lot's wife was overtaken by the raining brimstone and suffered the same fate as the inhabitants still in the cities.

James speaks of double-minded people, saying that they are "unstable in all [they do]" (1:8). Jesus summed up this idea in the Sermon on the Mount when he said, "No one can serve two masters. Either he will hate the one and love the other, or he will be devoted to the one and despise the other" (Matt. 6:24a). It is the picture of a person torn, wanting to go two opposite directions.

In Paul's imagery of the armor of God in Ephesians 6, he speaks of the belt of truth. In the Roman soldier's attire, the belt was the first thing put in place because all the other pieces of the armor attached to it. *Truth* here has the sense of integrity or truthfulness, and *integrity* implies wholeness or oneness, much as in mathematics we speak of whole numbers like 1, 2, 3 as integers. The soldier of God, therefore, is not double-minded, not one who possesses a fractious mind.

We cannot properly engage the battle with one eye on our enemy and the other looking elsewhere. Similarly, we cannot serve the Lord with our mind on him and our heart on our worldly desires. We must be fully dedicated soldiers. Truthfulness—integrity, single-minded-ness—must be the belt that holds everything else in place. Without truth as our belt, the rest of our armor will fall off. Double-minded believers are ill-fit to serve in the Lord's army, but so many of us suffer from split allegiances. As such, we do not possess the necessary commitment Christ desires and deserves.

## ARE WE PLOWING A STRAIGHT LINE FORWARD?

The imagery Jesus uses in Luke 9 echoes the idea of lukewarm com-mitment and double-mindedness. "No one who puts his hand to the plow and looks back is fit for service in the kingdom of God." Those in the first century who came from an agricultural background found many of the examples used by Jesus to be familiar and understandable; but today, in our mostly industrial society, we might miss the verbal pic-tures Jesus created. My travels to parts of Africa, especially Ethiopia, have made these biblical images easier to understand.

Consider the idea of plowing while looking backward. The farmer stands behind one or two beasts that are pulling the plow. As the ani-mals move forward, the farmer must place incredible pressure down-ward on the plow. This is no simple task; it involves great strength and coordination. Not only must the farmer push the plow downward, but he must also steady it from moving horizontally. If the plow is not ver-tically steady, the plow line will be uneven. If he does not push down hard enough, the plow line will be too shallow.

Furthermore, he must make sure the animals are moving properly. This normally means employing a whip to keep them moving and in line. Considering again the words of Jesus, it is really impossible to plow in a straight line and control the animals while looking backward.

If we need a more modern analogy to convey the same truth, con-sider driving down the highway while fiddling with the children in the backseat. It takes little imagination to envision the catastrophe that would ensue. If I may paraphrase the words of Jesus, "No one who puts his hand on the steering wheel and looks back is fit for service in the kingdom of God."

This is what Christ calls us to do. A commitment short of this ideal—a steadfast fixity of purpose—is a commitment unfit for his service. Let us commit—or recommit—ourselves to Christ. Let us begin to view *all* of our life as devotional, entrusting every facet of it to God and his glory. Only in this way can we plow a straight line forward for Christ.

> This, indeed, is no ordinary matter, no common casualty of the law of nature; but it is that illustrious devotion, that fighting for the faith, wherein whosoever loses his life for God saves it, so that you may here again recognize the Judge who recompenses the evil gain of life with its destruction, and the good loss thereof with its salvation.[11]
>
> Tertullian (150-212),
> *The Five Books Against Marcion*

# 4

# THE ART OF
# SPIRITUAL SELF-CRUCIFIXION

*If anyone would come after me, he must deny himself and take up his cross daily and follow me.*

JESUS CHRIST, LUKE 9:23

*But the believing soul longs and faints for God; she rests sweetly in the contemplation of Him. She glories in the reproach of the Cross, until the glory of His face shall be revealed.*

ST. BERNARD OF CLAIRVAUX (1090-1153),

*ON LOVING GOD*

*It is impossible for a human heart, without crosses and tribulations, to think upon God.*

MARTIN LUTHER (1483-1546), *TABLE TALK*

I often wonder what it was like when Abraham was commanded to sacrifice his son Isaac. The account in Genesis 22 is told with Abraham as the main character, and Isaac is hardly noticed save for a few lines of speech. But what was going through the boy's mind? I can only imagine my own son, who is roughly the same age Isaac is thought to have been at that time, walking with me to a place where we planned to kill an animal. Only upon arriving there do I tell him that he will be killed rather than any animal. I visualize the trust draining from his eyes. His father, whom he knows loves him dearly and in whom he has placed his childlike faith, is ready to kill him. I picture the look of terror in his eyes as I lay hands on him to do the terrible deed.

# TEN THINGS I WISH JESUS NEVER SAID

We normally consider the anguish from the perspective of the devastated father Abraham, but what about the equally devastated son Isaac? Did he attempt to run away? Did he put up any resistance as his father bound him with rope and lifted him up on the altar? When he saw the knife pulled from his father's belt, did he cry out? As his father slowly moved the weapon toward his throat, did Isaac try to squirm away?

In my office is a piece of reproduced art that I treasure. It is a painting by the great Dutch artist Rembrandt, *The Sacrifice of Isaac.* Rembrandt did not use vivid colors, and the entire portrait is more drab and brownish than anything else. Still the imagery is powerful. Isaac lies on his arms bound behind his back, propped up on a fagot of wood, with Abraham's left hand entirely over his son's face. The picture is dreadful as Abraham's hand pushes Isaac's head backward, exposing the boy's tender throat. Above Abraham is the angel, grasping the patriarch's right hand at the wrist as the knife falls to the ground. I cannot discern if the look on Abraham's face is more of shock than relief, but he certainly would have felt both of those emotions at that moment.

When I gaze at that portrait, the item I most ponder—the one that always catches my eye first and to which my eyes naturally wander—is Abraham's full hand over the entire face of Isaac. Did he place it there so the boy could not see the knife? Or did he put his hand there so Abraham himself would not have to see the look of horror in his son's eyes?

Questions continue to flood my mind as I contemplate Rembrandt's masterpiece. Did Abraham go about his business with a cold detachment, a man of unwavering faith who had absolutely no doubt in his mind about the terrible deed he was about to perform? When Jesus faced his great act of faith in the Garden of Gethsemane, he certainly felt the pain and anguish. Did Abraham feel similarly as he was about to sacrifice his only son, the son of the promise?

Unfortunately, the account gives us no record of emotions. But when I put myself in the place of Abraham and this awful position, tears always well up in my eyes. I cannot imagine the severe trial it would have presented me had I been asked to sacrifice my son on that dreadful altar.

What about Isaac? How often do I put myself in *his* place when I contemplate the story? Not often enough. But this is precisely what God is asking me to do. He is asking me to willingly position my body across the altar of sacrifice. There is no second party forcing me onto the wood and kindling; I am asked to place myself there willingly.

When I realize I am the one intended to be sacrificed, I begin to kick and scream and fight for freedom. But it is precisely in the act of sacrifice that I am most free. Jesus teaches that if I greedily hold onto my life, I will lose it.

I suppose there was no one happier to see that ram caught in the thicket than Isaac. He certainly would have remembered that day the rest of his life, and I assume his father was not lax in reminding him of the great provision of the Lord.

Several chapters in this book are interrelated. The idea of carrying one's cross encompasses self-mutilation (chapter 2), absolute spiritual commitment, even when it hurts (chapter 3), and self-loathing (chapter 8). In the attempt not to be redundant, I have separated certain aspects of cross-carrying into these individual chapters. In fact, this chapter and the next will have much to say concerning the related topic of suffering. Therefore, not everything associated with carrying one's cross will be covered in this chapter.

I intend to deal with the topic in three simple steps. First we will investigate what it meant at the time of Jesus to carry a cross. Then we will evaluate how we are called to do it; lastly, we will examine why.

## A HORRIFYING IMAGE

When Jesus told his disciples to carry their cross, what went through their minds?

In the past public executions were commonplace. Few people had not witnessed one sometime in their life. Even in America half a century ago, it was not uncommon to have a public execution. Now, however, only a select few people will witness one, usually the families of the victims. Although I am not advocating that we go back to a time of public hangings and electrocutions, it is unfortunate that most people today have no real sense of what Christ means when he speaks of a cross.

Instead of a piece of jewelry hanging from a person's neck or an icon in a place of worship, the cross was a despised and fearsome object in first-century Rome. The cross symbolized absolute pain and agony. The Romans knew how horrible it was to die in this fashion, thus limiting this cruel form of execution to non-citizens of the empire. (The evil of men is best seen in our devising instruments of torture, which we reserve for all but ourselves.)

In many cases, people not only witnessed the crucifixion, but they witnessed the procession of the criminal as well. As in the case of Jesus, this often involved carrying one's own crossbeam to the place of death. Imagine if today the one to be executed were told that he had to plug in all the electrical conduits or fill the needle with the lethal fluid before sitting down into the chair of death.

In the processional leading to the execution, all could see the fear in the eyes of the dead man walking. For some, this was a welcome sight, usually because the man deserved it or because some people were bloodthirsty. Even today many people revel in the raucous scenes of talk-show guests flinging chairs and foul words at each other or professional wrestlers inflicting cruel blows upon one another. Like the participants at the games in the Coliseum, too many people today cannot wait to see another victim's flesh devoured by the wild beasts.

But the fearful eyes of the criminal also spoke to other people of more sensibility. You do not watch such a gruesome event and eagerly want to become a participant. Rather, you endeavor at all costs to avoid it.

Once again, Jesus turns our natural inclinations upside down. Not only should we not avoid such a horrifying affair, but we should willingly subject ourselves to it. Imagine that long walk to the executioner's platform or up the hill of crucifixion. All earthly hopes are gone. Every dream you had, every comfort you desired—all of it has passed away. This is what Jesus's calling requires of each of us who would deign to wear the title Disciple of Christ.

> Denying oneself is not a matter of giving up something, whether for Lent or for the whole of life: it is a decisive saying "No" to oneself, to one's hopes and plans and ambitions, to one's likes and dislikes, to one's nearest and dearest, for the sake of Christ.
>
> F. F. Bruce (1910-1990),
> *Hard Sayings of Jesus*

## THE SACRIFICE OF THE SELF

Consider an animal sacrifice. The creature is lifted up and placed on the altar, where it is bound and its blood spilled. Of course, we do not come from a society where animal sacrifice is common, but in biblical times the picture of sacrifice was familiar.

Paul commands believers to "offer your bodies as living sacrifices" (Rom. 12:1). Unfortunately, like the example of a cross, much of the imagery of this powerful figure of speech is lost on us today. However, try to picture what a *living* sacrifice must be like. The sacrifice squirms and fights and claws. It does not want to be thrust upon the altar where its throat is customarily slit. Willingly carrying a cross is like willingly climbing up on the altar to be slaughtered.

As often happens in Christianity, a certain catchword or phrase gets thrown around so often that we lose sight of its original meaning. In this case, "carry your cross" can fall into that category, and we may find ourselves wondering what it means. The idea of carrying one's cross has become trivialized. It has developed into one of those evangelical slogans like "I am saved from my sins," or "Did you ask Jesus into your heart?" Neither of these statements is all that bad, but in the attempt to distill the gospel message into an easy-to-remember phrase, such statements have become somewhat inaccurate and imprecise.[1] The same applies when it comes to bearing our cross. Often we hear someone speak of a difficulty as "the cross that I must bear." Perhaps it is putting up with a persnickety or prickly workmate or an automobile that consistently breaks down, but this is hardly what Jesus meant. We have watered down the impact of this command by making it a slogan of evangelicalism.[2] But cross-carrying was hardly meant to be a catchy motto. It was intended to be a lifelong, life-changing practice. In line with what we saw in the three patterns of temptation (1 John 2:16), I want to investigate how carrying our cross is meant to counter those tactics of the Evil One.

*Crucify the Sexual Self*

Sexual sins are sadly common in the body of Christ. While we rarely revel in them like the immoral brother in Corinth did (1 Cor. 5), they are present. In a society that saturates us with sexual images, too many believers have fallen prey to this effective tactic of Satan.

There are few drives of human nature more powerful than the sexual drive. Unfortunately, with the growth of technology has come the greater ability to slake the thirst of this beast than ever before. The lust of the eyes can be satisfied via rented videos, pornographic software and magazines that seem ubiquitous, and now most effectively by means of the Internet. In the past, virtually all ways of meeting the urges of this monster involved looking someone else in the eye, either when buying a magazine over the counter or in renting a video. For some people, getting over the hurdle of that embarrassment was enough to keep them from the sin. But today a person can sit in the privacy of his or her own home and indulge in these "pleasures" without ever having to account to anyone else.

The insidious lie in this is that we can fool ourselves into believing that no one is getting hurt; but we forget Paul's injunction concerning sexual sin: "All other sins a man commits are outside his body, but he who sins sexually sins against his own body" (1 Cor. 6:18b). We primarily destroy ourselves whenever we sin sexually.

When Jesus said in the Sermon on the Mount that we must pluck out our eye if it causes us to sin, it was no mistake that this command followed his comments on adultery. In fact, if we recognize the progression in that teaching, Jesus noted that adultery starts in the heart, but can rapidly move to the eyes and then the hands. This provides us with valuable insight into how to fight and conquer this beast.

In chapter 1, I noted that material poverty is a means to spiritual poverty. Specifically, if we can curb our natural urge for food via the exercise of fasting, we can learn to better control other natural impulses. In chapter 3, we looked at areas of commitment, one involving the mind. What we dwell upon in our minds will ultimately bear fruit in our actions. For example, too many people believe the lie that they can look at pornography, and it will end there. It will not lead to greater evils. But what addict of pornography can honestly say his addiction did not first begin with a small, seemingly harmless glance? We foolishly believe that we can open the door for Satan just a crack, and it will remain there, but Satan will certainly not be satisfied with standing out in the hallway peeking in. He will only be content when he is fully standing in the room with us.

Not only is this spiritually foolish reasoning, but it does not even stand up to worldly wisdom. It is clear that people who were promiscuous before marriage have a much higher chance of becoming adulterers than those who remained chaste before marriage. Rarely does Satan hit us squarely between the eyes with the grossest of sins. He prefers to tempt us in more subtle ways, and before we know it, we have done things we would never have dreamt of doing a short time earlier.

What do we allow our eyes to dwell upon? If I see a pretty woman walking down the street, my eyes might naturally gaze for a moment at her. If my gaze ends there, then I have not sinned. But if I decide to take a further, longer look to absorb all the details, and further, if I begin to dwell on those details in my mind and allow myself to dream unmentionable thoughts, I have committed adultery in my heart. Once I allow such things to enter my heart, it may be a short time before they seep into my mind on a regular basis. Once my mind has become corrupted, my actions will soon follow.

> For evil thoughts will hold sway in us just so long as they are hidden in the heart.
>
> John Cassian (360-435), *Conferences*

David Robinson, the MVP basketball center who played over a decade for the San Antonio Spurs, set an example in this regard that other Christians should note. Whenever the scantily-clad cheerleaders for the Spurs came onto the court to dance, Robinson stared down at his feet. He said he did this for two reasons: to honor and respect his wife and to guard himself from temptation. This is wisdom we should all take to heart.

Let us not also make the mistake of thinking that sexual sin only involves raw lust. In many instances, the driving force of sexual sin is not lust but pride. We are flattered that others find us attractive, and often we can allow this to go to our heads. Everyone enjoys adulation, especially if it involves how we look. The woman who feels neglected by her husband, or the man who has reached an age where attracting younger women means he still has "it," can be driven more by ego than lust.

We must crucify the sexual self. We must make our bodies our slaves, not allow them to enslave us with their passions and urges. Such crucifixion begins with our eyes, just as much temptation does. Strict self-control in what we allow ourselves to look at will go a long way in guarding us from sexual sin.

## Crucify the Material Self

A theme runs throughout the first three chapters of this book, and that theme has to do with the love affair many Western Christians have with material wealth. As a lecturer in an African seminary, I am often confronted with difficult questions that surround how Christ and one's culture interact. Not wanting to be another paternalistic, white missionary from the West who only criticizes African culture, I have had to take a hard look at my own culture and upbringing. I have taught my students that the gospel confronts *all* cultures.

Americans have a distinct worldview formed by our culture, as surely as the African from a particular tribe or people group does. Often we Americans look at other peoples and are puzzled as to why they think and act the way they do, but the exact questions are asked by others who are perplexed by Americans and the things that seem so important to us.

I have asked myself the same questions I have told my students to ask: "What in my culture or society is contrary to the gospel? What does my society or culture desire that conflicts with Scripture?" The first thing that comes to my mind when I consider my American culture is material wealth.

Living overseas can have a dramatic effect on one's perspective. In our first four-year term in Namibia, we lived with very little. Our mission's mind-set encouraged a simple-living mentality, and for those four years I was even afraid to buy a microwave oven. In the first several months in the small town where we were stationed, we had a bookshelf, a table, and two plastic chairs in our living room. It was only four months later that I purchased a sofa for my wife's birthday. Only after a year did we have a television, and it was nearly two years before we bought a VCR. This was considerably different from our life previously in the States where we owned all of these things and much more.

After our first term we moved back to America for a year of home assignment. At the time people we knew were moving, and we came for a visit shortly after they had occupied their new home. I was shocked by all the stuff they owned. Each room seemed jam-packed with possessions. Four years earlier I would not have even noticed it, but after living in Namibia, things became more obvious to me.

Unfortunately, we Americans teach our children to become comfortable with excess. One Namibian friend refers to the USA as the United States of Abundance, and that is certainly true. The United States has been materially blessed by God in ways greater than any other nation on the planet and perhaps any nation in history. But with this great blessing comes great responsibility. God cares deeply about how we use the resources he has given us, both as individuals and as a nation. For example, we are the most obese people in the world. We also spend more money each year on entertainment (cinema and sports) than the bottom third of the countries in the world spend on anything, period.

Now before you think I have become one of those missionaries who arrogantly bashes his home country and who ultimately becomes anti-American by extended overseas living, let me defend myself with a brief story. In my early twenties, I was in a Sunday school class when missionaries from Afghanistan came to visit and share their ministry. After a short teaching, for the last fifteen minutes of their time this couple blasted Americans and our opulent lifestyle. I remember the pointed chastisement: "Americans spend billions of dollars each year feeding pet dogs and cats while there are millions of people in the world who are starving."

I yawned. *Just another one of those arrogant America-bashing missionaries,* I thought. That was more than fifteen years ago. Only now do I see why they were complaining.

Granted, I do not think they went about communicating their point in the best manner. I certainly did not think feeding my pet kitten was such a crime as they made it out to be. In fact, five years later when I was leaving for the mission field with my family, I told my closest friends that if I ever returned with that same snotty attitude, please put a bullet in my head.

Now, though, I see what they were getting at. Of course, if all Americans stopped feeding their pets, I do not think world hunger would automatically disappear. But as Christians we do need to evaluate our priorities. How much stuff do we need? Do we really need a DVD collection that big? Would we have died if we did not purchase the recent music CD from the latest up-and-coming pop star? What do we teach our children about godly use of possessions when we get them private phone lines and televisions for their bedrooms? Would it not be better to teach them self-control and restraint in these areas rather than unreserved indulgence?

As an American, at times I am patriotic to a fault, especially if there is a war somewhere that we need to either start or finish. But I must declare that I am first and foremost a Christian. My allegiance to my country, no matter how strong it is, cannot usurp my allegiance to Christ. Unfortunately, the ideals of my culture are often contrary to those of Jesus. In that case, I must choose to follow Christ and abandon my traditional values, just as surely as I tell my African students to do the same when faced with similar conflicts. I cannot allow the ideals that define my American culture to turn me away from my allegiance to Christ. The materialism of our society is certainly one area in which we regularly are torn between cultural norms that seem natural to us and following Jesus, which often involves crucifying those norms within us.

> For when Scripture enjoins us to lay aside private regard to ourselves,
> it not only divests our minds of an excessive longing for wealth, or
> power, or human favour, but eradicates all ambition and thirst for
> worldly glory, and other more secret pests.
>
> John Calvin (1509-1564),
> *On the Christian Life*

## Crucify the Worldly Self

I have already addressed the worldly ideals of the accumulation of wealth and pleasures of sensuality. Here I want to specifically address other worldly ideals that often secretly mold us and give direction to our lives.

In some instances, those ideals can be helpful. A capitalist model often engenders a positive work ethic, albeit normally driven by the desire to make money and acquire possessions. Still, there are many hard-working Americans who provide for their families simply because our culture tells us hard-working people become successful people. This is a positive aspect of our culture, even if it can be driven by less-than-stellar goals.

However, our society also is strongly individualistic and "me-centered." We have a tendency to "look out for number one" and often have less regard for others. Whereas in many of our organizations and structures individuality is encouraged, there is little place for it in the body of Christ. Can you imagine an arm proclaiming its independence from the rest of the body? Not only would the arm become gangrenous and rot away, but the body would be damaged by its absence. While the world tends to teach us to be self-focused, as believers we must endeavor to be others-focused. This is expressed in Jesus's command to deny ourselves.

The world also trains us to be now-focused. We seek instant pay-offs and quick fixes. This is seen in how we view sex (often trading the long-term benefits of commitment and monogamy for the short-term pleasures of immediate gratification) and how we use our possessions (often wasting money on frivolous or mindless activities or items instead of investing with longer-term goals in mind).

> The principal use of the cross is that it in various ways accustoms us to despise the present and excites us to aspire to the future life.
>
> John Calvin (1509-1564),
> *On the Christian Life*

Cross-carrying has a wonderful way of moving our focus from temporal concerns to eternal matters. As we noted earlier, our view is frequently myopic, and we often make decisions based on this shortsightedness. God wants us to focus on greater ideals than just what exists in this life. We love this world too much and do not recognize that we are only strangers and sojourners here. Our true, eternal home is elsewhere. Thus Paul can say, "If only for this life we have hope in Christ, we are to be pitied more than all men" (1 Cor. 15:19).

In many respects, this is what is embodied in the pride of life. We become so arrogantly caught up in our present accomplishments, excitements, and preoccupations that we lose sight of what is beyond and far greater. We cannot love both the world and God (James 4:4; 1 John 2:15). The fallen systems and powers of this rotating ball are coming to an end. Yet even as Christians who possess eternal truths, we pathetically run after the world and its ideals. We pant and puff for more wealth, greater power, and increasing privileges, and in so doing, we despise the cross.

> For there is no medium between the two things: the earth must either be worthless in our estimation, or keep us enslaved by an intemperate love of it.
>
> John Calvin (1509-1564),
> *On the Christian Life*

## Crucify the Egotistical Self

In his *Confessions*, Augustine often speaks about his pre-conversion days and how he had an almost insatiable need to achieve. Many Christians are the same today. We may claim to put Jesus first, but the simple fact is, we are just as driven by the world's goals and desires as anybody else. This is perhaps no better seen than in our aim to exalt ourselves.

In the *Spiritual Exercises* of Ignatius of Loyola (1491-1556), founder of the Jesuits, Ignatius envisioned his prescriptions as "spiritual exercises to conquer oneself." In an age when we are taught to actualize ourselves, conquering ourselves is not an option. The people who overcome adversity are the ones we laud, not the ones who are overcome by it.

I intend to speak more about this crucifixion of the egotistical self in chapter 8, so I will not dwell on the point any further now.

> This is the principal part of the great Christian duty of self-denial. That duty consists in two things, viz., first, in a man's denying his worldly inclinations, and in forsaking and renouncing all worldly objects and enjoyments; and, secondly, in denying his natural self-

**97**

exaltation, and renouncing his own dignity and glory and in being emptied of himself; so that he does freely and from his very heart, as it were renounce himself, and annihilate himself.

Jonathan Edwards (1703-1758),

*A Treatise Concerning Religious Affections*

## LESSONS FROM HISTORY

This time, instead of concentrating on people from the distant past, I want to consider those in the near-term history of the church. Perhaps there is no better example of this godly attitude of cross-carrying than in the body of men and women who serve as missionaries. I do not say this because I am a missionary, for I know full well that my self-denial has been meager when compared to many of my compatriots.

Namibia, and especially the capital Windhoek, is a first-world location in many respects. I am not one to romanticize living in a mud hut with no plumbing or power. In Windhoek I have ready access to the Internet, drinkable water from the tap, and consistent electricity. So many comforts that we in the West take for granted, I also enjoy in Namibia. Even further, I have the benefit of working in a country that is decidedly Christian, with estimates reaching as high as 90 percent of the population professing allegiance to Christ.

However, many missionaries face very different conditions. In some instances, we cannot even publicly speak about their work because they labor in what missiologists call "closed-access nations." They face the daily pressure of living among people who are not simply closed to the gospel; in most cases, they have been taught to hate it.

Then there are those who can openly serve as missionaries, but in so doing they place themselves at great risk. Fellow missionaries who work in Somaliland do not simply fear expulsion from the country if they overstep the legal bounds of anti-evangelism of the land. They literally risk a bullet to the head. A series of executions in that hostile land—one of a missionary doctor, another a nurse who for more than

thirty years served that country's ill—caused the leadership of a prominent evangelical mission agency to begin to question the wisdom of
leaving missionaries there. In every instance, when asked if they wanted
to leave, missionaries said no. They had made their choice *before* going
to that area of the world, knowing the risks involved.

Martyrdom for them was not a hypothetical possibility as it was
before they went to the field. It was a bloody reality as they saw other
missionaries gunned down (in one case in front of her own home, the
other right in it). Yet they were willing to stand their ground. It was the
mission leadership who ultimately pulled them out, unwilling to accept
any more risks.[3]

I am always quick to point out to people, who errantly believe that
I must be an incredibly holy guy because I am a missionary, that I am
only serving where the Lord has called me to serve. But secretly I am
glad he has not called me to serve in the aforementioned places. In fact,
much of my early resistance to missions, when I began in my early twenties to investigate entering full-time ministry, was for this reason. I was
afraid God would send me to a place I would hate.

The fear of sacrifice and self-crucifixion is not unnatural, but if we
allow it to dominate our emotions, we will become feeble disciples. Two
problems present themselves in this respect. The first is that we make
supreme sacrifice the hallmark of the "super Christians," while the rest
of us reside in the "normal Christian" category. Only super Christians
have to endure persecution and severe trials, while the rest of us are left
to lead simple, unchallenged lives. Because we have a low view of the
demands of discipleship, we do not expect to carry our cross, let alone
to lay down our lives.

A worse problem, though, is that we begin to despise the notion of
sacrifice. Many in the prosperity movement today view persecution, trials, and hardships in the Christian life as beneath a believer's calling.
When difficulties come, it is due to a lack of faith, not the presence of
necessary discipleship training. Anything less than health and wealth is
unbecoming.

The Catholic humanist Erasmus (1469-1536) recognized this same attitude in the leadership of his day. In his *In Praise of Folly*, speaking of the clergy and particularly the popes, Erasmus noted:

> To work miracles is old and antiquated, and not in fashion now; to instruct the people, troublesome; to interpret the Scripture, pedantic; to pray, a sign one has little else to do; to shed tears, silly and womanish; to be poor, base; to be vanquished, dishonorable and little becoming him that scarce admits even kings to kiss his slipper; and lastly, to die, uncouth; and to be stretched on a cross, infamous.

We must guard ourselves from both errant views. Carrying one's cross is a command for *all* believers, not just the ones we label superlative. Similarly, we can never make it a sign of a lack of faith or Christian commitment. As we noted in our opening chapter, this was the mistake of Job's friends. Rather than being a symptom of sinfulness, hardships are often an indication of godly commitment.

*Jesus, I my cross have taken, All to leave, and follow Thee;*
*Destitute, despised, forsaken, Thou from hence, my all shalt be:*
*Perish ev-'ry fond ambition, All I've sought, and hoped, and known;*
*Yet, how rich is my condition, God and Heav'n are still my own!*

*Let the world despise and leave me, They have left my Savior too;*
*Human hearts and looks deceive me; Thou are not, like man, untrue;*
*And, while Thou shalt smile upon me, God of wisdom, love, and might,*
*Foes may hate, and friends may shun me; Show Thy face, and all is bright.*

Henry F. Lyte (1793-1847), "Jesus, I My Cross Have Taken," 1831

## OUR DAILY DUTY

Too often believers think once they have become converted, the job is done and they can bask in the glory. Fact is, the difficult work is just beginning. Our justification is clearly effected when we profess the simple faith of a child in the accomplished work of Christ, but our sanctification can be a bloody, excruciating process. This is why Jesus says we must *daily* take up our cross. Along with daily bread must come daily agony. Our conversion may have involved getting on our knees and praying the "sinner's prayer," but our sanctification will involve white knuckles, sweaty brows, and tearful cheeks. It should be a daily, painful process of purging, where we submit our wills entirely to the Lord's.

I once counseled a couple having marital difficulties. It boiled down to the husband acting selfishly and not caring properly for his spouse. He was more interested in her obedience than anything else, and when he perceived that it was lacking, he became verbally abusive. I explained to him that, whereas a wife must submit to her husband, a husband must love his wife like Christ loved the church. In fact, as a selfish husband myself, I know how difficult this command of Christlike love can be. The husband looked seriously at me and said that he truly loved his wife in this fashion. He explained that if a train were coming down the tracks, he would throw himself out in front of it to save her. This he envisioned to be the supreme expression of love.

We are often led to such heroic thoughts of love when we consider what it involves, but love is not only expressed in this way, nor is it necessarily expressed best via such acts of heroism. If I may speak bluntly, I would find it easier to put my life on the line to save my wife from a mugger or housebreaker than to lay down my life in the daily process of loving her. How many men during courtship run around to the other side of the car to open the door for their potential wife but are entirely unwilling to do it for her once they are married?

The same applies to my walk with Christ. I can envision myself making the final, great stand for Jesus, facing the axe of the executioner, boldly going to prison. But when it comes to the daily grind of following Christ, I often stumble. Our love and commitment for Jesus are usually better proved in the small, day-to-day choices we make than in that one fantastic act of heroism we occasionally imagine. Fact is, most of us in the Western church will never have to make such a dramatic stand. I would also hazard a guess that those who are not willing to make the daily commitments to follow Christ would not be willing to make the great, final commitment either.

Take the young, brash Peter, for example. He boldly proclaimed that he would follow Jesus anywhere, even to his death. But when the time came to make a stand, he cowered in front of a servant girl. This is one reason I like Peter so much. He spoke loudly but flinched when faced with a small stick. I am certain that as he watched Jesus bear his own cross, Peter became fearful that he might have to do the same thing.

And thus our problem. We do not fully understand what it means to bear a cross because the concept itself is so foreign to us. To be sure, Mel Gibson's movie *The Passion of the Christ* made it more real for those who saw the portrayal, but as a body corporate, we have trivialized what it means *for us*. That Jesus had to endure a bloody and painful cross is one thing. That *we* have to do the same thing borders on blasphemy.

In Peter's defense, once he was reinstated by Jesus, he showed the willingness Jesus demanded of his disciples. Peter put his hand to the plow and this time did not look back, even when faced with martyrdom. Sad to say, when I evaluate myself, I am more like the young Peter than the mature Peter.

## WHY MUST WE TAKE UP A CROSS?

Is there not an easier way, a shortcut to the fruitful Christian life that we can take instead? I am certain some readers think I am taking things too far. *Perhaps Kuligin is one of those fanatical types?* Maybe I am fanatical but not necessarily in the bad sense. I think Jesus was fanatical as well. When we see the Son of Man taking up cords to whip the moneychangers and knocking down their tables, some of us flinch. Too many of us, I fear, believe that incident to be an anomaly in the character of Jesus; but I think it was a defining moment. When it came to the character and will of the Father, Jesus was fanatical. Rightly so.

If the greatest commandment truly is to love God with all our heart, mind, soul, and strength, it seems perfectly acceptable to conclude that only fanatics need apply for such a mission. Of course, I do not mean the type of fanatic we envision today, one who straps a bomb to his chest. But I do mean the kind of fanatic willing to fasten a cross on his back.

If we take seriously the biblical teaching that we are all contemptible sinners in need of new creation, we must admit that the remedy must be drastic. Christians who are honest with themselves realize how much work is involved in taking a sinful creature and transforming him or her into the image of the perfect Son of God. Only a cross will do the job.

Crucifixion is painful. Many believers today envision the Christian faith as more of a picnic or a walk in the park than a bloody sacrifice of the self, but the former is not the biblical portrait. The biblical portrait is of a person being nailed to a cross. Nails pierce the flesh, and the body is hoisted whole upon the wood where it is left to perish slowly. It is this crucifixion of the self that is necessary to draw us closer to God. Why is a cross compulsory for Christ's disciples?

1) *It causes us to concentrate on God.* There are few things better than suffering to bring us to God. C. S. Lewis's famous statement, "Suffering is God's megaphone," is certainly apt. Luxury and prosperity tend to make us concentrate on possessing more of the same, whereas pain and distress cause us to run to God. Jesus knew this human trait all too well, and that is why he prescribed a painful remedy. Too many believers envision the Christian life as lounging on the beach, not laboring in a sweatshop. As a result, they become ineffective witnesses—salt that has lost its saltiness and light that no longer glows. Yet the backs of true disciples should be scarred with splinters, not dripping with suntan lotion.

The prosperity message has diverted our attention in the wrong direction. Instead of concentrating on God, we are concentrating on what he can give us or do for us. Abraham's great reward was to know the Creator (Gen. 15:1). Unfortunately, Satan has blinded the minds of many Christians today by making God more into the image of a cosmic Santa Claus than the Lord of glory. Shame on us for wanting more from God than simply himself.

# TEN THINGS I WISH JESUS NEVER SAID

> For although it be good to think upon the kindness of God, and to love Him and praise Him for it, yet it is far better to think upon the naked being of Him, and to love Him and praise Him for Himself.
>
> Anonymous, *The Cloud of Unknowing*, fourteenth century

Carrying a cross focuses our attention on what is really important. That is why it is impossible to become Christ's disciple without it.

2) *It causes us to trust God fully.* When faced with difficulties and trials, many Christians actually flee from God. This is a sign that their faith is weak, if not entirely dead. Self-reliance is an exalted state in our world today, but God wants dependent disciples, not independent mavericks. True believers are strengthened through adversity, not crushed by it. When we willingly walk the hill of self-crucifixion, we are telling God we want to trust in him, not in ourselves.

One of my favorite biblical expressions of this trust through adversity comes from Job. When lesser men would have been crushed beyond recovery by the tragedy that struck Job, this great man of faith articulated ultimate trust: "Though he slay me, yet will I hope in him" (Job 13:15a).

Again the ways of the world are turned upside down. The problem of pain and suffering is one of the classic counterattacks by atheists when they voice their objections to Christianity and the existence of God. While this is not a trivial protest, as believers we must recognize that trials and difficulties are not proof against the existence of God as much as they are proof for his existence. We must come to the realization that God will not mold us into the people he wants us to be without them.

Gold is only refined through the extreme heat of the crucible. It is only when we travel through that heat and come out on the other side better people that we realize God is trustworthy. Because he wants us to live by faith, he brings trials and obstacles into our lives; through them we can grow in our trust in him.

3) *It causes us to rely on his strength and not our own.* We often extol the maverick, the entrepreneur, the solitary person who steps out against the odds and forges ahead on his own. Often this is the picture

we think we see in the lives of great missionaries like Hudson Taylor and William Carey or the apostle Paul. But they did not accomplish their work in their own strength. In fact, they uniformly claimed the opposite, that without reliance upon God, nothing of importance would have been done.

Paul expresses this truth beautifully in his second epistle to the Corinthian believers. There we learn that Paul had a "thorn in the flesh" that he asked the Lord to remove, but God had something greater in store for that difficulty. The following words perfectly express the notion of cross-carrying and why it is necessary:

> *To keep me from becoming conceited because of these surpassingly great revelations, there was given me a thorn in my flesh, a messenger of Satan, to torment me. Three times I pleaded with the Lord to take it away from me. But he said to me, "My grace is sufficient for you, for my power is made perfect in weakness." Therefore I will boast all the more gladly about my weaknesses, so that Christ's power may rest on me. That is why, for Christ's sake, I delight in weaknesses, in insults, in hardships, in persecutions, in difficulties. For when I am weak, then I am strong. (2 Cor. 12:7-10)*

What is most interesting in this passage is that Paul asked for the thorn to be removed, but God would not allow it. God could do more with Paul if the thorn were present than if it were absent. Some may errantly find here a justification in their desire *never* to have hardships in life, but this would be a mistaken application of the passage. To be sure, it is not a sin to ask that particular difficulties be removed from our life, but it is wrong to expect never to have any, or to think that only Christians of weak faith have them.

Carrying a cross is meant to break us. It breaks us of our self-love and conceit, our selfish desires and sinful cravings, and our stubborn will. Only upon being broken and taught that there is nothing in ourselves worthy of God's favor can we be used by God. Just as Christ was broken, battered, and bruised by his cross, so must we be crucified. Self-reliant people are not fit for following Jesus. As John Piper wrote, "A cross-centered, cross-exalting, cross-saturated life is a God-glorifying life—the *only* God-glorifying life. All others are wasted."[4]

## TAKING UP OUR CROSS

We must evaluate ourselves to determine which areas in our own lives need self-crucifixion. Are we overcome by lust and sexual desires? Do we yearn for worldly wealth and allow its tempting lure to consume us? In what ways have we adopted worldly ideals that cause us to shirk our cross-carrying mandate?

The following verses speak of crucifying some aspect of ourselves. It is no small point that this image of self-crucifixion and carrying one's cross is one of the most frequent images of Jesus used by the apostle Paul.

### Crucifixion of Our Bondage to Sin

*For we know that our old self was crucified with him so that the body of sin might be done away with, that we should no longer be slaves to sin— because anyone who has died has been freed from sin. (Rom. 6:6-7)*

### Crucifixion of Our Will

*I have been crucified with Christ and I no longer live, but Christ lives in me. (Gal. 2:20a)*

### Crucifixion of Our Nature

*Those who belong to Christ Jesus have crucified the sinful nature with its passions and desires. (Gal. 5:24)*

### Crucifixion of the World

*May I never boast except in the cross of our Lord Jesus Christ, through which the world has been crucified to me, and I to the world. (Gal. 6:14)*

Carrying one's cross is often shameful, frequently exhausting, and always painful. However, it is something we are commanded to do daily if we desire to be disciples of Christ. In the next chapter, we will look more pointedly at the issue of persecution and suffering for one's faith, which are encompassed in carrying one's cross. For now, let me end with my own prayer in this regard:

> Oh Lord, help me to endure the pain of the nails as they pierce my self-ish desires, the crown of thorns as it penetrates my selfish pride, and the sword as it is thrust through my selfish motivations. With each pang and spasm help me recognize that you are creating good out of what is evil. You are reforming my sinful body, mind, and heart. You are transforming me into a new creation. You are conforming me to the image of your perfect Son. Give me the faith to trust you as each morsel of my being is cut and sliced and perforated. Amen.

# 5

# THE ART OF
# SPIRITUAL MARTYRDOM

*Blessed are you when people insult you, persecute you and falsely say all kinds of evil against you because of me.*
JESUS CHRIST, MATTHEW 5:11

*True suffering is a mother of all the virtues.*
MEISTER ECKHART,
FOURTEENTH-CENTURY GERMAN MYSTIC

*To be near Jesus is dangerous. It offers no prospect of earthly happiness, but involves the fire of tribulation and the test of suffering. . . . Only through fire may the kingdom be attained.*
JOACHIM JEREMIAS (1900-1979),
*THE PARABLES OF JESUS*

I once led a group Bible study through the book of Hebrews. In this epistle are several instances that speak of suffering, and at some point I introduced to the group what I thought was a relatively obvious conclusion: Suffering for Christians is not only to be expected, but it is also necessary.

The group consisted of people mainly in their twenties, both married and single, but one member was older, a leader in the church and in his community. He piped up that he did not believe suffering for a believer was necessary at all. To my comment from Paul concerning the sharing of the sufferings of Christ to also share in his glory (Rom. 8:17), this man said that we share by having faith in him. He likened it to dialing on the Internet, where we plug into the sufferings of Jesus. In other words, Jesus has already done all the suffering for us; we do not need, nor should we expect, to suffer now.

I was shocked by his comments, and to be honest, I did not know entirely what to say. I did not want to embarrass this man in front of the others who viewed him as a leader. On the other hand, I did not want to leave his comments as they were, for fear that others would think by my silence I was approving them. I trod the ground lightly as I attempted to voice my disagreement and give solid, biblical reasons. Still he was not deterred, and it became apparent that he cared far less about embarrassing me, if possible, than I did about preserving his dignity. Regardless, I explained the reasons I believed Jesus expects us to suffer, much as our Lord had done.

To be honest, though, there is something about the man's position that I find appealing. Let's face it, who likes suffering? I have a friend who says there is no honor in pain; so if at all possible, try to avoid it. Considering his comment in the wider human experience, is it not natural for us to avoid difficulty or suffering? Generally speaking, only crazy people or fanatics go looking for it, right? Let me be the first to admit that if I am faced with the choice of enduring pain or avoiding it, I will always choose the latter. That being said, is it not a fair question to ask if I am made of the right stuff to be a disciple of Jesus?

## CHARTING OUR COURSE

What I intend to do with this chapter might appear overly ambitious. Admittedly, I have lofty goals for what I want to cover and for that reason, I would like to provide a brief explanation of where we are heading.

I classify suffering in two broad ways. The first is the more general topic, which can involve sickness or other ailments of natural human existence. This I call common suffering. However, I also think a more specific type of suffering needs to be addressed, that of suffering for the sake of Christ, what I will call special suffering. Liver failure or heart disease is not properly considered in this category, but persecution by unbelievers because of one's faith certainly is.[1]

Even within the category of special suffering a distinction can be made between voluntary and involuntary suffering. What I mean by voluntary suffering is that suffering to which a believer knowingly submits himself or herself as a result of Christian vocation or choices, such as missionaries who give up the blandishments of living in America to live in more difficult environments. By involuntary suffering I mean suffering that is not willfully chosen but comes from one's faith in Christ. This latter type is where I would categorize persecution. We do not make a choice: "I am going out to be persecuted today," but the fact that we are following Christ may result in persecution.

The title of this chapter speaks of *spiritual* martyrdom, but obviously physical martyrdom is also a possibility. However, unless we live in countries like Sudan or North Korea, the likelihood is slim. For those living in democratic countries that allow freedom of religion, a faith that leads to death is most likely not going to happen. That is why I have decided to concentrate on spiritual martyrdom—something all Christians should experience—but I will not ignore physical martyrdom in the process.

To one degree or another all people suffer. This common suffering is the universal experience of human beings, but I am more concerned with the special kind of suffering that Christians are meant to experience. Therefore, my intention in this chapter is not to spend much time on suffering in the general sense, but more specifically in the sense of suffering for Christ and his kingdom.

In the following sections, we will first look at several issues concerning suffering that are shared by both common and voluntary, special suffering. Next we will address three aspects of suffering that every Christian must recognize. After these more general considerations, we will spend the remainder of this chapter talking about the involuntary suffering embodied in persecution for our faith.

Suffering is unnatural to us, and therefore calls for the surrender of our will.

Andrew Murray (1828-1917),
*The School of Obedience*

## TEN THINGS I WISH JESUS NEVER SAID

## SURPRISED BY SUFFERING

The idea of willingly facing persecution or accepting suffering is odd to most people, even Christians. In fact, it is downright avoided by many believers. Perhaps this comes in part from our culture's constant attempts at evading it.

Philip Yancey notes that books on pain can be neatly divided into two categories. The older ones, by people like Augustine, Luther, Bunyan, and so on, "ungrudgingly accept pain and suffering as God's useful agents." The modern books on the topic move God to the position of a defendant who must answer to man for his inability to remove pain from our lives. Either God's love or his ability to overcome evil is questioned by many of the more recent authors. This Yancey wrote fifteen years ago, and it is not difficult to imagine that such attitudes have only grown stronger since that time.[2]

I am sure Americans by now are tired of hearing that they do not have any idea what is involved in true suffering. Unfortunately, I am going to say some similar things in this chapter, so be forewarned. We in the West do not understand it entirely because we live in societies that normally do not allow religious persecution or that enjoy comforts greater than people elsewhere even dream of having.

Whereas millions of people in the world today are worried about food to eat and shelter from the elements, Americans as a whole have fewer concerns in these areas. If we speak of evangelical Americans, there are few demographic groups in the world that enjoy the plenty that we experience.

In Namibia, for example, UNICEF estimates that nearly 50 percent of the population lives in poverty. Whereas numerous Americans deliberate over what movie to watch this weekend, many Namibians do not know where their food will come from tonight. "Only in the West do we need to be reminded that Christians are called to suffer."[3]

To our shame, there are even segments of the Christian community who think suffering and persecution are sure signs of the absence of God's favor on one's life. In chapters 1 and 2, I noted that those who hold to the prosperity gospel are living by sight and not by faith. Much like Lot, they have traded the idea of eternal rewards for ones that are temporal and immediate. This health-and-wealth message sells well in our affluent American society, but it becomes increasingly difficult to peddle in cultures and countries where persecution for one's faith is experienced.

However, the prosperity proclamation is nothing new. In chapter 4, I quoted Erasmus who observed this same attitude among the clergy of the Catholic church during the fifteenth and sixteenth centuries. Even as early as A.D. 100, we find in a letter commonly known as *Second Clement*[4] that the idea of persecution and hardship for believers struck some as unacceptable. The author of the letter wrote:

> But do not let it trouble your mind that we see the unrighteous possessing wealth while the servants of God experience hardships. Let us have faith, brothers and sisters! We are competing in the contest of a living God, and are being trained by the present life in order that we may be crowned in the life to come. None of the righteous ever received his reward quickly, but waits for it. For if God paid the wages of the righteous immediately, we would soon be engaged in business, not godliness; though we would appear to be righteous, we would in fact be pursuing not piety but profit.[5]

Each time I read that quotation, I am cut to the quick. Of course, I am using it to criticize those preachers of prosperity in our own day, and rightly so. But I would be remiss if I did not take it to heart myself. How often have I wanted quick rewards from the Lord? Or conversely, how little do I value eternal rewards when compared with the ones I perceive I can obtain in this life? When I contemplate my own avarice in this regard, my soul cries out, "Lord, have mercy on me!"

What incredible wisdom the author of *Second Clement* imparts to us. I want to glean three points from this quotation. The first is that we must have faith. Too many times we evangelicals throw this word around and yet do not comprehend it. The opposite of living by faith is living by sight. In his eternal wisdom God has purposefully ordained that we would not receive everything in this life. That is why the Holy

Spirit is considered a "deposit guaranteeing our inheritance" (Eph. 1:14), and why Abraham "was looking forward to the city with foundations, whose architect and builder is God" (Heb. 11:10). The author of Hebrews, in that great chapter cataloguing the heroic deeds of the saints of old, can say that "none of them received what had been promised" (v. 39). God calls us to believe in things not seen, to hope for future glory, not present payoff.

So many Christians today want the opposite. They want to live by sight, not faith. As a result they remain immature babies, believers who can only suckle milk and whose throats have not properly developed to swallow spiritual meat. The 2,000-year-old truths of the faith are not good enough for them. "If God spoke to Peter and Paul, why can he not also speak to me directly?" they arrogantly demand. If they do not have a constant menu of miraculous signs and wonders, their faith becomes weak and brittle. They move from one spiritual fix to the next, all the time believing themselves to be spiritual giants when they are feeble infants.

Persecution and hardship have a way of driving us to faith. Prosperity rarely can do that, and in fact more often than not it becomes a stumbling block. That is why Jesus can say it is nearly impossible for a rich man to enter the kingdom of heaven. As sinful humans, we have a tendency to trust in what is seen more than in what is not seen.

King David expresses this truth. "As for me, I said in my prosperity, 'I shall never be moved.' By your favor, O LORD, you made my mountain stand strong; you hid your face; I was dismayed" (Ps. 30:6-7, ESV). David's prosperity dulled his spiritual senses, and only after God "hid his face" from the king did he recognize error. When prosperity reigns, we have a tendency to trust in ourselves. When suffering is supreme, our natural inclination is to turn to God.

The second thing we can learn from *Second Clement* is that hardship trains us. The modern adage "No pain, no gain" shows that we implicitly recognize this truth, even if we look for ways around it. However, get-rich-quick schemes still work, in large part because there are enough people unwilling to perform the hard work necessary to make a solid living. Gambling houses and casinos are packed with people of similar sentiment.

A common scam, originally created in Nigeria, still succeeds in duping people the world over who are looking for an easy way out. E-mails are sent out by a person who supposedly is related to a recently deposed or deceased leader or government official, with the promise that millions of dollars can be made available to people willing to help this relative. It amazes me that there are people falling for this nonsense, but what it tells me is that people don't want to do the hard work necessary to succeed, and that in looking for an easy way out, they are easily hoodwinked by such cons.

The apostle Paul recognized the importance of suffering as producing greater qualities in us when he wrote, "Not only so, but we also rejoice in our sufferings, because we know that suffering produces perseverance; perseverance, character; and character, hope" (Rom. 5:3-4). It may be wrong to say that character cannot be created without suffering, but experience has shown us that few people possess character who have not also had to endure suffering. In fact, we often extol the saints of old—and refer to them as saints—precisely because they endured incredible hardship and yet did not turn away from their faith.

> My tribulations are more necessary for me than meat and drink.
>
> Martin Luther (1483-1546), *Table Talk*

Even Jesus was trained through suffering. The author of Hebrews makes this intriguing statement: "Although he was a son, he learned obedience from what he suffered and, once made perfect he became the source of eternal salvation for all who obey him" (Heb. 5:8-9, cf. 2:10). These two passages have caused consternation with those who know Jesus to be fully God. How, if he already possessed perfect deity, could he be made perfect through suffering? The answer is found in the understanding that Jesus was also fully human.

Jesus was not morally or spiritually imperfect, but in experiencing suffering, he participated in our humanity to its fullest extent. Consider what would have happened had Christ not suffered. He would have become a man and lived a glamorous life of ease. He would not be able to relate to us nor we to him. Only by suffering could he learn experientially what it was truly like to be human.[6]

In the same way God's adopted children must undergo suffering. In Hebrews 12 the author speaks of suffering and persecution as God's disciplining of his children. This might be hard for us to accept, especially when persecution can result in death, but God even uses physical martyrdom to bring the body of believers into increased fellowship with him. Without suffering, we cannot be made useful to God. As Oswald Chambers wrote, "If you are ever going to be wine to drink, you must be crushed. Grapes cannot be drunk, grapes are only wine when they have been crushed."[7]

The third thing we learn from this early church letter is that immediate rewards can cause us to lose sight of the important things we should focus on. Much like the idolaters Paul chastised, who worshiped the creature and not the Creator, so we often become focused on the gifts and not the Giver. How many of us run after profit but not piety? We are willing to trade heavenly treasures for worldly waste. How often have we striven for possessions later stolen by thieves or ruined by rust or eaten by moths when we could have labored for possessions that cannot be robbed, corroded, or devoured?

> There remains the pleasure of these eyes of my flesh. . . . Let not these occupy my soul; let God rather occupy it, who made these things, very good indeed, yet is He my good, not they.
>
> Saint Augustine (354-430), *Confessions*

In summary, then, we see that suffering is to be preferred over prosperity if we want to know God and become more Christlike. Prosperity rarely produces faith in us, and more often than not turns us away from it. Second, we grow in character through suffering, and this character leads to other qualities that make us serviceable for God. Lastly, suffering focuses our attention on matters that are more important and lasting than the immediate accoutrements of life.

## THREE ASPECTS OF SUFFERING

Now I want to briefly point out three aspects of suffering that all Christians should be alerted to. Again I am not necessarily referring to common suffering, which as human beings we can all expect to experience, but I am concentrating on suffering for the sake of Christ and his kingdom.

1) *Suffering for Christ is to be expected by all believers.* Jesus said that because the world hated him, it will hate his disciples (John 15:18-21; Matt. 10:21-22). This is when we begin to realize that proclaiming one's allegiance to Christ can be dangerous. The closer we stand to Jesus, the closer we stand to the firing squad. Conversely, if we find the world is happy and at peace with us, perhaps something is wrong with our faith.

Too many Christians think that by being friends with the world they will make the gospel attractive. Of course, I am not advocating that we become spiteful and mean-spirited, spitting epithets at sinners like the Pharisees did. Still we need not become bosom buddies with the world either.

The common understanding among many Christians that if we truly become Christlike, the world will be attracted to us does not hold up to close scrutiny. A more biblically accurate statement is that the more Christlike we become, the more we will be hated by the world. I want to be clear here. I am not saying that the more loving we become, the more the world will hate us. But being more loving does not encompass all that Christlikeness entails. Christ was not hated so much for the fact that he healed the lame and gave sight to the blind as much as he was hated for proclaiming the judgment of God and his hatred of sin.

Unfortunately, many Christians have been duped by the common portrayal of Jesus created by the world, not by the Word. In it Jesus is a namby-pamby, tolerance-loving sage who loved everybody and never,

ever condemned them. To be sure, Jesus loved us so much that he stretched himself out on that cruel cross, but this is not the whole picture of Jesus. The same Jesus who loved to the point of death is also the Jesus who turned over the tables of the moneychangers and whipped them. The same Jesus who taught us not to condemn others himself condemned sin in others. The same Jesus who healed the wounded also cursed the fig tree.

Our world is in love with "Jesus-lite," not the real Jesus. If all we ever do is tolerate the evil around us, the world will love us to death for it. But we should not fool ourselves into believing that *Jesus* will approve of us. I have known Christians who pride themselves on never talking about sin or judgment, or who will never speak a harsh word against anybody or anything, no matter how heinous the heresy or the heretic. This they boldly proclaim is what it means to follow Jesus, but that is hardly the case. Tolerance of virtually every evil is what the world loves, not hates. If we become Christians like that, we are salt best trampled upon, not salt that is tasty and preserves the meat on which it is sprinkled.

Does the world hate us? If not, then we might have a discipleship crisis on our hands. If Jesus were to come to earth today in the same manner in which he previously came, teaching the same things he taught and doing the same things he did, would the world love him or hate him? I'm not even sure that if Jesus came and spent a year in my church that we would like him. I have a feeling that in time I would be bothered by him to the point of asking him to leave or hoping that he would move on to another church.

If our message to the world is simply, "God loves you," we will have little problem with the world. But if our message is the message of Christ, that we are sinners dead in our trespasses, mortally depraved and unable to save ourselves, I guarantee you the world will hate us. If we add to that the message of faith in Jesus Christ as the only Savior and Lord, one who not only saves but also expects to be our master, our pluralistic planet will look for ways to silence us.

Suffering for Christ is to be expected by believers, not avoided. So often, though, the latter is precisely what we do. We do not take a proper stand for the faith, and we might even participate with the world and its sins, thinking we are making the gospel attractive. What we are doing, though, is becoming more worldly, not making the world more Christlike.

We should stop treating suffering as if it is unexpected. We should cease expressing surprise when a child of God suffers. Suffering for the Christian is not to be startling but rather predictable. One cannot expect to be made into the image and likeness of God's perfect Son without experiencing suffering. While the old man is being crucified, we cannot expect him to feel no pain. Yet apart from suffering and the consequent product of perseverance, no believer will be made holy.

> Now there is no one who approaches God with a true and upright heart who is not tested by hardships and temptations.
>
> *On Cleaving to God*, attributed to Albertus Magnus (1193-1280)

2) *Suffering for Christ is necessary for all believers.* In Augustine's apology for why the Roman Empire had experienced heavy military losses to the barbarian Germanic tribes, the North African bishop argued that God uses hardship and trials to build character in his people. *The City of God* contains some of the most eloquent statements from Augustine on this difficult topic. Consider this one passage:

> For, in the same fire, gold gleams and straw smokes; under the same flail the stalk is crushed and the grain threshed; the lees are not mistaken for oil because they have issued from the same press. So, too, the tide of trouble will test, purify, and improve the good, but beat, crush, and wash away the wicked. So it is that, under the weight of the same affliction, the wicked deny and blaspheme God, and the good pray to Him and praise Him. The difference is not in what people suffer but in the way they suffer. The same shaking that makes fetid water stink makes perfume issue a more pleasant odor.[8]

The author of Hebrews notes that if we are not experiencing the discipline of God that comes through suffering, we cannot be considered his children. "If you are not disciplined (and everyone undergoes discipline), then you are illegitimate children and not true sons" (Heb. 12:8). Literally, this passage means that we are bastard children, ones who do not know our true father.

Suffering is the universal experience of all believers, and as Jesus taught, if the Master had to suffer, so too will his servants. When we suffer, our character is strengthened. Suffering burns away the dross, much like walking on a treadmill burns away fat.

The image of pruning a tree is a frequent analogy for this idea in Scripture. We prune a tree so the good branches can grow better. The tree can mature stronger and healthier if the weak portions are cut away. Conversely, if a tree is never pruned, it grows into a misshapen plant that produces little fruit.

How a person handles suffering can say much about that person's character. Greater so, how a believer handles suffering speaks volumes about his view of God. If we truly believe God to be the sovereign Lord of all, when suffering comes into our lives, we will not curse its arrival but rather welcome it.

> Sickness is the acid test of spirituality, because it discloses whether our virtue is real or sham.
>
> Saint Alphonsus de Ligouri (1696-1787)

Rather than viewing suffering as a nuisance to be avoided or even as a necessary evil, we should embrace it. We should also note the advantage of suffering in encouraging the faith of others. Suffering is not a benefit only to ourselves. It can serve as an encouragement to those who are undergoing similar trials. Consider how often you have been encouraged through your difficulties because others can empathize with you.

In one of the enduring classics of Christian literature, John Bunyan's *The Pilgrim's Progress* recounts the martyrdom of Faithful and how it encouraged the other believers to press onward.

When they were gone from the townsmen, and when their friends had bid them farewell, they quickly came to the place where Faithful was put to death. Therefore they made a stand, and thanked him that had enabled him to bear his cross so well; and the rather, because they now found that they had a benefit by such a manly suffering as his was.[9]

This is precisely how we are told to view the suffering of Christ. "Consider him who endured such opposition from sinful men, so that you will not grow weary and lose heart" (Heb. 12:3). The suffering of other believers provides us with motivation to press onward.

To those who might not have to endure extreme, physical persecution for our faith, the idea of being blessed through it might strike us as odd or even worse, as reprehensible. But for those experiencing persecution, this command can bring encouragement and even joy. Instead of the persecution being viewed as an anomaly that should be removed if not avoided, we recognize it for what it is—a necessity and a privilege. What believer cannot be inspired by stories of courage and bravery in the face of opposition like the following?

A young man, blind in one eye, asked if he could go to teach the Babendi. Paul warned Tomais that they might beat him, starve him, perhaps kill him. "But Bwana," he replied, "The Lord Jesus suffered for me; certainly I can suffer a little for him." The Babendi Chief arrested Tomais, put a rope around his neck and commanded soldiers to force him to run to the government center. Wherever they rested, villagers enquired why he was detained. He replied, "for preaching the gospel of Jesus who died for your sins" and went on to tell them the way of salvation. Imprisoned at the government post, he passed on the same message to his guards. Next morning the judge ordered him to be laid on the ground and lashed with a hippo-hide whip. He thanked God for the soldier assigned to flay him. "My preaching the previous night made him friendly and he did not hit me as hard as he should." Released, he continued to preach, and God established churches among the Babendi.[10]

In suffering for Christ, we have the opportunity of inspiring others to greater acts of faith for the kingdom. God often uses his children in this way. One generation endures extreme hardship to the benefit of the numerous generations to come. When Tertullian (150-212) proclaimed his famous dictum, "The blood of the martyrs is the seed of the church," he was recognizing this fact.

3) *Suffering for Christ is the privilege of all believers.* Perhaps the most difficult aspect of suffering is that it should be viewed as a privilege. That we can expect Christians to suffer sometimes is not difficult to accept. That suffering is a necessary aspect of a Christian's life is a little more troublesome for many believers. But that suffering is a privilege, something we are *allowed* to experience—and something without which we are missing an opportunity (as the connotation of *privilege* portrays)—is difficult to swallow.

However, the biblical examples and teachings about suffering for Christ as a privilege are too numerous to list in full.[11] James says we should "consider it pure joy" when we face trials of many kinds (1:2), and Paul refers to this as the "fellowship of sharing in his sufferings" (Phil. 3:10). Every biblical writer views suffering for the sake of Christ in a positive light, and as such, expects it to produce joy in the believer. "For it has been granted to you on behalf of Christ not only to believe on him, but also to suffer for him" (Phil. 1:29).

Oswald Chambers (1874-1917), author of the devotional read by millions of people, *My Utmost for His Highest*, served in Egypt as a chaplain to British Commonwealth troops in World War I. The sweltering heat of the midday could reach 130 degrees Fahrenheit in a tent, and with no shade outside for protection against the scorching rays of the sun, inside a tent was the better option. Add to this the threat of malaria and the thousands of flies hatched in the waste of horses and other animals that frequented the area, and it takes little imagination to understand why service in this area of the war was hated by virtually every soldier. One soldier wrote:

> Few people know, unless they have experienced it, what a climate
> such as that of Egypt can mean. The effect of the climate and of the
> historic atmosphere of Egypt is psychically appalling to certain tem-

peraments, and to those who are spared this, there is yet the continual sapping of the physical forces by fever and the resultant lowness of par which makes it difficult to fight moral or mental battles.[12]

Chambers, on the other hand, found the place a blessing. He was constantly busy serving the spiritual and physical needs of the troops. His diary frequently records fits of exuberance during his time in that miserable place. How is it that Chambers's experience could be so different from that of the majority of others stationed there? If we consider Augustine's comments quoted earlier, we will see that for those people whom God is training and building up in character, suffering can be a joy and a blessing. But for others who endure the exact same difficulties and trials, it can crush them. "One man's curse is another man's blessing," or as a similar adage goes, "One man's junk is another man's treasure." Oswald knew the holy Lord of glory, and he trusted in this Lord's ability to bring good out of evil.

The biblical teaching shows us that suffering is not meant to be an occasional event in the Christian's life, but rather something familiar and frequent. Suffering for the Christian is not intended to be recreational but vocational. It comes with the job.

In Christ, God turned the evil act of crucifying an entirely innocent man into something life-saving and redeeming. We must begin to cultivate this outlook in our own lives so that suffering no longer becomes an evil to be avoided but something to be expected, necessary, and, yes, even a joy-producing privilege.

O ye poor souls, who exhaust yourselves with needless vexation, if you would but seek God in your hearts, there would be a speedy end to all your troubles. The increase of crosses would proportionately increase your delight.

*Autobiography of Madame Guyon* (1647-1717)

## A FINAL WORD ON SUFFERING

C. S. Lewis, one of the foremost apologists for Christianity in the twentieth century, penned one of the classic Christian statements on suffering, *The Problem of Pain.* In it he waxed eloquent about the benefits of suffering and pain. Several years later, though, when faced with the agonizing death of his wife, he wrote another book on the subject, *A Grief Observed.* This time he used a pseudonym because his practical experience of pain had shattered his academic musings on the topic written years earlier.

In all my gushing commentary on suffering and its benefits, I feel the need for further clarification. I want to be clear that I do not believe that suffering is no big deal or that suffering should not be viewed as really all that bad. On the contrary, only if suffering *is* bad can it rightly be called suffering.

Nor do I want my readers to think I jump for joy when suffering comes my way. All that I have enumerated above is quite academic. Emotionally speaking, my experience of suffering and my attitude toward it are quite removed from the biblical ideal.

Let me also foresee an objection to the notion that suffering is only truly suffering if it is experienced as horrible in its extent. Put another way, if all we ever do is rejoice whenever pain or misery come our way, can those experiences be categorized as painful and miserable? One might respond by saying, "But isn't our future glory not worth comparing to our present suffering?" In other words, when everything is said and done, the suffering accounts for little because the end product is far greater. But this would reduce suffering to something inconsequential, which it is not.

Jesus endured the cross for the joy set before him. Would we then conclude that because of the incredibly vast glory he now enjoys, his bloody death on the cross was inconsequential? If we do that, we begin to negate the suffering he did for us. Jesus already possessed glory before he became incarnate man. If the goal was merely to have glory, he already had it. But the goal of the incarnate Son was to enter into the state of man, to undergo the temptations and suffering that man undergoes, and to conquer them. He could only do that if his suffering was real.

The objection would also negate the element of faith involved in the process of suffering. We know the promises because we read them, but we do not yet experience all the promises. Only in glory will we truly understand that our temporary sufferings are not worth comparing to our eternal paradise. For now, we endure suffering and have faith that it will yield something far greater.

Lastly, I want to revisit the sin often committed by believers when suffering comes their way. Instead of viewing it as a privilege or a necessary positive, we often curse God for it. Perhaps this is why God brought suffering into our lives in the first place, to rid us of this despicable habit of calling God to task for how he chooses to run his creation. If the *only* experiences of our lives were suffering, God would still be the perfect, holy Lord. That suffering is not our constant experience speaks of God's love, because as sinners, we certainly deserve nothing better.

The suffering of Job serves as an example of God's sovereignty and his determination to use his creatures for his own good purposes. Job suffered because God had made a "cosmic bet" with Satan. Job lost virtually all his possessions and family and endured incredible physical pain, all because God had determined to test him as a challenge to Satan that God's faithful servant would not turn his back on his Maker. The remarkable aspect of the test is that nowhere do we find God explaining to Job why he suffered. In fact, when all is said and done, it is Job who is contrite and groveling before God, when one might expect the opposite to be the case, especially if the story had been written from our modern worldview. "God owes Job an apology," could well be words coming from the mouths of many Christians today, who view man as the determining agent when it comes to the relationship between God and man. But we must always affirm God's sovereign goodness, even in the midst of extreme anguish.

In prosperity, even sinners find it easy to unite themselves to the divine will; but it takes saints to unite themselves to God's will when things go wrong and are painful to self-love.
Saint Alphonsus de Ligouri (1696-1787), *Uniformity with God's Will*

# TEN THINGS I WISH JESUS NEVER SAID

## PERSECUTION AS A TYPE OF SUFFERING

For the remainder of this chapter, I want to address the more specific issue of persecution for one's faith. There will be parallels between persecution and our discussion above on suffering; so I have decided to cover topics where redundancy will be minimized.

In the following sections, I will address several issues concerning persecution for one's faith:

- How are we blessed because we are persecuted?
- If persecution is so great an experience, should I seek it out?
- Is there ever a proper time to flee persecution?
- If physical persecution is not a reality for me, because of my location and culture, what other forms of persecution should I expect?

## THE BLESSINGS OF PERSECUTION

First let us reconsider the statement by Jesus that forms the topic of this chapter: "Blessed are you when people insult you, persecute you and falsely say all kinds of evil against you because of me. Rejoice and be glad, because great is your reward in heaven, for in the same way they persecuted the prophets who were before you" (Matt. 5:11-12).

Why does Jesus say we are blessed if we are persecuted for our faith in him? Because the world hated Jesus it will hate his followers; if we are being persecuted by the world, that usually is a sign that we are following Christ.

Paul makes this rather shocking statement in his letter to young Timothy: "Everyone who wants to live a godly life in Christ Jesus will be persecuted" (2 Tim. 3:12). Note, he did not say, "might be persecuted"; he said, "will be." This is one instance when I would like to add or change one small word in a passage of Scripture to blunt its force and the pain of its blow. There is no "if" here. Persecution will definitely, positively, absolutely be the experience of every Christian who truly is following Jesus.

This being said, how can Jesus possibly say that we are blessed for enduring such things? Several of these matters we have already touched upon in our discussion concerning suffering; so I will only briefly mention them where appropriate. Let me suggest seven ways in which persecution for one's faith is actually a blessing. (This list is not exhaustive.)

1) *When we are persecuted for our faith, this is usually a sign that we are affiliated with Christ.* Paul quotes the psalmist in expressing the cry of God's faithful: "For your sake we face death all day long; we are considered as sheep to be slaughtered" (Rom. 8:36). Our affiliation with Christ brings us into danger's territory, at least in this life and this world. In God's overall plan of redemption, this may mean casting our lot with slaughtered sheep.

2) *Persecution has a way of causing us to rely more on God and less on ourselves.* This is especially the case when we are persecuted by those who hold power over us or whom we are unable to resist. Such persecution causes believers to run to God for refuge. When faced with overwhelming obstacles, the believer's natural inclination should be to flee to God.

3) *Persecution produces godly fruit in our life, something that might otherwise not be produced.*

4) *Persecution creates a godly joy in us that might not otherwise be present in times of prosperity.*

5) *Godly suffering is an encouragement to others and their faith.*

6) *God often uses persecution to build and strengthen his church.*

7) *Jesus says we should rejoice when persecuted for our faith because we have a heavenly reward waiting for us.* This seems to imply something other than salvation, as the reward is tied directly to something we do. In other words, there are heavenly rewards that await those who have endured persecution, while a lack of persecution might imply an absence of these specific rewards. Whatever the case may be exactly, one thing is clear. Jesus is telling us to lift our eyes beyond our earthly burdens, with a forward gaze to the eternal future.

If you are undergoing persecution for your faith, take heart! Don't lose sight of these blessings of persecution. God can take the grossest evil and turn it into blessing. If you are not experiencing persecution for your faith, commit these blessings to mind and heart. For if you truly strive to follow Christ, persecution for your faith will surely fall upon you.

## AVOIDING A MARTYR COMPLEX

With all this talk about persecution and suffering for Christ, would it not be logical that we actively seek such things? For example, St. John of Avila (1499-1569) was convinced that every right-minded person should desire death on account of living in peril of losing divine grace. In his reasoning, what could be more pleasant or desirable than dying a good death in order to have the assurance of no longer being able to lose the grace of God? (We noted in chapter 2 Origen's example as someone who actively sought martyrdom.)

It seems that this is not what Christ had in mind. Even though as his disciples we should expect persecution, this does not mean we should go looking for trouble or picking fights. Walking around with a martyr complex is not what Jesus expects; nor would it make the gospel attractive. If we are following Jesus, rest assured persecution will come our way. We will not need to go hunting for it or purposefully creating it.

## FLEEING PERSECUTION

When we face persecution, often our inclination is to flee. Is it ever right or wise to run from persecution? If persecution is to be expected and even a privilege, would it not be better to always endure it? In line with the notion of a martyr complex, some may think fleeing persecution is never right. However, I'd like to argue against that idea.

Athanasius (296-373) gave a defense of "timely flight" in his *Apologia de Fuga* (*Defense of His Flight*). Five times during his archbishopric in Alexandria, Athanasius was sent into exile by the emperor. This normally was at the hands of the Arian sympathizer Constantius, who opposed Athanasius's strong stance for Nicene Christianity and the belief that Jesus was fully God. Athanasius provided a defense of his flight from Alexandria when Constantius put a death sentence on his head. He argued that there is a proper "time to flee and a time to stay."

Athanasius certainly had biblical support for such a notion. The prophet Elijah fled from the evil Queen Jezebel when she sought to kill him (1 Kings 19), and even the courageous apostle Paul found it proper in one instance to flee persecution in Damascus, soon after his conversion (Acts 9:25; 2 Cor. 11:33).

There seems to be biblical warrant for fleeing persecution to preserve oneself to fight another day. Even Jesus "escaped" martyrdom at times, until the time was right for his death. For example, John makes it clear in his Gospel that Jesus was moving toward an appointed destiny, so that even when people attempted to lay hands on him—in one case attempting to throw him over a precipice, in two other cases wanting to stone him—Scripture tells us Jesus "escaped." We are not told how he did this. In Luke's account of one such instance, all he says is that Jesus "walked right through the crowd." But it seems clear that Jesus knew his time to die had not yet arrived. Therefore, he was not going to submit himself to a martyr's death until the right time.[13]

This requires great discernment. I can imagine some Christians who possess a martyr complex never looking to escape persecution, while others who do not want to ever endure it will use the above instances as their justification for flight. However, it seems clear from several examples in Scripture that there is wisdom in knowing when to stand your ground in the presence of persecution and when to flee it to fight another day.

## TYPES OF PERSECUTION

Even though many Christians might never have to endure physical persecution, I hesitate to skip the topic. Not only has it been the common experience of Christians in ages past, but it is seen in many areas of our world today. Dallas Willard notes that more Christians died as martyrs in the twentieth century than in all the previous centuries combined leading up to 1900.[14] Therefore, after this section, I will note several instances of martyrdom in our "Lessons from History" section.

Physical persecution can take several forms and may not necessarily lead to death. In several places, the author of Hebrews catalogues various forms of persecution, most notably in 11:32-38 and in the following passage:

> *Remember those earlier days after you had received the light, when you stood your ground in a great contest in the face of suffering. Sometimes you were publicly exposed to insult and persecution; at other times you stood side by side with those who were so treated. You sympathized with those in prison and joyfully accepted the confiscation of your property, because you knew that you yourselves had better and lasting possessions. (Heb. 10:32-34)*

Although we tend to elevate martyrdom as the highest form of persecution, other varieties can be equally devastating. The pagan Roman Empire devised ingenious ways of eliciting a recantation of one's faith, but unfortunately so did the medieval church with the Spanish Inquisition. Scalding with hot oil, flogging with blunt or sharp instruments, even the purposeful breaking of bones were all used to cause believers to recant.

Jesus says we are blessed if people insult us or slander us. I want to be clear here. Often we are insulted because we are worthy of insult, not just because we are believers. Creating our own problems through our ill behavior, and then claiming spiritual martyrdom and persecution because of it, is not what Jesus has in mind. The type of persecution Jesus envisions has everything to do with our confession of faith in him, not for other mundane reasons. In chapter 7 I will recount my experience of being slandered, but that situation was what we might call general slander, as opposed to being slandered specifically because I am a Christian.

As Americans we may never have to endure the confiscation of our property, or imprisonment and torture, or martyrdom because of our faith. But we can endure other kinds of persecution. For example, many believers suffer emotional persecution. When they profess their allegiance to Christ, they may be shunned by family and friends, ridiculed by co-workers, even divorced by spouses. High-profile believers in America are frequently denigrated by politicians and preachers, by people of other faiths, and by those with no faith at all. Christians can be labeled fanatics or homophobes, all meant to belittle them and engender hatred. This kind of emotional persecution can ruin our relationships and careers, our mental as well as our physical health; so it never should be taken lightly. Living under a cloud of false accusations and slander is never easy.

Jesus endured persecution in a variety of forms: physical, emotional, mental, verbal, even spiritual. Spiritual persecution can be considered in the broader discussion of spiritual warfare. Because we have affiliated ourselves with Christ, Satan and his minions will target us for attacks. There is a spiritual battle brewing in the heavens, and the children of the light are being bombarded by the forces of darkness. When a person becomes a believer, that person enters a war. Previously that person had been a bystander, but now he or she is an active participant in this confrontation. So these various forms of persecution can come to virtually any believer.

## LESSONS FROM HISTORY

In the early centuries of Christendom, it was easy to tell the genuine Christians from pretenders. When persecution came, genuine believers stood their ground while pretenders lapsed. Physical martyrdom was often a sign of authentic Christianity, even to the point where many Christians coveted it to prove their faithfulness to Christ.

The early accounts of Christian martyrs are well known to most of us. In Acts 7 we read the account of the first martyr for the faith, the deacon Stephen. Some of the most important early church fathers of the first centuries of Christianity were martyred for their faith: Polycarp, Clement of Rome, Ignatius of Antioch, Justin Martyr, Irenaeus, and Cyprian. If we add to this list all the original apostles except John, while including Paul, we have an incredible list indeed. Why God would determine to have some of his best servants killed is an enigma to most of us, but it seems that doing so has always produced greater fruit in the end.

After Constantine the Great brought Christianity to the forefront of the Roman Empire, the threat of physical persecution waned. Faithful Christians found themselves in a sea of pretenders because it became fashionable to be a Christian. With the crucible of physical persecution gone, authentic believers sought other ways of proving their faith. Thus arose the institution of monasticism, a means of "spiritual persecution" of oneself.

However, throughout the centuries and continents, physical maltreatment has been the lot of many believers. For example, the introduction of Christianity in East Africa in the nineteenth century came with violent persecution, despite the fact that this part of the world had enjoyed a Christian presence nearly from the beginning.[15] However, with the strong Muslim occupation of parts of the coastal area along the Indian Ocean, reintroducing the faith was wrought with difficulty. Mark Shaw traces much of this opposition and the ensuing martyrdom, and then quotes Ludwig Krapf's observation: "The victories of the church are gained by stepping over the graves of her members."[16]

When considering the vast amount of unfair treatment and suffering God's children have endured through the past 2,000 years, we are left to conclude either that God is really impotent and cannot protect his people, or he must have a greater plan for us that involves persecution. Clearly, I choose the latter answer, although many of my contemporaries unfortunately have opted for the former.

## SINGING THE PRAISES OF SUFFERING

How many of the hymns we sing today reflect a positive attitude toward suffering? Often we sing praise and worship songs that rightly exalt God and who he is; but our repertoire is paltry when it comes to melodies that applaud trials and suffering and how God works through them. The songs we sing in churches frequently reflect the theology we have adopted. Too many churches have become anemic when building a theology of suffering, and our hymns reflect that feebleness.

Here are sample verses of three hymns written in an age when suffering and difficulties were viewed in a proper, biblical light:

## The Art of Spiritual Martyrdom

*Ye fearful saints, fresh courage take,*
*the clouds ye so much dread*
*Are big with mercy and shall break*
*In blessings on your head.*

William Cowper,
"God Moves in a Mysterious Way," 1774


*When thro' fiery trials thy pathway shall lie,*
*My grace, all sufficient, shall be thy supply;*
*The flames shall not hurt thee, I only design,*
*Thy dross to consume, and thy gold to refine.*

Rippon's *Selection of Hymns*,
"How Firm a Foundation," 1787


*Be still, my soul: the Lord is on thy side;*
*Bear patiently the cross of grief or pain;*
*Leave to thy God to order and provide;*
*In every change he faithful will remain.*
*Be still, my soul: thy best, thy heavenly Friend*
*Thro' thorny ways leads to a joyful end.*

Katharina von Schlegel,
"Be Still, My Soul," 1752


For many, the existence of suffering is the single greatest argument against a holy and sovereign God. (I am not just referring to atheists.) Many Christians find it the most difficult topic to consider, and this is normally the result of the bitter reality of trials and ordeals. There is perhaps no other topic in Christian theology that can produce arguments and opinions that look so different on paper than in the light of harsh experience.

As believers, we realize Christ also suffered, and this should be the basis upon which all subsequent commentary on suffering and persecution is built. He shed tears. He sweat drops of blood. He was mocked, ridiculed, slandered, and abused. But he persevered and triumphed. "In this world you will have trouble. But take heart! I have overcome the world" (John 16:33b). What is proper for the Master to experience also must be true for his servants.

Do I like any of this? Not one bit. But now I am faced with the same decision I always must make when confronted with Christ and his teaching. Do I submit my will to his, or do I continue in my stubborn, mule-like ways?

In the next chapter, we move to a logical consequence of persecution—the existence of enemies. If we have people in our lives who are intending to do us harm, how should we relate to them? As should be expected, the answer Jesus provides to this question is not the same that the world would offer.

> All that is not beautiful in the beloved, all that comes between and is not of love's kind, must be destroyed.
>
> George MacDonald (1824-1905), *The Consuming Fire*

# 6

# THE ART OF SPIRITUAL LOVE

*You have heard that it was said, "Love your neighbor and hate your enemy." But I tell you: Love your enemies and pray for those who persecute you, that you may be sons of your Father in heaven.*

JESUS CHRIST, MATTHEW 5:43B-45A

*All men are frail, but you must admit that none is more frail than yourself.*

THOMAS À KEMPIS (1380-1471),

*THE IMITATION OF CHRIST*

One crisp January evening in Windhoek, the capital city of Namibia, two men sneaked up behind me while I was getting into my car. A brief noise startled me, and as I wheeled around, I took a rock in the face. The next thing I knew I was on the ground with both men on top of me, going through my pockets. Only then did I realize that one had a large homemade knife in his hand.

They stole my wallet, shoes, shirt, jacket, and a few things out of my car, like my sunglasses. They did not steal my car most likely because they could not drive, which was fortunate for me, since had they stolen my car, they would have killed me. At the time, Namibia ranked number three in the world for countries with the highest per capita murder rate.

They ran away and left me lying on the ground, covered in my own blood. The incident was stunning to say the least, and the blow to my face caused me to move in and out of consciousness during the ordeal. After they left, I moved to a sitting position on the ground, hoping it was all a bad dream. I had taken the rock square in the nose and mouth, and as I rubbed my tongue over my front teeth, I could feel that one was broken and the other severely bent inward.

I got up and went to my car. There was the knife lying between the front bucket seats. Evidently one of the bad guys had forgotten it there as he unsuccessfully tried to remove my radio. I turned on the dome light and tried to look at my face, but then a shiver came down my spine. "What if they decide to come back?" I put the keys in the ignition and started the car. Only then, when I put my right hand on the steering wheel, did I see the big gash across the back of my hand. Sometime during the attack, I had taken a knife wound that laid my hand entirely open.

I muttered, "Don't go into shock. Drive yourself to the hospital. Don't go into shock." The hospital was about a mile and a half away, and there I received five stitches to my upper lip, and my right hand was temporarily patched up. Miraculously my nose was not broken, just scuffed by the rock.

The cut on my hand had severed the tendons running from my third and fourth fingers. The next morning the tendons were repaired, and I received fifteen stitches. That same week came a root canal on my one broken tooth, which had been shattered to the root; a composite filling was used to make it appear whole again. There was still hope that the other one would survive, but not until two years later was it found that a root canal was needed on that tooth too. I have yet to get caps on the teeth, but it is only a matter of time before I will have to.

My hand was in a cast for six weeks, running to the tips of my fingers so the tendons would heal. I am right-handed, which made for a most inconvenient month and a half. As a professor, I do a fair amount of typing. I must say, I became good at typing with only my left hand. Other things were not so easy, like trying to wash my left armpit or flossing my teeth. I could hold nothing at all with my injured hand, and I couldn't wait until the cast was off.

Unfortunately, the really hard part was yet to come. As the orthopedic doctor told me, if you take a perfectly healthy hand and totally immobilize it for only one week, the ligaments tighten up, and you will not be able to move it at all. After having my hand in a cast for six weeks, I could expect nothing less.

My fingers had been tightly wrapped in the cast with no space between them. After the doctor removed the plaster, he gently spread my fore- and middle fingers apart not more than a quarter of an inch. I wanted to throw up. He had told me I might feel a little nausea, but I did not believe him. How wrong I was.

I was referred to a physical therapist, who for the next several weeks attempted to restore movement in my hand. I am convinced physical therapists exist to do to your body what you would never do to yourself. The pain was unbearable at times; yet she mercilessly continued. Slowly I regained movement, first just the bending of the fingertips, then moving them downward toward the palm, later approaching a fist. Each step was excruciating.

It took several months before I could write with my hand, or throw a football, or pick up and grab something tightly. I play the piano, and I feared such an injury would permanently prohibit me from doing so, but thankfully that was not the case. Still I cannot make a full, tight fist, and on rainy days particularly I get an aching pain in my hand. Even as I type, there is a dull ache that runs up my tendon to my elbow.

I must admit, I am fortunate. Just two weeks before I was mugged, a man was driving in one of the suburbs of Windhoek and stopped at a stop sign. Another man came running out of the bush along the road and hit him in the face with a rock through his open window. The blow destroyed his right cheek bone, and he eventually lost his eye. The thug stole fifty dollars and a cell phone in the exchange.

I had been jumped by two men who had similar intentions. It did not matter where they hit me in the face, so long as they hit me. I could have just as easily been hit in the eye, but I wasn't. Then there was the knife, a blade about ten inches long, a homemade item obviously intended to do harm. I have kept the knife, much to my wife's chagrin. While I lay on the ground, they could have easily slit my throat or punctured my body with holes.

Still as much as I like to try to find silver linings in every dark cloud, the fact remained: I was angry. I replayed the scene over and over in my head. From the moment I had heard the noise until I turned around had hardly been five seconds, but what if I had reacted better? I envisioned fighting back and giving those guys a good whipping.

I was just at the wrong place at the wrong time, so the saying goes. Thankfully, I had little issue with God in all this. I know bad things can happen, and we must weather the storms; and I was more thankful that things were not worse than they turned out to be. God had allowed the mugging to happen, but he also did not allow it to be worse than it was.

But those muggers. Oh, boy, I would have loved to get my hands on them. For several weeks I walked through town looking at shoes, hoping I would spot my stolen pair. Then I imagined beating the living you-know-what out of them, and a smirk of satisfaction would appear on my face as I reveled in the daydream.

As I shared the mugging with my students, they would inevitably ask what I would do if I found one of the men. The sinful part of me knew clearly that I would seek revenge, but the Spirit within me knew better. One student suggested I go to a witchdoctor who could quickly divine the culprits, and for a split second I found the offer tempting.

Pagans look for revenge, but not the disciples of Jesus. Our Master calls us to a higher ideal, a more noble model of behavior. At times I think that really stinks, and I downright hate it.

In my early twenties I attended an adult Sunday school class in my home church. The teacher asked us if we could cut out any one passage in the Bible and simply ignore it, what would it be. My answer almost immediately was, "Love your enemy." It seemed to me then, as it still does now, to be one of the most stringent commands from the mouth of Jesus.

Why on earth should I love my enemy? If a person is opposing me, don't I have the right to push back? At the least isn't neutrality acceptable—neither intending harm nor offering blessing?

## TWO TYPES OF ENEMIES

There are two kinds of enemies, and this is where the problem lies. One kind of enemy is produced by me for no other reason than my own sinfulness, my failings and selfish ways. My personality may grate on some people; with others I may have spoken gossip or treated them poorly in a bout of anger. Rash words were spoken, and I created—through my own obnoxious behavior—an enemy.

Many Christians like to think themselves persecuted for the sake of Christ, but in reality they are persecuted because they deserve it. They are rude, hateful people, the kind who show up at funerals of homosexuals with "God hates gays" signs. They revel in the prospect of unbelievers going to hell, and they frequently pray for the judgment of God to come quickly. Little do they realize that they may be praying for something they can ill afford to bear themselves.

Paul speaks of his Jewish brethren in such a way in his Epistle to the Romans. There he tells them God is blasphemed among the Gentiles because of the poor behavior of the Jews (Rom. 2:24). Those who claimed to know God and follow his commands consistently broke them, producing in the Gentiles a hatred for their hypocrisy and the God they claimed to serve.

Many Christians act similarly today. They go around driving people from the kingdom of God, looking for fights, and proudly proclaiming they are being persecuted for their faith in Jesus. Hardly. They are being persecuted for being obnoxious, nothing more. Jesus had strong words for the religious leaders of his day who behaved similarly: "Woe to you, teachers of the law and Pharisees, you hypocrites! You travel over land and sea to win a single convert, and when he becomes one, you make him twice as much a son of hell as you are" (Matt. 23:15).

Many Christians unfortunately produce the same effect when, instead of sharing the truth in love with unbelievers, they pound people over the head with it. There is no compassion or concern for the lost. Rather, there is only the shrill screaming of a "Bible thumper" who displays little of the love of Christ while dripping venomous epithets for sinners. Should we speak out against sin? Of course. But let us do it from a position of love, not one of judgment; for surely a day will come when we too will be judged with the same measure we used on others (Matt. 7:1-2).

Other Christians produce enemies when they hypocritically live in unrepentant sin, all the while condemning others for similar transgressions. For example, the sin of homosexuality is a common whipping boy of modern evangelicals while the sin of wanton divorce is hardly spoken about. Jesus teaches that improper divorce can lead to adultery, which certainly is a sin God does not take lightly.

Some reports put the divorce rate in the Christian community at over 30 percent, equal to or even higher than even some non-Christian demographics.[1] Surely here is an instance where the church is little different than the world. We have begun to allow our moral foundation to erode, and hence our moral authority to speak out against sin in our society. Who can take seriously a person speaking out against sin in the lives of others when he is all too willing to tolerate it in his own life?

Again Paul notes that his fellow Jews did the same thing: "You, therefore, have no excuse, you who pass judgment on someone else, for at whatever point you judge the other, you are condemning yourself, because you who pass judgment do the same things" (Rom. 2:1). This hypocritical living not only results in the storing up of wrath for themselves, but also the blaspheming of God by the Gentiles. Paul's words are harsh in this regard, and he uses the specific examples of stealing, adultery, and idolatry to expose the hypocrisy of the Jews. Much like Jesus referred to the teachers of the law as "blind guides" (Matt. 23:16), so Paul makes a similar allusion. Christians who are persecuted, ridiculed, and belittled for their hypocritical living are rightly persecuted, ridiculed, and belittled.

The second kind of enemy is produced by a Christian who genuinely strives to follow Christ and, in so doing, arouses animosity from those thoroughly steeped in the world and its values. This enmity comes in a variety of forms: from the materialist, who mocks the superstitious views of the Christian worldview; from the relativist, who rejects any idea of objective, religious truth binding on all men; from the hedonist, who despises the killjoy attitude of the believer; from the naturalist, who only sees in a quest for heaven a cavalier approach to Mother Earth; from the religionist, who sees a threat in Christianity as competition for his brand of faith; to the pluralist, who scorns the claim that Jesus is the only way to eternal bliss.

For all these, Jesus as the incarnate God-man, the only Mediator and Savior who through his vicarious atoning death has paid the penalty for sins committed against a holy God, is an offensive Jesus. This biblical picture of Jesus will quickly produce enemies in a tolerance-loving, relativist world. The reason so many Christians and churches have found "Jesus-lite" so appealing is because the world finds it so appealing. Declaring a warm, fuzzy Savior is not a problem; you will get little opposition from the world on that score. Declaring that this Savior demands to be Lord is where the problem lies.

We have already seen that followers of Jesus will be persecuted. We have further noted that if a Christian is not being persecuted at least to a certain degree, that Christian may not be following Jesus as he or she should. If we take a stand for Christ, persecution will surely come.

Persecution, then, produces enemies. Show me a person who is out to harm me, and I will show you my enemy. It is that simple. It might be someone at the workplace, or in my church, or even in my family. Ask yourself the question, "Who is my enemy?" and someone will most likely come to mind. If no one does, you are indeed blessed.

Or perhaps not. If persecution produces enemies, and all Christians should expect persecution in varying degrees, then all Christians should have enemies. We are not meant to go looking for and purposefully creating enemies, but if we are genuinely taking a stand for Christ in a world that hates him, we can fully expect to have an enemy or two lurking about. If we do not, perhaps we are not truly standing for Christ.

Most likely, we have both kinds of enemies in our lives, and yet our attitude toward both must be the same. Herein lies the difficulty in the teaching of Jesus.

## THE MISTAKE OF THE PHARISEES

This teaching from Jesus comes in the Sermon on the Mount. Jesus has established the radical call for his disciples in the Beatitudes, some of which we already have discussed. After declaring his intention to fulfill the law, Jesus tells his disciples that they must have a righteousness that exceeds that of the Pharisees if they expect to enter the kingdom of heaven. He then gives six concrete examples of how this surpassing righteousness is meant to be expressed.

First, Jesus covers murder; then adultery, divorce, oaths, retribution; and last, love for enemies. In each case Jesus attacks the common misperceptions of the teachers of the law when it comes to faithfully obeying the law's requirements. In each instance he exposes their lack of understanding and their improper application of the law. This is most clearly seen in the sixth example, the focus of this chapter: "You have heard that it was said, 'Love your neighbor and hate your enemy.'" There are two parts to this verse. The first comes from the Old Testament law, the other from the teaching of the Pharisees. "Love your neighbor as yourself" is the command found in Leviticus 19:18a. The verse says: "Do not seek revenge or bear a grudge against one of your people, but love your neighbor as yourself."

There is a simple principle involved in Leviticus 19:18. How do you want people to treat you? Do you want them to hold grudges against you? Have you ever been confronted by a person who simply will not forgive you for some wrong you committed, even if it was years ago? We should not take vengeance into our own hands. We should not look for ways to retaliate against someone who has harmed us. But the command in Leviticus 19:18 not only addresses our actions; it addresses our attitudes as well. We should not even harbor a grudge against somebody else. Love that person as yourself. In other words, treat that person the way you want to be treated.

The Pharisees, though, interpreted this love for one's neighbor as a license to hate those who were their enemies. In fact, the Pharisees made two mistakes in this regard. The first was to understand the word *neighbor* to only mean someone close to them—a friend, companion, or fellow countryman.

This errant understanding of *neighbor* was exposed by Jesus in the parable of the Good Samaritan. Samaritans, hated and despised by the Jews as half-breeds, were in no way considered neighbors by the Jews. For this reason Jesus chose a Samaritan to make his point in that parable. *Neighbor* really means anyone with whom you come into contact.

The second mistake the Pharisees made was to conclude that if they were commanded specifically to love their neighbor, they did not have to love their enemies. If you are not required to love your enemies, what is left really but to hate them?

If you sit back and think about it for a moment, what the Pharisees did was incredible. In a command that tells us to love people, they found the right to hate others. "By Jesus's time, this hatred of foreigners was so institutionalized that the Jews thought they were honoring God by despising anyone who was not Jewish."[2]

## WHAT? NO ABJECT INDIFFERENCE?

It is against this backdrop that Jesus interjects his interpretation of the law: "But I tell you: love your enemies and pray for those who persecute you." Immediately our minds should recall what Jesus said in the Beatitudes at the beginning of Matthew 5. He said we should rejoice when we are persecuted. We may find ourselves saying, "Okay, so I must rejoice when I'm persecuted, but that doesn't mean that I have to *like* the people persecuting me." And we may make the error the Pharisees made, reading too much into a passage of Scripture and trying to find reason to keep harboring ill will in our hearts.

Jesus allows us no such liberty. In later manuscripts of the Bible, verse 44 is actually expanded and reads, "Love your enemies, bless those who curse you, do good to those who hate you, and pray for those who persecute you."[3] What an incredibly insensitive thing for Jesus to command us to do.

This insensitivity of Jesus is made all the more striking when the command to love our enemy is understood in the context of the verses immediately preceding it (Matt. 5:39-42). There we find four equally stringent commands about not resisting an evil person: 1) "turn the other cheek"; in other words, do not retaliate when someone insults you; 2) give up your cloak in addition to the tunic you were sued for; 3) go an extra mile if forced to go one mile; and 4) do not refuse to lend to someone who asks to borrow from you.

First, I have to endure insult and open myself to greater insult by offering my other cheek. Then I have to give up my property rights, my legal rights, my personal rights, and my financial rights. And now I must love my enemy? I'm not even allowed to be indifferent toward him, let alone to hate him? I must love him? What does Jesus expect of me, the moon?

In a way, yes, he does. We find Jesus commanding his disciples not only to love their enemies but to pray for them. This does not mean the sort of prayer that says, "Dear Lord, help my enemy; change his heart so he will no longer persecute me." That is a prayer for me, not for my enemy. When Jesus commands us to pray for our enemies, we are meant to ask for God's blessing for them, to ask that good and not evil befall them, and so on.

This is an issue of trust. Knowing that we are being insulted or opposed or harmed by our enemies, God still asks us to pray for them. God is just. In praying for our enemies, we are displaying absolute trust that God will judge justly, much as Christ did (1 Pet. 2:23).

## LESSONS FROM HISTORY

As I pored through the writings of great church leaders from the past, I was amazed at the paucity of material on loving your enemy. To be sure, there was a great amount on the love of neighbor as yourself, and love of enemy could rightly be categorized under this section, but Jesus makes a distinction between the two in his teaching, obviously recognizing the qualitative difference entailed in loving those who hate you. Even in the mystics, who often speak of love in such palpable, sentimental ways, there was virtually nothing concerning love of enemy. This is especially surprising when many of them speak of "perfect love" or degrees or kinds of love.

In the monastic rules of the father of Western monasticism, Saint Benedict of Nursia (480-547), seventy-one "instruments of good works" are enumerated, starting with love of God and neighbor, mirroring the teaching of Jesus about the "greatest commandment."[4] Love for our enemies is number thirty, and praying for our enemies is near the end of the list at sixty-nine. We see a distinction made between love of neighbor and love of enemy, and thankfully Benedict recognized this important command by Jesus and included it in his list.

Reformer John Calvin bemoaned the fact that during his day, many prominent "schoolmen" had turned this command of Jesus into a "counsel" that was then only meant to be followed by the most rigid of Christians, normally the monks. This Calvin tells us was done because the command to love one's enemy was thought to be too burdensome for the average Christian to obey. Calvin noted Thomas Aquinas and Philip Melanchthon as two of the culprits in this regard.[5] In essence, Calvin cited the most influential Catholic theologian in the Middle Ages and arguably the most significant Lutheran scholar after Luther. So it is reasonable to conclude that much of sixteenth-century Christianity was influenced to think this way about this command of Jesus.

Martin Luther, who ranks among the greatest Christian leaders of the past two millennia and who is at the top of my personal list of theologians who have influenced my beliefs, serves as an excellent example of a Christian who bit back. I am certain that if someone wanted to compile a list of all the personal attacks, hateful comments, and name-calling that Luther engaged in, such a list could fill a small book. Luther's temper and distemper are well known, despite the fact that few have positively influenced Christianity more than he.

Just a small sampling should suffice. Luther had specific words for his enemies in *Table Talk*.[6] Among the choice comments include calling Tetzel, Cochlaeus, and Lemnius "detestable," referring to Martin Cellarius as an "impious knave," and teaching his followers to "despise" Campanus, not just his teaching, but the man himself. Luther referred to Erasmus of Rotterdam as "the vilest miscreant that ever disgraced the earth."

Then, of course, we could include in such a study Luther's comments about the pope as antichrist, or even about other reasonably likeminded Christians such as the Swiss reformer Ulrich Zwingli, with whom Luther bickered over the proper understanding of the Lord's Supper. Luther referred to Zwingli's teaching on that score as the doctrine of Satan. Is the above a proper Christian example to be followed? More pointedly, does it violate the command of Jesus to love our enemies?

In Luther's defense one could point out similar strong language used by biblical characters. How about Jesus calling people hypocrites and a "brood of vipers," the latter echoing a denunciation of John the Baptist? Or his comment to Peter, "Get behind me, Satan," an obvious rebuke for an errant belief Peter spoke.[7] Of course, we could always claim that what was proper for the sinless Son of Man is not necessarily so for us. But consider the apostle Paul's execration of the Judaizers in his Epistle to the Galatians, in which Paul wished that these teachers of circumcision would completely emasculate themselves (5:12). He even hoped people who preach a false gospel would be "eternally condemned" (1:8-9).

I must admit that when I read such biblical condemnations, I feel more comfortable making my own. "Jesus condemned his enemies with harsh language; so I can too." But I may find myself quickly falling into the error of the Pharisees and finding scriptural justification for hatred of my enemies. Perhaps it is best never to say anything negative toward others. In this way is not the cause of Christ best served?

I have encountered well-meaning Christians who *never* have a harsh word to say. Even when faced with false doctrine and outright heresy, they neither condemn nor censure. Many unbelievers find such an approach acceptable, if for no other reason than that they do not find their anti-Christian views opposed. But how Christian is such an approach, really? Jude, Peter, Paul, and even Jesus did not practice it. We consistently find throughout Scripture words of condemnation for those who would warp and distort the truth of God. To well-meaning Christians who exude tolerance in the face of ungodliness, the incidents of Jesus clearing the temple and cursing the fig tree must seem strange indeed.

There is a well-known aphorism that goes like this: "The only thing that needs to happen for evil men to succeed is for good men to stand by and do nothing." The problem, then, is how we properly balance a defense of the gospel with the words of Jesus that command us to turn the other cheek and to love our enemies.

Here the wisdom of Luther is most helpful:

A Christian, for the sake of his own person, neither curses nor revenges himself; but faith curses and revenges itself. To understand this rightly, we must distinguish God and man, the person and cause. In what concerns God and his cause, we must have no patience, nor bless; as for example, when the ungodly persecute the gospel, this touches God and his cause, and then we are not to bless or to wish good success, but rather to curse the persecutors and their proceedings. Such is called faith's cursing, which, rather than it would suffer God's Word to be suppressed and heresy maintained, would have all creatures go to wreck; for through heresy we lose God himself, Numbers xvi. But individuals personally ought not to revenge themselves, but to suffer all things, and according to Christ's doctrine and the nature of love, to do good to their enemies.[8]

Luther is onto something here. As ambassadors of the message of reconciliation between God and man, we can expect both the message and the messenger to be attacked by those who oppose God's truth. However, we must make the active delineation between attacks against our own person (which must be ignored) and those attacks that seek to belittle the message.[9]

If I defend myself for no other reason than that I do not like to be falsely accused, or if I find myself attacking others because I feel my own character has been disparaged, I am not acting in the way Christ expects me to act. However, if I am defending the truth of the gospel and at times use condemnatory language toward those who despise the gospel, then I am not overstepping the bounds of Christian decorum. Again, if the issue is my own character and person, then I should take the blows like Jesus did. But if the issue is the gospel, I am called to provide a rigorous defense.

Perhaps the best biblical example is found with Jesus and his clearing the temple of the moneychangers. This incident often causes perplexity with believers because we are accustomed to the meek and mild image of Jesus. Picturing him making cords and whipping people while overturning their tables strikes many of us as out of character. It is behavior we find more familiar with a madman than the Son of Man.

However, it shouldn't surprise us. The character of God was at stake, and Jesus made no mistake about communicating that fact. Whereas we might be shocked at the blatant disregard Jesus showed for personal property, he was more concerned with the character of his Father and defending it. As we noted in chapter 4, rather than an anomaly with respect to the character of Jesus, the temple-clearing is a defining moment.

Yet Jesus was willing to undergo extreme insult and persecution when it came to his own person. Mocking him, spitting in his face, and even physically assaulting him was met with mild complacency, as were the constant personal jabs and attacks on his character that he experienced throughout his ministry. Evidently, Jesus clearly saw the difference between attacks on his person and attacks against God the Father.

My problem, of course, is making a distinction between the two kinds of attacks. Frequently, in sharing or defending the truth of the Christian faith, I find myself personally attacked. Often it is easier for people to make *ad hominem* attacks than to address the substance of the issues. This is perhaps no better evident than in the modern debates over abortion and homosexuality. At times both sides merely make personal attacks ("baby killers" versus "women haters," or "depraved perverts" versus "bigots and homophobes"), without addressing the substance of the issues. Neither side is above such tactics.

The true disciple of Christ is called to great discernment and self-control in this area. If we are personally attacked, the teaching of our Lord is crystal clear: We should not retaliate. As difficult as it is for me to separate my religious convictions from my person—because what I believe is who I am—I must do so. I have come across people who despise me for no other reason than because of my faith in Jesus, but when their attacks are hurled at my person, and not simply at my beliefs, I become defensive. I am what I believe. If you say my beliefs are nonsensical and uneducated, you imply the same thing about my person.

I have been falsely attacked and slandered, my views caricatured and twisted, and things I do not believe wrongly attributed to me, all in an attempt to disparage my character and hence my Christian beliefs. I have been called names from the mildly amusing "idiot" to the much more vulgar.

And I fought back with equal vehemence. I defended myself, pointing out the lies and slander, often with my own derogatory name-calling thrown in, and I received back in my face, "You call yourself a Christian? Christians aren't supposed to act that way." At times I wonder how many people I have driven from the kingdom in this manner.

This "message versus the messenger" approach requires extreme caution and prudence. Just as surely as I have a problem distinguishing between my message being attacked versus my person, those in the world will feel similarly. In other words, condemning sin can easily be confused with condemning sinners, and when we condemn sinful behavior that is near and dear to the heart of unbelievers, we should expect to be strongly attacked, often personally. In these instances we must endeavor to continue to be loving, never denying the gospel truth, but at the same time not taking personal assaults to heart.

"Do not repay evil with evil or insult with insult, but with blessing, because to this you were called so that you may inherit a blessing" (1 Pet. 3:9). We are not even allowed to be indifferent but must instead bless when we are personally attacked.

## WHY MUST WE LOVE OUR ENEMIES?

As noted earlier in the Sermon on the Mount, Jesus expects the righteousness of his disciples to surpass that of the Pharisees. He provides two reasons why.

### Sons of Our Father

The first reason is that as children of God we should emulate the character of our Father, "that you may be sons of your father in heaven." God "causes his sun to rise on the evil and the good, and sends rain on the righteous and the unrighteous" (Matt. 5:45). God does not show favoritism in this respect; if we want to be his children, we should not show favoritism either.

An example comes from the sixteenth-century Protestant Reformation. The Anabaptists, a group of Protestant Christians, were hated and despised by Catholics and other Protestants alike. For several decades, Anabaptists endured terrible persecution at the hands of other Christians. One account involved an Anabaptist man running for his life from several Lutheran Christians who wanted to execute him. The flight of the Anabaptist took him over a frozen lake. At one point, one of his pursuers fell through the ice, and the Anabaptist stopped, ran back, and saved him from drowning. He was captured as a result.

We may find this odd or even foolish behavior. But the question is, if it were your friend who fell through the ice, would you not attempt to save him? So why, now that it is your enemy, do you not do so?

A reasonable objection might pop into our heads: Doesn't God punish evildoers? So the sun and the rain come upon them, but that doesn't negate the fact that he also punishes them. We may even revel in that saying, "God is enacting judgment, and I am his instrument of vengeance." In other words, if I am called to imitate God, can I not also imitate him in judgment? But there is a vast difference between what we are commanded to do and what God does. In short, he does not allow us to take vengeance or retribution into our own hands. So why does Jesus use the example of the sun and the rain when he commands us to love our enemy?

I think the answer is found in the idea of repentance. We are limited in our understanding, and we are not privy to what God intends to do in the future. It could well be that God intends to draw people to himself through our meekness and gentleness and willingness to endure mistreatment. "The Lord is not slow in keeping his promise, as some understand slowness. He is patient with you, not wanting anyone to perish, but everyone to come to repentance" (2 Pet. 3:9). If God allows room for repentance, so must we.

If all we ever do is insult back when insulted, strike back when being struck, or hate those who hate us, the only thing we can expect from those people are more insults, more blows, and more hatred. Repaying evil with evil will only continue the evil. An old Zulu proverb teaches this same truth: "Those who bite get bitten."

God shows his grace in some form to all people. Theologically we call this "common grace," and from it can come two different reactions. The first is that people will respond to that common grace, repent, and be saved. The other is that they will continue to harden their hearts toward God and will then endure the inevitable punishment.

How do you and I know who is who? How do we know if our enemy will eventually repent or will continue to remain hard-hearted? Do you want God to tell you one day that you had something to do with your enemy's continued hard-heartedness? Or would you rather hear from God how your meekness and non-retaliatory manner was instrumental in drawing that person to Christ? I hope the choice is obvious.

*Do not repay anyone evil for evil. Do not take revenge, my friends, but leave room for God's wrath, for it is written: "It is mine to avenge; I will repay, says the Lord." On the contrary: "If your enemy is hungry, feed him; if he is thirsty, give him something to drink. In doing this, you will heap burning coals on his head." Do not be overcome by evil, but overcome evil with good. (Rom. 12:17a, 19-21)*

Because God shows his common grace to all people, we should do the same.

### A Surpassing Righteousness

The second reason Jesus gives for why we must love our enemy is found in Matthew 5:46-47: "If you love those who love you, what reward will you get? Are not even the tax collectors doing that? And if you greet only your brothers, what are you doing more than others? Do not even pagans do that?" Jesus expects his disciples to have a surpassing righteousness. If all we do is act like pagans, how can we consider ourselves to be salt and light in the world?

We are not called to indifference toward our enemies and love toward our brothers, neighbors, family, or friends. We are called to love all people, even our enemies. We act as salt, preserving the world from its increasing decay and hatred, and we act as light, drawing people to the love of Christ. If all we do is repay evil with evil, we will only drive people away from Christ.

Of course, we may ask, "Who is my enemy?" I assume each of us could individually give a solid answer to that question. It could be the boss at work who mistreats you, or someone who hates you and spreads vicious lies about you, or even the family member who abused you or belittled you for years. Corporately, we as Christians might consider as our enemies those who oppose Christianity, or those who oppose the morality and Christian ethics we hope our society would maintain. Our enemies could be the people who in general oppose the people of God. We are commanded—this is not a suggestion from Jesus as if we have a choice in the matter—to love our enemies and to pray for them.

King David had a clear enemy early in his life, King Saul. At one point, Saul took three thousand men to hunt down and kill David in the desert. Incredibly, while David was hiding in the back of a cave, Saul came in to relieve himself. David had the opportunity to sneak up on Saul and end his troubles by killing him. Instead, he cut off a corner of Saul's robe and later showed it to Saul, proving that he did not intend to harm the king.

Here is what David said to Saul:

> May the LORD judge between you and me. And may the LORD avenge the wrongs you have done to me, but my hand will not touch you. As the old saying goes, "From evildoers come evil deeds," so my hand will not touch you. . . . May the LORD be our judge and decide between us. May he consider my cause and uphold it; may he vindicate me by delivering me from your hand. (1 Sam. 24:12-13, 15)

Incredibly, David had another opportunity to kill Saul, this time taking Saul's spear and water jug as proof, and yet again did not kill the king. This time Saul seemed to have a moment of repentance when he cried out to David, "You are more righteous than I" (1 Sam. 24:17), but as we know, his repentance was short-lived. David had hoped his actions toward Saul would cause Saul to relent, but even if Saul did not, David entrusted his cause to God.

There is practical wisdom in loving our enemies. If we hate them back, they will always remain our enemies. As Abraham Lincoln once said: "The best way to eliminate your enemies is to make them your friends." Hating our enemies and attempting to bring them harm makes us no different than the pagans, who do the same thing. Jesus expects more from his disciples.

There is also great liberty in loving your enemy and praying for him. Just consider the opposite. Consider the amount of wasted emotional energy when we stew in bitterness and anger toward others or when we plot their demise. I must admit, for a short while such conniving can bring me pleasure, but in the long run, all it does is tap my spiritual vitality. I eventually realized what a waste of time it was walk-

**153**

ing around downtown Windhoek looking at shoes, hoping to get my revenge on those muggers. Much greater peace comes in handing the matter over to God, who alone can judge rightly and has the ability to do so.

Our world is filled with hatred. Can you imagine if all Christians throughout the world began to behave in the way prescribed here by Jesus? Can you imagine the transformation that would take place, both in the lives of those faithful Christians and in the lives of unbelievers? Certainly, there will always be evil men who view love and forgiveness as a sign of weakness, particularly when shown by their enemies, and they will move to exploit it. But this would not even begin to negate the revolution that would take place in humanity if we learned to love our enemies and woo them.

Two twentieth-century examples, both from South African men not avowed to be Christians but who nonetheless displayed this type of love, demonstrate how attractive such a love can be. Mahatma Gandhi attributed his nonviolent resistance to the teaching of Jesus. Many saw in it a remarkable strength not otherwise displayed by those who violently oppose their enemies.

The other example is Nelson Mandela. After over two decades of false imprisonment at the hands of the Apartheid regime, Mandela emerged as the leader of South Africa and its first democratically-elected president. With the reins of power in his hands, he easily could have struck back at his enemies, but Mandela took the high road. He instituted a time of reconciliation unheard of on the African continent, and the world now rightly esteems him. Although not a professing Christian, Mandela certainly was influenced by the Christianity of his homeland.

A final twentieth-century example can be found in the person of Martin Luther King, Jr., who clearly was influenced by this teaching of Jesus. Other black leaders in the civil rights movement called for violent confrontation with those who opposed their freedom, but Dr. King did no such thing. Today we honor his nonviolent opposition with a public holiday.

## DEGREES OF LOVE

The simple truth is, hatred of our enemy diverts us from the love of God. If we truly want to be called children of God, then this command of Jesus stands at the forefront of Christian discipleship, not as an appendix. We cannot say we love God when we hate our enemy.

Scripture recognizes different types or degrees of love. On one level is the simple love of family, perhaps the easiest type of love. This love comes naturally to us and normally does not need to be manufactured. It is this kind of love that Jesus refers to when he states that his disciples must "hate [their] father and mother," a matter we will come to in a later chapter.

The next level is the love of your brother, the common term used throughout the New Testament to refer to fellow believers. This love might not come as naturally as familial love and may be more difficult to conjure. We can all think of times when we have come across other believers with whom we instantly have a common bond through Christ. I have had contact with many believers from vastly different cultures than my own, but a love between us is immediately present due to our shared faith. Still, love of brothers can be difficult, especially in a church setting where conflict can result between believers who have differing viewpoints. John's first epistle is the quintessential statement on brotherly love, especially 4:20-21, where he tells us we cannot claim to love God if we do not love our brothers.

Love of neighbor is a more general type of love that extends to all those with whom we come into contact in our community, in the workplace, in business, or in recreation. In some instances easy, at other times more difficult, neighborly love is usually expressed in the adage, "Do unto others as you would have them do unto you."

Next is love of enemy, which is perhaps the most difficult level of love. In this instance, there is no instinctive love present as with familial love, nor is there the common bond that accompanies brotherly love. Further, it is not as easy as neighborly love that, although at times difficult, still does not involve a person who is actively opposing you or harming you. The love of our enemies, then, is perhaps the most unnatural love of all.

Lastly, of course, is love of God. In a strange way, the love of our enemies trains us to better love God, by guiding us in emulating his character. If God did not show love for his enemies, as Paul argues in Romans 5:6-11, we would be without hope. The love of our enemies is one of the ways we become "imitators of God" (Eph. 5:1).

Jesus tells us that pagans love their families and friends, and if his disciples do so, they are not doing anything out of the ordinary. But love of your enemies, ah, that is a surpassing love. It is a love that does not come naturally but must be received through the power of God's Spirit. "To return evil for good is devilish; to return good for good is human; to return good for evil is divine."[10] At the end of his teaching on this subject, Jesus told his disciples to "be perfect as your heavenly Father is perfect" (Matt. 5:48). Is it an accident that this command falls right after his teaching on the love of enemy?

## PERFECT LOVE

Miraculously, I find in this harsh command to love my enemy a perfect peace that transcends all understanding. As I begin to love my enemy and pray for him, a wonderful transformation takes place—not necessarily in my enemy but in me. I begin to move farther along the spectrum of transformation into the image of God's Son. Concerning those muggers, I moved in my thinking away from the hope of evil befalling them to the hope that they would genuinely repent of their sin and trust God for forgiveness. Pagans hope for evil to befall their enemies, but the disciples of Jesus Christ hope for blessing to come upon them.

However, to attain this perfect love, I must submit myself to the power of the Holy Spirit. It is not something that can be attained in my own strength. My natural inclination is not only to hate my enemy but to hate this command as well.

The issue is one of trust. Do I trust God enough to submit to this teaching, or do I prefer my own way? In submission I move along the path of humility, learning the art of spiritual love.

This is my calling. Our Lord Jesus Christ commands it. To condone anything short of this perfection is to condone sin in my life. I am convinced that if I take this teaching seriously, I will be transformed into the godly person Christ desires me to be. I should not act like a pagan. Christ calls me to a higher calling. May God give me the grace to live as I should.

Do we flinch from the test? Do we find it impossible to do good to our enemies? If that is the case we may be sure we have yet to be converted.[11]

J. C. Ryle

# 7

# THE ART OF
# SPIRITUAL FORGIVENESS

*But if you do not forgive men their sins, your Father will not forgive your sins.*

JESUS CHRIST, MATTHEW 6:15

*There are few duties so strongly commanded in the New Testament Scriptures as this duty is, and few whose neglect so clearly shuts a man out of the kingdom of God.*

J. C. RYLE (1816-1900),
ANGLICAN MINISTER, *MATTHEW*

*A man can as well go to hell for not forgiving as for not believing.*

THOMAS WATSON (1620-1686),
PURITAN PASTOR, *THE LORD'S PRAYER*

My wife Rachel and I have spent several terms as missionaries in Namibia, first arriving in 1994. A term is five years, with four on the field and one for furlough or home assignment back in the States. Because of the expense of travel from Namibia to America, only in rare instances would we consider traveling to the States before our furlough year.

One such instance occurred in 1997 when Rachel went home for her sister's wedding. At the time we had three children, and the youngest was a little over a year old and had yet to be seen by anyone in our families. It was a good opportunity, then, for Rachel to take her back to the States for the three weeks she planned to remain there. I stayed in Namibia with our two older children, who were then five and three.

One Sunday morning I went to church with my two little munchkins and was asked by a young lady whom we knew where Rachel was. I told her about the trip to the States, and she seemed mildly interested. Later that afternoon I heard a voice calling from outside the fence of our home, and it was the same woman. She said she was in the neighborhood and thought she would stop by to say hello. I let her in, and she visited us for a little while, then departed. Outside of church or the chance occasion where I bumped into her in town, I never saw her again.

A year later our first term in Namibia ended, and we returned for a year to the States. In 1999 we came back to Namibia to begin our second term. Only several months after our return did a friend from church tell me that rumors had spread about me in my year of absence. I was shocked by the rumors, but when asked, other friends told me similar stories. It seemed that during our furlough the young lady visitor from our church began to tell people that I had tried to make sexual advances on her.

The rumors were disturbing. Fortunately, I had several friends to whom this woman had gossiped who did not believe the stories, and they were kind enough to tell me about them. Each story had a different twist on how I supposedly made advances; no two stories were alike.

Fortunately, and rather ironically, one of the women to whom she told these lies was intimately familiar with something comparable. Back in 1997, the year this young lady had come to my home unexpectedly, she had made similar accusations against my friend's husband. One afternoon this same woman unexpectedly visited his home while his wife was away, and he let her in for a brief visit. Later she began to spread the rumor that she had had an affair with this man. All people involved went to the same church, and the elders launched an investigation into the matter. They concluded it was a lie, and they disciplined the young lady.

During our year of absence, she took the opportunity to spread the same vicious lies about me when I was not around to contest them. By the time I was able to piece all the puzzle together, it was nearly two and a half years after that one visit she made to our home.

I was faced with a difficult decision: dredge up the matter in an official capacity with the church or let it drop. Taking into consideration that her visit to my home was now thirty months in the past, and realizing everyone she had gossiped to about me (with whom I had spoken) did not believe the allegations, I decided to drop the matter.

Incredibly, it was not until 2002 when our mission field director asked to talk to me privately that the issue came up again. Evidently the woman was still slandering me, now five years later, and he had heard about it from a friend. By this time the woman was well known for her lying ways, and she had tried the same thing with several other married men, to the point where she was banned from the church for a year. Still, my mission boss wanted to know about the matter and what I thought should be done about it.

To make matters worse, there had been incredible tension between the mission and the national church for several years. Some in the church's leadership felt the mission had served its purpose and needed to leave the country. Fortunately, many of us in the mission were involved in other ministries outside the church, and the idea of the mission leaving the country altogether was questionable at best. It was in this atmosphere that my field director wanted to know about the rumor he heard concerning my sexual misconduct with a young woman in the church.

Once again I faced the problem of what to do. Taking a formal complaint to the elders of the church would accentuate the problems that existed between mission agency and church, but doing nothing might make it appear that there was some truth to the allegations. The choice was difficult.

I must admit there was bitterness in my heart during the ordeal. Rachel and I discussed the matter, and at times my anger would well up to such an extent that I did not care what would happen, just so long as I could shut up the slanderous woman. Irrationality surfaced in my thoughts, and I spent many sleepless nights pondering the evil that I could do to her.

Still, deep within my soul I knew I could not retaliate or take any steps that would flow from vengeance. The best course, and the one most biblical, was to first confront the woman personally before going to the church. However, in light of sexual allegations of misconduct, I could hardly do that alone; so my wife and I decided to meet with her to discuss the matter. A time was set, and we went to visit her.

She was taken aback that I had brought my wife with me, even though I told her I would. Further, I brought along a tape recorder and placed it between us; so she knew everything she said henceforth would be recorded. I then asked her specifically about the rumors I had heard and the comments attributed to her. With each one she denied having said them.

At the end of our meeting I told her I never wanted to hear these rumors again, but that I was satisfied with her answers. I have never had a conversation with her since.

As I write, it is three years after that meeting. Last month I heard from a friend that the slanderous woman lied about the meeting my wife and I had with her, attempting to disparage the tape recording and what was recorded on it. I still have the tape, but I have decided to drop the issue no matter what else I might hear about her slander.

But have I *forgiven* the woman? Part of me can say yes to that question, but was that forgiveness just a product of the passage of time and memory? Last month when the topic came up about the woman and the tape recording, within moments bitterness welled up inside me again, and I became angry. It is now eight years since I let that woman into my home, and still she has this sick desire to slander me. When will it end?

There is a natural overlap between this chapter and the previous one. The ability to love your enemy normally has the prerequisite of forgiving him. In this sense, then, the present chapter might more logically have been covered before the last chapter. However, I see the issue of forgiveness as much broader than the matter of loving your enemy.

The act of forgiveness does not necessarily involve an enemy although it often does. In those times when we are hurt or harmed by someone, at that moment those people become enemies, and much of what we said in the previous chapter can apply to the context of forgiveness. However, as a general distinction, I see an enemy as someone with whom there is an ongoing struggle, whereas forgiveness is often a one-time issue and may even involve those we love the most. There is enough difference between the two that a specific discussion about forgiveness is warranted. For starters, Jesus speaks often about forgiving others, and it is here where many Christians fail.

## "FORGIVE THEM, FATHER"

How easy it is for us to harbor ill will toward those who hurt us, often finding good justification for doing so. Sometimes, under the guise of self-respect, we hold a grudge because it would be beneath us to allow the infraction to slide. Or we can be as crass as seeking revenge simply because we are able to do so.

A study of the Gospels reveals the prominence of forgiveness in the teaching of Jesus. For example, it is the only item from the Lord's Prayer that Jesus expands upon. Several well-known parables employ it as their main theme (e.g., parable of the unmerciful servant, parable of the prodigal son). There are also other instances from the teaching of Jesus that express this command in didactic form ("forgive seventy times seven"). It is one of the most prominent elements in the teaching of Jesus, as we would expect.

Perhaps the most incredible instance of forgiveness is from the Lord himself. As he hung on the cross, blood pouring from his battered body, he spent some of his limited energy and breath to pray for those who crucified him: "Father, forgive them, for they do not know what they are doing" (Luke 23:34a).

This example must be firmly implanted in our minds as we begin the difficult task of understanding what it means to be a forgiving person. Remember, Jesus never asks us to do something he was not willing to do. In this case, if he asks us to forgive people even when they perform the most heinous and horrible acts imaginable to us, he is not asking us to do something foreign to his own experience. Jesus suffered insult, mocking, ridicule, scorn, and the worst type of execution known in Roman times—and he was guilty of absolutely nothing. The sinless Son of God received abuse from rotten sinners and yet was willing to forgive.

If this is the example he set for us, how can we, who due to our own sinfulness often play a part in the alienation and confrontation we experience with other sinners, claim that we need not be forgiving people? In fact, as we will see, the command of Jesus is not intended to be an occasional practice, or to be performed in select instances. It is a command for *unlimited* forgiveness on our behalf, the kind Jesus is willing to give us.

## IT'S ALL IN THE PARABLES

The parable of the prodigal or lost son warms our hearts because of the forgiving spirit the father showed toward his wayward son. Had Jesus ended the story by telling us that the father demanded that the son repay every cent he frivolously wasted of his inheritance or that it took several months or even years before the father warmed back up to his son, we would have a parable few people would find touching. Yet I am certain many people would still find the parable satisfying, thinking, *That worthless son got exactly what he deserved.*

The thing is, if all of us got what we deserved from God, none of us could bear it. I am consistently amazed by believers who proclaim that God has not dealt fairly with them or who have the audacity to speak the words, "I demand justice from you, God." If that is what we want from God—fairness and justice—none of us would appreciate the results. For a holy God to deal fairly and justly with sinners, he would have to punish us. Fairness would mean hanging on that cross in the place of Jesus.

Fact is, what we have received from God is mercy. Pure, unadulterated mercy. We have received what we did *not* deserve. Fairness would have been to have us endure our own punishment and penalty for our sins against an eternal God. Mercy is what we actually obtained. God's Son came and bore our penalty for us.

The parable of the workers in the vineyard (Matt. 20:1-16) is instructive here. There we find men who have agreed to work for a day's wage and who put in twelve hours of labor. Because the vineyard owner realizes that he needs more workers, he goes out and hires extra hands at different points during the day. Some of the workers come quite late and work only one hour.

When it comes time to pay all the workers, the vineyard owner gives them all the same wage. The early-arriving workers, who have "borne the burden of the work and the heat of the day," get paid the same amount as those workers who only labored for one hour. The former complain, and we can understand why, because on the surface the situation seems unfair.

Yet Jesus will not allow such an understanding. In the parable, the vineyard owner represents God the Father, and we are told that the men who have worked the whole day got exactly what they initially agreed to receive, a full day's wage. To their complaints the vineyard owner responds that the men should not begrudge his generosity to the late-arriving workers: "Don't I have the right to do what I want with my own money?" In the parable, the full-day workers receive fairness (they get exactly what they deserved) while the late-arriving workers receive grace or mercy (they get what they do not deserve).

We need to get beyond the false dichotomy of fairness and unfairness when it comes to God's dealings with humanity. No such separation exists. God never deals unfairly with sinful humans. Rather it is fairness and mercy. We must put aside our man-made ideas of justice and fairness because they do not apply to God. God's generosity transcends human ideas of fairness.

Too many Christians have the attitude of the early-arriving workers. They believe they deserve God's grace, which of course would not make it grace at all. Grace is unmerited favor shown to those who only deserve punishment; by definition grace is unwarranted and unearned.

If a man comes and works in my yard, I pay him because he has earned the pay. This we call merit. It is the opposite of grace. If a man comes and steals my car, and I catch him but let him go, then he has received grace. Grace and merit are opposites.[1]

On a larger scale, we must understand that our salvation comes entirely as a free act of grace by God. If we want to rely on our works, then we can rely on them straight to hell. Those who work, work themselves to hell. Entrance into heaven is by grace; entrance into hell is by works. Being saved by grace means that the entire process of salvation is by grace.

- We are saved by grace, but continuing in our salvation is not a product of our works.
- We cannot add to grace, as if our salvation is a cooperation between ourselves and God.
- We cannot lose our salvation, which would imply an ability to work to keep it.

This understanding of grace is instructive concerning forgiveness because we must understand that everything we receive from God is undeserved. *Everything.* We will always have a tendency to harbor bitterness and grudges as long as we misunderstand God's mercy shown to us. Once I believe all I have is mine, and what I have is deserved by me, I will be less willing to show mercy to others. After all, if they have harmed me, I deserve recompense for my suffering.

Conversely, if I realize my spiritual poverty and destitution, understanding that I receive all I have as if I am a beggar, then granting others forgiveness becomes easy. Yes, I said easy, not easier. When we recognize that our entire relationship with God is undeserved grace—favor shown to us when all we deserve is punishment and God's wrath—granting forgiveness to others should be easy for us.

Did someone harm us, slander us, or abuse us? What they deserve, of course, is punishment. What they deserve is to endure that same treatment from others. But Jesus expects his disciples not to think that way. We have an unholy propensity for desiring mercy when we have harmed others but being stingy in offering it to those who harm us. An unforgiving spirit is almost always the product of a false view of ourselves and our salvation, placing ourselves on a pedestal above others.

But when we realize God has shown us unmerited favor, we will be quick to show it to others.

## THE PARABLE OF THE UNMERCIFUL SERVANT

It is difficult to rank the parables in order of degree of judgment and dread, but if we were to attempt to do so, the parable of the unmerciful servant (Matt. 18:23-35) would rank near the top. That verdict is driven not so much by the details of the parable as by the concluding comment: "This is how my heavenly Father will treat each of you unless you forgive your brother from your heart" (v. 35). With this, we get a clear teaching about how God will act toward us if we are unforgiving people.

The details of the parable are subject to hyperbole. For effect, Jesus contrasts the great amount of money the servant owed the king[2] to the amount a lesser servant owed the first servant, which amounted to less than a day's wage. So great was the debt of the servant to the king that the king had determined to sell the servant's wife and children into slavery as well as confiscate all his material possessions. The point Jesus is trying to make, of course, is that the servant could not possibly repay such an incredible debt. The parallel to our own lives is that we have a similar debt to pay to God, one we could not possibly repay.

Begging for mercy, the servant is shown it by the king who cancels all his debt. This inconceivable act of kindness should cause the servant to act accordingly, should he find himself in a similar situation. If the servant had done that, we would not have a parable. However, the forgiven servant finds another servant who owes him such a pittance of money that it is not even worth mentioning. Demonstrating a lack of awareness of the great mercy he had been shown by the king, the servant physically accosts this other servant and throws him into prison, even though the servant begs for more time to pay back the small debt. Thus the title of this parable. The servant who was shown great mercy is himself unmerciful.

We are rightly shocked when we see such an attitude, and we may, like King David did upon hearing the report from the prophet Nathan, want to strike out at such a man. That is, until we find out that the man is us. The debt we owed to God was so great that it would be impossible for us to pay it back. But God, in sending his Son, cancelled the debt. Now, in the light of such mercy, we should act likewise.

The character of the king in the parable exudes mercy—up to a point. Upon hearing about the actions of the unmerciful servant, he seizes him and has him thrown into prison to be tortured until he can pay back everything he owes. Of course, once in prison, the man will not be able to pay back anything, and that is the point. He was forgiven a debt he could never have paid back and now, due to his own unforgiving heart, he will experience firsthand just how much he had been forgiven.

Jesus is telling us that as forgiven people we should in turn be forgiving people. It is ludicrous for us to have a debt forgiven that amounts to our lives and then turn around and be unmerciful to those who owe us what amounts to far, far less. Who can rightly hold a finite debt (sins against other sinners) as unforgivable when he recognizes he has been forgiven an infinite debt (sins against the eternal God)?

As citizens of the kingdom of heaven, we should not only forgive, but do it exhaustively. Jesus provided this parable in the context of a question asked by Peter: "Lord, how many times shall I forgive my brother when he sins against me? Up to seven times?" Peter's opening question about forgiving someone seven times stems from the Jewish tradition that, once a person sinned against you more than seven times, you were not required to forgive him anymore. Jesus contradicts this Jewish tradition by telling Peter that he must forgive "seventy times seven" (Matt. 18:22). This is not to imply that after 490 times he need not forgive a person. Rather Jesus is telling Peter in a poetic way that he must always forgive.

This verse echoes the teaching of Jesus found in Luke 17:3-5: "If your brother sins, rebuke him, and if he repents, forgive him. If he sins against you seven times in a day, and seven times comes back to you and says, 'I repent,' forgive him. The apostles said to the Lord, 'Increase our faith!'"

I love the response of the disciples because it is so honest. I can relate with their exasperation: "Increase our faith!" The weight of this teaching was not lost on the disciples, and it should not be lost on us.

> Do not seek to avenge yourselves on those that injure you. . . . Let us make them brethren by our kindness.
>
> Ignatius of Antioch (35-107), *The Epistle of Ignatius to the Ephesians*

## "FROM YOUR HEART"

The parable of the unmerciful servant ends with these words: "This is how my heavenly Father will treat each of you unless you forgive your brother from your heart." This command by Jesus would be made much easier if only three words were excised from it: "from your heart." These three words move us from false forgiveness to a forgiveness that is genuine and real—and almost impossible to manufacture. If I were only commanded to forgive, with no further stipulations, I could go through all the external motions of forgiveness and not really forgive.

I could smile and wave nicely to the person, shake his hand or give her a hug, even have a polite little chat—and still harbor unforgiveness in my heart. My sepulcher could look spanking white while inside it houses contempt and bitter animosity. "From your heart" guards against false forgiveness, going through the motions, and pretending you do not hold a grudge. What wonderful imposters we can be, but Jesus will allow none of that.

Whenever I think about this command by Jesus and its seeming harshness, I think of my uncle. He was a tough man who served as an Air Force pilot in the Vietnam War; I have always respected my uncle and still do. Unfortunately, at age forty-five he died of a massive heart attack.

When he was fifteen his mother walked out on the family. My mother, his younger sister, was only twelve, and my grandfather, their father, served as a minister of a Baptist church. My grandmother left a seventeen-year marriage, took the oldest daughter who was sixteen at the time, and moved to the big city, Philadelphia, to sow her wild oats.

# TEN THINGS I WISH JESUS NEVER SAID

My mother has told me the story, and it still brings her pain, especially the part about her running down the street as her mother drove away, begging her to come back. My grandfather, who is now deceased, also related the pain that situation brought to him. It brought him problems for the ministry as few churches think highly of a pastor whose wife has left him.

For five years my grandfather waited for his wife to return. When everyone said he was crazy and should file for divorce, he did no such thing. He hoped and prayed that she would come to her senses and return home, but she never did.

As for my uncle, he vowed never to forgive his mother. Never. My mother, on the other hand, consistently attempted to reach out to her wayward mother and sister with relative success for several years. Particularly at the time of my birth, my mother's first child, the relationship was fairly strong, especially between the two sisters.

In my teen years, my aunt and grandmother fell on hard times. After a series of failed marriages they were both in financial straits and needed to move from Philadelphia back to southern New Jersey. My grandfather, who had since remarried a single missionary nurse, was instrumental in finding them an affordable place to live; he even physically helped relocate them from Philadelphia. There were people who thought my grandfather was just plain nuts for giving them a helping hand; I must admit, even now I have similar thoughts. My uncle, on the other hand, did not lift a finger to help them, and to his dying day he proclaimed he would never forgive his mother for what she had done.

I have often contemplated my uncle's attitude when I read the command of Jesus to forgive others from the heart, and anxiety creeps into my heart. I even hesitate to use it as an example for fear that the conclusion I must have is too much for me to accept. To be sure, my uncle was a Christian who loved the Lord very much, but harboring an unforgiving spirit is never right for a disciple of Jesus.

What did my uncle gain by remaining bitter his whole life? As is usually the case with the teaching of Jesus, there is practical wisdom to this command. Just like the command to love our enemies, who will always remain our enemies if we hate them back, so too harboring an unforgiving spirit only hurts us in the final analysis.

To my mother's credit, she always sought reconciliation to the best of her ability. My aunt and grandmother are still alive and are still bitter people who have shut out virtually everyone who ever loved them. I think Jesus is proud of my mother and her constant attempts at reconciliation, even though it has cost her much emotional anguish. Often my mother has had to relive that horrible feeling of rejection whenever her attempts at reconciliation have been rebuffed, as was the case with her most recent attempt. But of this I am certain: If my aunt and grandmother ever did seek forgiveness from my mother, she would give it to them. For this I think Jesus smiles down on my mother.

I have never been hurt to such a degree. The unforgiving spirit I have often harbored over far less grievous infractions is to my shame, but a comparison such as this is wrongheaded. I am not called to compare my level of forgiveness to others such as my mother. Rather, I am called to compare it to that of my heavenly Father.

## DOES GOD COMMAND US TO DO THE IMPOSSIBLE?

I once had a student complain about this teaching, noting that God is perfect and we are sinful humans. How can we be expected to forgive as God has forgiven? I know some readers concur: "That's easy to say but much harder to do." I would go even farther than that and say it is impossible to do. Flatly impossible. And that is why Jesus commands it.

If you have read this far, you will see that I believe the Christian life to be a struggle. Martin Luther once quipped, "Show me a Christian who is not struggling with sin, and I will show you someone who is not a Christian." I think Luther's comment has value. Walking from the darkness to the light is agitating, especially if you were hunkered in a pitch-black cave of sin and must now be exposed to the blinding, pure light of Christ. Taking a sinner and making him or her into the image of the sinless Son of Man will be a difficult, painful process, no matter how many prosperity preachers tell us the opposite.

My hunch is that God purposefully commands things that are

impossible for us to accomplish, simply because he wants to humble us. That being said, he does not command something impossible for *him* to do. He commands us to do things that in our own strength we will find impossible to perform. Yet through his Spirit, these things can be achieved. The command to forgive from the heart is, I believe, one such command.

So many people have been harmed by others. I think of women who have been raped, people who were abused as children, others who have been financially ruined by men of greed. Living over a decade in Africa has exposed me to some of the worst behavior of humanity. We often have refugees as students at our seminary, and the stories they tell of the atrocities they have seen and experienced are pathetic.

Jesus expects that we will forgive all such sins. The man who sexually abused you as a child must be forgiven by you. So many senior citizens today are targets of scam artists, and in many instances they have lost all their life's savings, with little chance of earning it back. Yet they must forgive the scam artist from the heart. That woman who slanders you wherever she goes must be forgiven by you. There is no choice in the matter if you deign to be Christ's disciple. To harbor an unforgiving spirit against such a person is to not be Christian in your behavior.

Christ says we must forgive. I must admit, at times I find that command impossible to obey, at which point I am left with two options: ignore it or submit myself to it and seek the Spirit's miraculous power to overcome my bitterness and anger.

## LESSONS FROM HISTORY

One of the great literary works of Christian history is John Wesley's *Journal*. The original existed in twenty-six bound volumes and chronicled the last fifty-five years of Wesley's life. Reading it is a remarkable eighteenth-century journey with "one of the most strenuous ethical figures in history," says the editor of the *Journal* in his preface. How did a Christian leader, evangelist, and founder of one of the largest Protestant denominations in the world act when opposed? To be sure, Wesley had many enemies, and opposition against him was a constant throughout his ministry—opposition from fellow Christians, excommunication by his own church, attacks by angry mobs who refused to allow him to preach. Wesley knew antagonism and hostility. He endured riots, the stoning of his congregation during a service, derision by the press, and opposition from government officials and clergy alike. He was slandered in the pulpit by fellow pastors; threatened; beaten; arrested; pelted with mud, stones, and rotten eggs. He was even burned in effigy.

Wesley somehow rose above it all. This man who "devoted all his powers in defiance of obloquy and derision"[3] remained at peace. Unlike many other great church leaders throughout the history of Christendom, Wesley rarely struggled with bouts of depression or despair. Perhaps it was his ability to forgive even his enemies, as his own perception of himself ran along those lines. "If I have any strength at all (and I have none but what I have received), it is in forgiving injuries; and on this very side am I assaulted more frequently than on any other."[4]

In fact, more than mere forgiveness, perhaps it was Wesley's love for his enemies that constantly drove him in his ministry. He tracked over 250,000 miles crisscrossing the British Isles on horseback, driven by love for his countrymen, many of whom despised him.[5]

Likewise, consider this explanation for true heartfelt forgiveness from a second-century document, *The Testament of Gad against Hatred*, for which the author and exact date are unknown:

If a man sin against thee, tell him of it gently, and drive out the poison of hatred, and foster not guile in thy soul. And if he confess and repent, forgive him; and if he deny it, strive not with him, lest he swear, and thou sin doubly. Let not a stranger hear your secrets amid your striving, lest he hate and become thy enemy, and work great sin against thee; for ofttimes he will talk guilefully with thee, or evilly overreach thee, taking his poison from himself. Therefore, if he deny it, and is convicted and put to shame, and is silenced, do not tempt him on. For he who denieth repenteth, so that he no more doeth wrong against thee; yea also, he will honour thee, and fear thee, and be at peace with thee. But if he be shameless, and abideth in his wrongdoing, even then forgive him from the heart, and give the vengeance to God.

## VENGEANCE IS NOT MINE

The opposite of forgiveness is vengeance. Certainly, some people adopt indifference toward those who have harmed them, seeking neither reconciliation nor retaliation. But even indifference is wrong if we are commanded to pray for those who harm us. Worse still, many of us see the road of vengeance as quite a delectable option. Yet we are called to avoid it completely.

This lesson was brought home to me in a powerful way during a visit I made to Ethiopia. There I learned of a Christian man whose wife had committed adultery and become pregnant. Her husband intended to do what was expected of the people of his tribe. He took his gun, loaded it with bullets, and set out to find the adulterer. Along the way he realized that this was not the proper Christian thing to do, and he returned home.

Had he carried out his original intentions, there would have been no legal ramifications from the Ethiopian government, and such vengeance was expected by his people. At least in the short term, the husband would have felt good about what he did. I am also certain many Christians would have sympathized with him and openly or secretly expressed desires to act similarly if faced with a comparable situation. But the husband chose another path, one that was initially more difficult and required more self-control and maturity.

The long-term outcome of the situation was that he adopted the child, his wife eventually came to be a believer in Jesus Christ, and they have a strong and healthy marriage today. The one choice—his culturally acceptable first option—would have resulted in death. The second choice—the one Jesus approves—resulted in life. Who in their right mind would say that this man did not make the best choice? Yet at the basest level of our sinful instincts, the first option woos us nonetheless.

When I was a young man out of college, my company sent me away for several weeks of training. There I met a young lady, and we hit it off immediately. The first week I was there we spent a considerable amount of time together, laughing and joking with each other. As the British say, "We got along famously." To be honest, I even thought things were going so well that this might be a long-term relationship, and we had been talking about how to keep in touch once the weeks of training were finished.

The Saturday of the end of the first week, after short training sessions in the morning, she and I spent the afternoon walking around town. We spent six hours together talking and teasing. Near the end of the day, just before we were going to part for the evening, I made a little poke of fun at her. Immediately her face changed expression, and I knew I had said something I should not have said. She said good-bye quickly and departed.

Sunday we didn't see each other, but Monday morning, we were again together in the meetings. It was the cold shoulder all morning, and she made it a point to let me know that she wanted nothing to do with me. It was only Tuesday when I was able to get a moment alone with her and apologize for what I had said on Saturday. However, I also wanted to know why it offended her. Again I received the cold shoulder, and she was not interested in explaining what had bothered her.

For the next couple of days I made it a point whenever I could to simply tell her I was sorry and to ask for her forgiveness, but she continued to be aloof. The fact that she would not accept my apology or grant me her forgiveness caused me anguish during those days, but I finally gave up. Others even recognized that something was wrong because in the first week we seemed inseparable, but afterward we were hardly together. The situation became a bit embarrassing for me, and I could feel myself becoming bitter over her unreasonable behavior.

Incredibly, after the weeks of training were completed, she came to me on the last day with a piece of paper. On the paper was her mailing address, and she asked me if I would write her. I was shocked. I took the piece of paper, crumpled it into a ball and handed it back to her. "I'm not interested," was the last thing I ever said to her.

To this day I am embarrassed I behaved that way. To be sure, her unforgiving spirit caused me considerable pain, especially being a young man initially enamored with a fine young woman. If only she had forgiven me of my misstep and allowed us to start afresh. But as a follower of Jesus Christ, I had no business being mean back to her, no matter how good it initially made me feel. It is eighteen years later, and I am still ashamed of my behavior, despite the fact that I believe she treated me unfairly.

## WHAT FORGIVENESS DOES NOT MEAN

I feel the need to clarify finer points on this issue. Let me start with an incident that occurred some years ago in America when a young girl disappeared and was found dead weeks later, her body severely abused. After a high-profile search was conducted, the perpetrator was found. Through the long process of the trial, the parents of the young girl came to forgive the man of his wicked act.

As Christians, they believed it was the right thing to do. Even after the man was convicted and awaiting his sentencing, the couple went on national television and asked that the man not be given the death penalty. They proclaimed their faith in Jesus and their forgiveness of the criminal and asked that the State forego the most severe punishment.

I thought they were nuts. It was only later that I realized how brave this couple was and how much of an example they served as Christ's disciples. Yet I am going to disagree with an aspect of their understanding of forgiveness. In fact, I think three misunderstandings concerning this matter of unlimited forgiveness must be addressed.

1) *It has nothing to do with penalties of law and the State.* The State has an obligation to punish lawbreakers. If it did not carry out that mandate, we would devolve into anarchy. That said, I applaud this couple for offering *personal* forgiveness. Still, the State is obligated to deal with crime in the best way it can, and we must be content with having the State punish lawbreakers, even if personally we have forgiven them.

2) *It does not negate church discipline.* I have often seen churches that believe that because the church is a place of grace and forgiveness,

sins committed by its members must go unpunished. Ironically, whereas individual believers are called to forgive, the church as a corporate body of believers is called to discipline its membership. I find it interesting that in Matthew's Gospel the parable of the unmerciful servant comes directly after the well-known passage about discipline in the church (Matt. 18:15-17). There we learn of the escalating sequence of events in dealing with sin, first on a personal, one-on-one level; then employing witnesses; and lastly involving the whole congregation. Then, "if [the offending party] refuses to listen even to the church, treat him as you would a pagan or a tax collector."

The teaching of Jesus on forgiveness, then, can hardly be used as a blanket statement dealing with all infractions when it comes to the governing of church affairs. How many high-profile church leaders have been caught in gross misconduct, only to proclaim that the church does not have a right to punish them because the church is meant to be a place of grace? Yet we find Paul chastising the Corinthian believers for not properly disciplining a brother in self-professed sexual immorality (1 Cor. 5), and we find other instances in the Epistles of disciplining within the church body (e.g., 1 Tim. 5:19-20; Tit. 3:10-11).

3) *Forgiveness does not mean I act as if nothing has happened.* What about the adage, "Forgive and forget"? Interestingly, this proverbial statement is not new. The second-century church father Tertullian had this to say on the matter: "For His will is, not that you should forgive an offence, but forget it" (*Five Books Against Marcion*). How often have we heard the biblical teaching on forgiveness characterized in this manner? If we are to take this command of Jesus seriously, is it not proper for us to adopt this forgive-and-forget attitude?

Yes and no. The fact is, the relationship I had with the person before the infraction is not the same as afterward. New information has been introduced into the relationship, such that I know the person differently than I did previously. A relationship built on unquestioning trust may now be compromised, and it would be foolish to pretend that things have not changed.

For example, I may find out that a certain person has sexually abused one of my children. Both my child and I must forgive that person, no matter how difficult that will be. Yet new information about the person has been revealed, and I cannot act as if I do not know it. To live as if I do not have this new information—as if the person exists in the state previously to this new information—would be lying to myself. Would anyone seriously argue that I must "forgive and forget" and allow my child to spend time alone again with this person? To do so would be lunacy.

Some may ask, "But if you treat the person differently than you did previously, are you not still holding a grudge and hence not forgiving that person?" I would make a clear distinction between holding a grudge (maintaining an unforgiving spirit) and behaving differently in the face of new information about the person in question.

If I return to my opening example about the woman who slandered me, I can forgive her for the slander, but I can hardly spend time alone with her again. That would be the height of foolishness, especially in light of her sexual accusations. So if my behavior toward the person has changed, how can I seriously say that I have forgiven that person?

Let me use a quote from Puritan pastor Thomas Watson (1620-1686) to get us thinking about this matter. Here is what he envisioned to be the ideal goal of forgiveness:

> When do we forgive others? When we strive against all thoughts of revenge; when we will not do our enemies mischief, but wish well to them, grieve at their calamities, pray for them, seek reconciliation with them, and show ourselves ready on all occasions to relieve them. This is gospel-forgiving.[6]

An incredible task indeed. Watson identifies both positive and negative aspects of forgiveness. Negatively, we will not intend to do harm to people who have harmed us. This involves our actions, words, and thoughts. The latter is obviously the hardest to control; yet we must strive against unforgiving thoughts, as Watson states. We must not seek revenge or payback of any kind. If we have been slandered, we must not slander in retaliation. If people have stolen from us, we must not make plans to steal from them in return.

Positively, we must look to help those who have harmed us. Much of this ground we covered in the previous chapter, but it is worth repeating. We cannot call ourselves Christ's disciples if all we do is pay back evil with evil or insult with insult. We all can understand the man who walks into a courtroom and blows the head off of the pervert who sexually abused his child, and many of us not only understand such emotions but approve of them. And yet we can hardly say such a man is acting in a Christian way. If we want to be followers of Jesus, we must pray for that man, not look to harm him.

If I found that slanderous woman from my opening story on the side of the road needing assistance, I can honestly say I would help her. But it would end there. I would not stay for a chat or in any other way encourage conversation with a woman who has falsely accused me of sexual misconduct, simply because that may encourage further slander. But if I do not pray for her, I cannot call myself a believer.

> To forgive is one of the highest evidences of grace.
> Thomas Watson (1620-1686), *The Lord's Prayer*

The relationship after forgiveness also depends on the person whom you have had to forgive and the type of relationship you have with that person. If it is my wife whom I must forgive, I certainly should attempt to live as if the offense never happened. To do otherwise might result in holding a grudge against my wife, and then our marriage would suffer. But I can hardly pretend that a child molester is not a child molester or that it is acceptable to share my darkest secrets with someone I have recently learned to be an incurable gossip.

## THE MANY WONDERFUL BENEFITS

I have promised myself never to turn away someone who seeks my forgiveness, no matter what pain or harm that person may have caused me. In the specific case of the slanderous woman,

- I have determined not to slander or gossip about her;
- I have determined to only say good things about her should she ever come up in a conversation; and
- I have determined to forgive her should she ask to be forgiven.

Concerning the mugging I recounted in the last chapter, I eventually came to a resolution in my mind. Two things would happen: Either 1) the muggers would repent, at which point I could hardly hold anything against them, or 2) they would not repent, and God would judge them. He could certainly do a better and fairer job than I could ever do. And so I let it go.

This approach forms the heart of my dealings with similar issues. Either the offender will repent, at which time I am obliged to forgive, or the offender will remain stubborn and unrepentant, at which time God will deal with it. Consider these words of wisdom from *The Homilies of Chrysostom* (350-407):

> Hath thy neighbour wronged and grieved thee, and involved thee in a thousand ills? Be it so, yet do not prosecute vengeance on thine own part, lest thou do desire to thy Lord! Yield the matter to God, and He will dispose of it much better than thou canst desire. To thee He has given charge simply to pray for the injurer; but how to deal with him, He hath ordered thee to leave to Himself.[7]

Some may object to this understanding of the command to forgive. "But doesn't this open us up to the possibility of extreme abuse?" Certainly this can be the case, but this has always been the case for the followers of Christ. It is why Paul can unapologetically say, "All day long we are like sheep to be slaughtered." Frequently, submission to the will of God brings with it certain discomforts in this world, a world that often despises God and his people. But this can hardly be an excuse for not obeying our Lord.

Practically speaking, this line of action also guards us against that gnawing bitterness that taps our spiritual vitality and causes us greater grief at times than did the original ill against us. A supernatural peace comes when we submit our will to the Father's, especially in this command of forgiveness. Allowing bitterness to fester with an unforgivable grudge, we also will find it increasingly difficult to approach God. Is this not the reason Jesus commands in the Sermon on the Mount not to approach the altar if we have an unreconciled issue with our brother or sister in Christ (Matt. 5:23-24)? I find it instructive that this teaching from Jesus comes in a section of the sermon dealing with hatred and murder.

> He could not have God at peace with him, who through envious discord had not peace with his brother.
>
> Cyprian (200-258), *On the Unity of the Church*

Harboring an unforgiving spirit is also supremely foolish given what Jesus says in the Lord's Prayer: "Forgive us our debts, as we forgive our debtors." The irony of the Lord's Prayer, something many if not most of us pray many times a year either privately or in our churches, is that we are signing, as it were, our own judgment. The clear stipulation in the prayer is that we are shown the same level of forgiveness we show others.

> Wherefore, we are not to ask the forgiveness of our sins from God, unless we forgive the offenses of all who are or have been injurious to us. If we retain any hatred in our minds, if we meditate revenge, and devise the means of hurting; nay, if we do not return to a good understanding with our enemies, perform every kind of friendly office, and endeavour to effect a reconciliation with them, we by this petition beseech God not to grant us forgiveness. For we ask him to do to us as we do to others.
>
> John Calvin (1509-1564), *Institutes of the Christian Religion* (3.20.45)

Perhaps this is why Jesus expanded on this item in the prayer. How often do we treat this prayer as a mindless formula that we chant? Yet in it we find self-incrimination of the worst kind if we are wont to harbor an unforgiving spirit.

> The prayer of the vindictive for forgiveness is mockery, like the prayer for daily bread from a wheat-cornerer.
>
> P. T. Forsyth (1848-1921), *The Soul of Prayer*

Harboring an unforgiving spirit is one of the worst sins we can ever commit. Again Chrysostom's words are prudent:

> For a man when he has committed fornication, or adultery, at the same time that he hath accomplished his lust, hath also completed the sin; and should he be willing by watchful living to recover from that fall, he may afterwards, by manifesting great penitence, obtain relief. But he who is resentful worketh the same iniquity every day, and never brings it to an end.[8]

What Chrysostom rightly identifies is that a person may have sinned against me, but that sin is in the past. However, if I harbor an unforgiving spirit against that person, I sin each day I allow that merciless spirit to exist.

I am not perfect, and evil thoughts can occasionally pop into my mind against those who have harmed me. It is then and there that I must deal with them, confess them to God, and ask for forgiveness. Harboring such thoughts will allow them to fester, providing a foothold for Satan and ultimately yielding more sin than perhaps was committed in the original infraction.

One of the most important lessons I want to teach my children is the art of forgiveness, both seeking it and granting it. A principle that underlies much of the teaching of Jesus, what we often call the "golden rule," is to treat others in the way we want to be treated. There have been instances when I have wronged another person, have come to recognize my error, and have sought forgiveness and reconciliation, only to be rejected. No matter how often I tried to express my remorse, it was met with a hard heart. There are few things more painful than knowing you have harmed someone and finding that person unwilling to accept your apology for the wrongdoing. In a few instances, I have had good friends who have decided not to forgive some misstep on my part, and our relationship was never the same. Even here I must be careful, as bitterness can be created in such situations. If I do not watch out, I might find myself not forgiving someone for not forgiving me.

## BUT WHAT IF I DON'T FEEL LIKE IT?

I wonder what my attitude would be if that woman who slandered me ever came to me and asked for forgiveness. I know part of me would simply not trust her, but I also know I would have an obligation to tell her I forgive her—and do so from my heart. To do otherwise would be unchristian.

But let me go even further. There should be part of me that wants and hopes that she would give me the opportunity to do so. Let me say that again. I should consider it an opportunity and privilege to forgive her. Such situations provide us a wonderful occasion to prove our faith in Christ.

Forgiveness is a choice we make, not necessarily a feeling we have. As is often the case with our Christian walk, raw obedience is the order of the day, even when our emotions are not in step with our will.

> Never say: I feel no love; I do not feel as if I can forgive this man. Feeling is not the rule of your duty, but the command, and the faith that God gives power to obey the command. In obedience to the Father, with the choice of your will, and in faith that the Holy Spirit gives you power, begin to say: I will love him; I do love him. The feeling will follow the faith.
>
> Andrew Murray (1828-1917), *The New Life*

I have encountered believers who act meanly toward someone who has hurt them, using the argument that they must do so because of their integrity. To act as if nothing is wrong is, to them, contrary to behaving honestly; so they feel obliged to treat the offending person with disrespect. After all, if you do not *feel* like being nice to someone who has harmed you, is it not dishonest to act as if you do?

We are so adept at finding justifications to avoid a clear teaching from Jesus. An incredible chunk of the teaching from Jesus covers this topic, and we see it supremely worked out in his life and specifically in his substitutionary death for us. Often this command does appear impossible for us to obey, and yet it is in the act of obedience that we find peace and freedom—freedom from bitterness, hatred, and festering anger that derails us from fellowship with God.

God does command us to do what is impossible in our own strength, in order to cause us to humble ourselves and rely entirely on him. Only if we possess a poverty of spirit can we hope to attain the level of forgiveness Christ requires of us. Without it, we will have a tendency to drive people away from his kingdom, not draw them toward it.

> There are no virtues wherein your example will do more, at least to abate men's prejudice, than humility and meekness and self-denial. Forgive injuries; and "be not overcome of evil, but overcome evil with good."
>
> Richard Baxter (1615-1691), *The Reformed Pastor*

# 8

# THE ART OF
# SPIRITUAL SELF-LOATHING

*If anyone comes to me and does not hate his own father and mother and wife and children and brothers and sisters, yes, and even his own life, he cannot be my disciple.*

JESUS CHRIST, LUKE 14:26, ESV

*No one, however, is more wealthy than such a man; no one is more powerful, no one freer than he who knows how to leave all things and think of himself as the least of all.*

THOMAS À KEMPIS (1380-1471),

*THE IMITATION OF CHRIST*

*Whoever is utterly cast down and overwhelmed by the awareness of his calamity, poverty, nakedness, and disgrace has thus advanced farthest in knowledge of himself.*

JOHN CALVIN (1509-1564),

*INSTITUTES OF THE CHRISTIAN RELIGION, 2.2.10*

The distraught mother and father sat across from the talk show host. They recounted the difficulty they were having with their teenaged daughter, who had become increasingly disrespectful and aloof. The discussion turned to drug or alcohol abuse, but when those possibilities were exhausted, it turned more pointedly to the father and his role in the family.

Enter the daughter. Replete with typical marks of rebellion—body piercings, dyed hair, and a tattoo—she sat separate from her parents with arms folded. Hers was a body language of defiance and scorn, especially as occasionally she shot a glance at her father. There was no sexual or physical abuse to account for the animosity that existed between the daughter and father. Rather, it was the fruit of an estranged, strained relationship. The father always wanted his way, and when he did not get it, he became angry and aggressive. The daughter, increasingly impatient with her lack of autonomy, fought back the only way she knew how—with hatred.

Few things appear more unnatural and pathetic to us than to see a child hate his or her parent. In our day of trash television, where dysfunctional people are trotted out onto the stage and screen to be ridiculed by the studio audience and viewers at home, we often are exposed to families with deep emotional scars. Who cannot feel sympathy for a parent who has a child spitting venomous epithets his or her way? Conversely, who cannot feel a knot in the pit of the stomach on hearing stories of parents abusing their children? Horribly, many children are safer from abuse out on the streets than in their own homes.

So when Jesus tells us we must hate our mother and father, a natural opposition wells up inside us. We can understand suffering for the gospel or putting away sinful pleasures, but hatred of one's flesh and blood? Surely Jesus has gone too far.

For those of us who come from healthy, loving homes, this teaching may be all the more difficult to process. I have much to be thankful for when I think of my parents and my upbringing. To consider the prospect of hating them is anathema to me, and I assume many of you feel similarly. When it comes to my own children, few things are more offensive than to be told I should hate them.

With this chapter we will investigate this complex teaching of familial hatred. Jesus notes several types of love in this command: love of parents, love of siblings, love of spouse, love of children, and love of self. I will address these broadly by speaking about familial love and self-love.

## MUST I REALLY HATE MY MOTHER?

It would indeed be an anomaly if Jesus literally expected us to love our enemies and hate our parents. We have already seen in chapter 6 what it means to love our enemy and how this love brings us to closer communion with God. Why, then, should we hate the ones we are supposed to love and love the ones we most naturally should hate?

Jesus loved hyperbole. We have already seen his use of it in chapter 2, and we see it again in this hard saying. After hearing the teaching of Jesus, if you did not come away scratching your head in bewilderment, you probably did not think hard enough about what he said. By using shocking statements and juxtaposing common wisdom with truths that seemed incongruous, Jesus made his listeners think. The same should be the case for us today.

Note in chapter 6 that we referred to familial love as the easiest and most basic type of love. It is natural to us to love those with whom we have lived or by whom we were raised. Loving our enemy is difficult if well-nigh impossible, but to love my mother—unless she is commanding me to eat my vegetables—is inborn. It is precisely for this reason Jesus uses this kind of love as a test of our commitment as disciples.

In chapter 3 we noted that even the desire to bury one's father must be placed secondary to our commitment to live the life of a disciple. Our familial love must pale in comparison to our love for Christ.

Perhaps an example might help in cracking open the meaning of this teaching. In nations dominated by Islam, conversion to Christianity can be a painful, even deadly choice. Extreme ostracism is common from the community at large and from family members. In most instances, a person who converts to Christianity is cut off from the family and considered dead. Whole nations have laws against evangelism and proselytism, many with severe penalties attached. So Muslims who have heard the gospel and want to commit their lives to Christ face a dilemma.

Many of us, particularly in the West, may meet certain hardships as a result of choosing to trust Christ, but rarely are they as intense as in the Muslim world. Few in the West will be confronted with the possibility of death for choosing to convert to Christ.

## TEN THINGS I WISH JESUS NEVER SAID

After all this talk about radical commitment to Christ, you might expect me to decry those Muslims who balk at the idea or who "recant" their professions of Christian faith when faced with acute pressure. Actually I have nothing but sympathy for such people; I am glad I never had to face such choices. In most cases, Muslim conversions mean a complete break with everything near and dear. They can no longer frequent the same shops or hang out with the same friends; many lose their jobs and have to move from locations where they are well known; most will never have a prospect of a mate or any semblance of a normal existence. All of this for following Jesus.

And yet this is precisely what Jesus envisioned would happen. He knew that following him might involve the greatest turmoil imaginable. He recognized that faith in him would produce animosity and strife, not just between his disciples and those in the world, but even within families. In a passage that combines many of the themes we have already discussed, Jesus says:

> Do not suppose that I have come to bring peace to the earth. I did not come to bring peace, but a sword. For I have come to turn "a man against his father, a daughter against her mother, a daughter-in-law against her mother-in-law—a man's enemies will be the members of his own household." Anyone who loves his father or mother more than me is not worthy of me; anyone who loves his son or daughter more than me is not worthy of me; and anyone who does not take his cross and follow me is not worthy of me. Whoever finds his life will lose it, and whoever loses his life for my sake will find it. (Matt. 10:34-39)

One such case involved a Muslim mother who became intrigued with Christianity but was reported by her teenage son. The authorities locked her in prison until she recanted. My guess is prison was not nearly as traumatic for her as her own son's betrayal.

As much as I sympathize with the difficulties of Muslim conversions to Christ, I know Jesus expects them to persevere despite the opposition. I readily admit that I say this sitting in my Western cocoon of comfortable Christianity. Yet radical commitment is what Christ requires.

Christians in the West tend to have the exact opposite problem. Whereas Satan looks to deter Muslim converts to Christ via threats and overt means, he looks to dissuade Western converts covertly by lulling us to sleep with easy believism. Arab converts are scared to take the leap of ultimate commitment; Western converts are fooled into believing that following Christ is all prosperity and ease.

## CRUCIFYING THE EGOTISTICAL SELF

> You must know that self-love is more harmful to you than anything else in the world.
>
> Thomas à Kempis (1380-1471), *The Imitation of Christ*

What does hating oneself entail? In chapter 2, we noted that our love of sinful pleasures must be eliminated. In this sense, we hate ourselves by denying ourselves those things that we desperately want. In chapter 3, we spoke about absolute commitment to Christ and placing commitment to all other things, including ourselves, below it. In this chapter, I want to pick up a theme from chapter 4 and what it means to crucify the egotistical self.

I think it is safe to say that all temptations pale in comparison to the temptation of self-love. In fact, sins such as pride, greed, and even lust could be tied directly to self-love, or the idolatry of self. In his *Large Catechism*, Martin Luther writes, "Whatever you set your heart on and rely on is really your God." This understanding of idolatry is broader than the typical view of idolatry limited to blocks of wood or precious metals. Virtually anything can serve as an idol for sinful man, even oneself.

In fact, self-love is always a sin. Yes, I know such a statement can land me in hot water. How often have we been told we must first love ourselves before we really can love others, or that to truly accept the love of others, we must first love ourselves?

What about "love your neighbor as yourself"? Does not this passage show us that self-love is expected by God? This argument has often been used, especially by those in the field of psychology and other related behavioral disciplines. The line of reasoning normally goes: You cannot love others until you first love yourself. Those people who do not love themselves (i.e., are not happy with who they are as individuals) will not be able to love others. Therefore, you must first be content with yourself before you can give love to others.

> The reigning cliché of the day is that in order to love others one must first learn to love oneself. This formulation—love thyself, then thy neighbor—is a license for unremitting self-indulgence, because the quest for self-love is endless. By the time you have finally learned to love yourself, you'll find yourself playing golf at Leisure World.
>
> Charles Krauthammer, quoted in *Christianity Today*[1]

On the surface, there is much to appreciate concerning this view, and we know from experience that people who hate themselves find it difficult to express proper love for others. However, some have taken this too far and encouraged a self-love that is ultimately damaging to all other relationships. Secular society would have us believe, for example, that a woman cannot truly be happy as a housewife because she is forced to give of herself without putting her own needs first. Many people in relationships speak about "finding themselves" before they can care for the needs of others, and so on.

This attitude is often portrayed in television shows or movies that depict an empty-nest wife telling her husband that she wants a divorce. "All these years I have served others. Now I must go out and find myself." Implied is the fact that the woman cannot be content until she puts herself first.

Unfortunately, this attitude has crept into many of our churches when it comes to our relationship with God. We come to demand that God bless us, and when we perceive that he does not (in the ways we expect of him), we begin to question his loyalty and faithfulness. I have seen preachers on television programs seen by millions of viewers worldwide speaking about demanding a raise or promotion from God.

"I see everybody else around me getting a raise, Lord. Now it's *my* turn." Usually such messages are delivered in front of an audience that numbers in the thousands, all waving their hands and cheering loudly as the speaker tells them to insist on God's blessing in their lives. Of course, 99 percent of the time this is *material* blessing.

It seems we love ourselves so much that we have no time to really serve God or others. Let me be clear: Self-love does not make loving one's neighbor possible. In fact, self-love kills the love of one's neighbor. We are meant to put others first, not ourselves, so that we can then accommodate others. Once we put ourselves first, we have lost the ability to accommodate anyone else—even God.

## THE SIN OF SELF-RELIANCE

With self-love always comes the stepsister of self-reliance. Is it any wonder that many church leaders of the past spoke harshly about self-love? It is what Calvin called the "depraved confidence in the flesh" and "pernicious carnal confidence." As we continue to investigate this controversial understanding of self-love, we need to answer a fundamental question that will greatly determine the tenor of our relationship with God: Is God working with material that is basically good or basically bad?

As I argued in chapter 1, I do not think "healthy self-esteem" means always thinking positively about yourself. In fact, I believe you can think negatively about yourself and still have healthy self-esteem. I define healthy self-esteem as holding right and honest views about yourself. So healthy self-esteem must involve a realization of one's spiritual poverty, something we discussed at length in the opening chapter.

The opposite of spiritual poverty is self-reliance—the arrogant attitude that says we somehow earn God's love or favor, or in and of ourselves we can please God. It is the view that God owes us something or that heaven is a place where we deserve to live. It is the belief that if we work hard enough, we can somehow attain the righteous requirements necessary to live an eternity with our Creator.

I anticipate the objection that I am muddying the waters by speaking of earning one's salvation and the matter of self-love, but I think the two are intimately linked. Only in the realization that there is *nothing* in me that is good and commendable before God can I grasp the gospel and what Christ did at the cross. The notion that I am spiritually dead but am an otherwise good guy is false. There is nothing commendable in me if I am a sinner dead in my sins. That is why Paul can say that those who do not have God's Spirit living in them "cannot please God" and are "unfit for doing anything good" (Rom. 8:8; Tit. 1:16). How can I love someone like that, even when it is describing me?

A further objection may follow, though: that as believers we are now lovely and somehow worthy of God's love, but again I disagree. The moment we accept the notion that God loves us because we are inherently lovable, we have moved from the realm of grace to the realm of merit. In other words, God *must* love us because we are naturally lovable. Then God's choice of having a relationship with us hinges on something worthy in us—in other words, because we deserve the relationship with him.

I must strongly protest such an idea. God's relationship with us is always and only motivated by grace. Not one of us deserves his favor and his love or has a right to spend an eternity with him. All such benefits come exclusively via his grace, as shown in the vicarious sacrifice of his Son on the cross. No amount of effort on our part can ever commend us to God. Why? Because he is holy, and we are always sinners. As we noted in our discussion in the last chapter concerning the parable of the workers in the vineyard, God's dealings with humanity are only based on justice or mercy.

Spiritual self-reliance and self-love have no place in the body of Christ. Either you admit you are a sinner devoid of anything worthy or deserving in yourself, or you proclaim your ability to make yourself commendable to God. The first option—self-loathing—brings freedom from sin and life; the second—self-love—brings enslavement to sin and death.

I am more afraid of my own heart than of the pope and all his cardinals. I have within me the great pope, Self.

Martin Luther (1483-1546)

## LESSONS FROM HISTORY

Protestant reformer John Calvin produced one of the most significant documents of the Reformation, his *Institutes of the Christian Religion*. Few documents have influenced Christianity in the past four hundred years more than this one. Historians often note that Martin Luther was the most important of the first-generation reformers, whereas Calvin was the most influential from the second generation. His *Institutes* played a vital role in the spread of the Reformation to most European countries, and we see a general trend of early Lutheran dominance in several countries being supplanted later by the Reformed tradition of Calvin.

Calvin's *Institutes* are divided into four books, the first being "The Knowledge of God the Creator." What might strike some people as a bit odd, though, is that the first section of this book addresses the knowledge of oneself: "Without knowledge of self there is no knowledge of God," he writes.

On the surface, this may seem to be in agreement with the world's point of view, but if we look closer, we see why Calvin made such a statement. He wrote, "Thus, from the feeling of our own ignorance, vanity, poverty, infirmity, and—what is more—depravity and corruption, we recognize that the true light of wisdom, sound virtue, full abundance of every good, and purity of righteousness rest in the Lord alone."[2] The world tells us contemplation of self raises self to a higher level; Calvin and Scripture tell us contemplation of self drives us to God, because in contemplating ourselves, we see we are sinners in need of God.[3]

In *The Dialogue of Saint Catherine of Siena* (1347-1380), Catherine speaks of the "cord of self-contempt." What a strange notion for us today, but for Catherine, it was this cord that kept her connected to God. She recognized that to love herself automatically created a force that moved her away from love of God. St. Bernard of Clairvaux (1090-1153) saw something similar, speaking in his *On Loving God* of a "fourth degree of love," whereby we do not even love ourselves save for God's sake. Such ideas are foreign to those of us steeped in a self-absorbed culture.

# TEN THINGS I WISH JESUS NEVER SAID

> I am poor and needy; yet best, while in hidden groanings I displease myself, and seek Thy mercy, until what is lacking in my defective state be renewed and perfected, on to that peace which the eye of the proud knoweth not.
>
> Augustine (354-430), *Confessions*

It is no secret that the world tells us the foremost thing we should do is to know ourselves. This should be the primary contemplation of every person, and in so doing, we can then become successful in all other areas of life. For many, the sole aim of life is self: self-love, self-esteem, self-help, self-actualization. Well-known theologian Carl Henry said of his twentieth-century world that it embraced "the illusion that the human species is the sole crown of the cosmos, generator of the good, touchstone of truth, fashioner and designer of destiny."[4]

## ENLIGHTENED IDOLATRY

Where has this ideal of self-love come from? Of course, sinful humans have always had this inclination. Ever since the Garden of Eden, when Adam and Eve perceived that by disobeying God and eating the fruit they could obtain some hidden benefit, fallen humanity has consistently gravitated toward the idolatry of self. However, in the Western world we also have been influenced by the generations and movements that have come more recently before us.

On the heels of the Reformation came the "Age of Reason," also known as the Enlightenment. The Enlightenment, which most Christians thought was the worst thing to come along in Western civilization (that is, until postmodernism hit the scene), did much to foster the idealism of autonomy. It called for a movement away from authority, especially religious authority, and a "turn to the self." Consider this quotation by one of the "fathers" of the Enlightenment, Immanuel Kant (1724-1804):

> Let us endeavor to disperse those clouds of ignorance, those mists of darkness, which impede Man on his journey, . . . which prevent his marching through life with a firm and steady step. Let us try to inspire

him . . . with respect for his own reason—with an inextinguishable love of truth . . . so that he may learn to know himself . . . and no longer be duped by an imagination that has been led astray by authority . . . so that he may learn to base his morals on his own nature, on his own wants, on the real advantage of society . . . so that he may learn to pursue his true happiness, by promoting that of others . . . in short, so that he may become a virtuous and rational being, who cannot fail to become happy.[5]

Ironically, the Enlightenment also called us to know ourselves, but this was based on the supposition that humans are basically good. It is the same mentality today, what I call the "Olympic Spirit."

## WHAT THE UNITED NATIONS, TOWER OF BABEL, AND THE OLYMPICS HAVE IN COMMON

The commercials that accompanied the Olympic Games played in Sydney in 2000 and in Athens in 2004 gave great images of athletes in pain and in triumph—striving to cross the finish line first or stumbling before getting there. Men flying through the air, women sprinting to victory—"giants," the advertisements called them. We see a sprinter, for example, pull up with a torn hamstring and yet hobble to the finish line, minutes after all the other sprinters had crossed it. Or in the Winter Olympics we see a skier lose control on his descent down the slope and crash into the fencing around the boundary, a horrific accident as he topples head over heels down the hill. Then a caption comes up telling us that two days later he won two gold medals.

Such images cause us to well up with pride. These giants inspire us to greater things. The commercial shows men and women who have pushed themselves to the limits of their bodies, indeed, to the limits of humanity itself. Then, after a brief pause where no images are shown, a two-word caption appears at the end of the commercial: "celebrate humanity."

This is the Olympic spirit. There is nothing we cannot do as long as we put our minds to it. Press onward for bigger and better things. No matter how trying the circumstances, you can be a giant too.

## TEN THINGS I WISH JESUS NEVER SAID

Push yourself to the limit. Press on for the prize. This is the spirit of humanity.

This is also the spirit of humanism that claims if humans would join hands and come together, putting aside differences and problems, we could do anything. We may have different cultures and languages and skin colors and sexual orientations, but we are all humans. Through education, through empowerment of the lower classes, through the taking from the haves and giving to the have-nots, we can obliterate world hunger, forge world peace, conquer the AIDS pandemic, and rid the world of disease, war, pollution, and the threat of nuclear holocaust. Through the tolerant exercise of human rights that we all equally possess, there is nothing humanity cannot do. Corporately we can succeed in making this world a place where each generation after us can call it blessed, a place of peace and happiness.

It is the United Nations mind-set. When all the nations of the world begin to work together, sharing our resources equally with one another, ridding the world of rogue states that do not share humanitarian ideals, the world will be a place of prosperity and peace.

This humanist spirit pervades not only on a corporate level but on an individual level. Believe in yourself. Build your self-esteem. Be proud of who you are. Each of us can reach the pinnacle of self-actualization if only we believe we can. Dig deep down inside yourself, and there you will find "god." There is nothing you cannot do.

With this spirit of humanism comes a contempt for anything perceived to damage this spirit. If the church talks about sin and one's need for repentance and forgiveness before a holy God, it is castigated for belittling man. If a Christian speaks about an afterlife, he is ridiculed for cheapening *this* life. With this spirit of humanism comes an implied freedom from God. When man can do anything, God is no longer necessary. Who needs to turn to God when all that is needed comes from self?

This Tower of Babel mentality pervades our society. If we only work together, we can build a tower to the heavens, or better yet, build heaven on earth. Why look to God or to a future life when in this life we can play god ourselves?

At the heart of all three views lies humanism that places man at the center and either ignores or excludes God. "Celebrate humanity." A noble goal when humanity is celebrated for being created in the image and likeness of God. But when we move from God-centeredness to man-centeredness and have no mind for God at all, we are no longer celebrating humanity but destroying it. Celebrating humanity without celebrating deity is no celebration at all. Unfortunately, though, this is the state of our current world ethos and of many in our churches as well. If I might try my hand at a little poetry, my characterization of this attitude would be the following:

*Oh, blessed self-actualization.*
*That I may revel in my own ability,*
*Rest in my own self-assurance,*
*Be comforted by my own self-worth,*
*And be commended by my own self-righteousness.*

We still live in a world with Enlightenment ideals. Yes, postmodernism is here to stay, but many of the postmodern ideals found their seed in enlightened thinking. Notions that truth is relative and can only be truth once it is accessed by me, while flowering into a full-blown pluralism in postmodern times, grew from roots in the Enlightenment. Unfortunately, Christianity has not been immune to the scourge of rejecting absolute or objective truth. Dallas Willard says, "The 'Western' segment of the church today lives in a bubble of historical illusion about the meaning of discipleship and the gospel. We are dominated by the essentially Enlightenment values that rule American culture: pursuit of happiness, unrestricted freedom of choice, disdain of authority."[6] So more and more Christians—even evangelicals—are painting a religious mural of many saviors and mediators, thus diminishing the exclusivity of Christ and his work. All of this finds at its base a reliance on the self.

But Christ's radical idea of self-loathing involves radical trust in God. This may be the reason so many of the commands of Jesus are foreign to our way of thinking. We are taught to trust ourselves, to pro-

**197**

vide for ourselves, to worry about ourselves. The call of Jesus is to consider ourselves nothing, to forget ourselves, to always place others before us.

## AMERICAN SELF-RELIANCE

There is something appealing about the world's ideal of self-love. I find myself instinctively fighting Christ's ideal on this score. I *want* to love myself. Who likes to think lowly of himself? Do we not all prefer high opinions of ourselves, expressed either by others or by our own secret reflection?

It was only after I moved from America that I began to understand my homeland. For my first thirty years I lived in the United States, and except for a trip to Canada and a cruise to the Caribbean, I never laid foot outside its soil. Statistics show that over 90 percent of Americans will never hold a passport. At times our view of the world is incredibly myopic. I love my country, and it is hard for me not to wax patriotic about it, especially in the face of those who hate it. Living overseas has exposed me to the love affair many have with my homeland, as well as the hatred others have for it.

Americans are rugged individualists. Is it any mistake that the best-known American icon in the world is not the red symbol of Coca Cola, the golden arches of McDonalds, or the swoosh of Nike? It is the Marlboro Man—even in today's increasingly anti-smoking environment. We Americans love entrepreneurship, the individual's struggle against the forces of nature and commerce. We are the quintessential individualists, Americans *contra mundum*. We are big enough to do what we want to do, and we will not listen to anybody who appears to limit our autonomy, not even as influential an organization as the United Nations.

Perhaps you've heard the anecdote. What do you call a person who can speak three languages fluently? Trilingual. What do you call a person who can speak two languages fluently? Bilingual. What do you call a person who can speak only one language fluently? American. We don't need to speak several languages, and most of us don't want to.

I know I tread on sacred ground now, but consider the events of 9/11. Before that time, numerous terrorist attacks had occurred around the world, many even targeting Americans or American interests. I can think of two of them on African soil simply because I was living in Africa at the time. The attacks on the Kenyan and Tanzanian embassies in 1998 killed hundreds of people. Then there was the bombing of a Hard Rock Cafe in Cape Town, South Africa. This was close to home for me because I had eaten there two days earlier. Soon thereafter a major mall in the Cape Town suburbs changed its food court theme from "Mississippi Junction," replete with American flags, to something more mundane and neutral.

I was also living in Namibia at the time of the tragic events of 9/11. While I watched with horror as those airplanes plunged into the World Trade Center, I told my Namibian friends that the world would never be the same again. They thought I was just expressing American arrogance. "Sure, when it happens elsewhere, you guys don't lift a finger. But once it happens to you, then the whole world is falling apart." They were right, and I knew it. Terrorism overseas would not get our attention, but on our own soil? The whole world would never be the same again; we would make sure of that.

This seeming digression into American ethos is really no digression at all. Although Americans give more charitably than any other country—a subject I have written about in editorials in the major English newspaper in Namibia—we are nonetheless self-centered and egotistical. Until we admit this, there will be no hope of becoming proper disciples of Jesus.

We are all culturally conditioned individuals. This has become more apparent to me as I have lived in Africa where the mind-set is incredibly different. Americans are project-oriented; Africans are people-oriented. Americans are driven by time, Africans by events. Americans are individualistic, Africans communal.

When Jesus says we need to hate our father and mother to be his disciples, this offends the Africans more. When he says we need to hate ourselves, it offends Americans more. I do not like to be told that I must hate my mother and father either, but I made the choice to become a missionary. I already had to make the hard choice of moving overseas and separating myself from my family. I am not intending to extol myself in using this example. Rather, I want to recount what it is like to leave one's family to go overseas as a missionary.

My grandfather, who was in many ways my spiritual mentor, died two months after we first came to Namibia. He struggled for his last years with leukemia, but he always maintained a cheery disposition. I resigned myself to the fact that once I left for the mission field, I would never see him again, but that did not make it any easier to miss his last months or his funeral.

When we left for the mission field, we had two small children. We had three more born to us, all in Namibia; but for stretches of four years, virtually no one in our families could see the children. With e-mail and digital cameras, missionary work is not nearly as solitary as it used to be, but a picture on the computer screen can hardly replace the warm body of a grandchild sitting in your lap. When I think of the sacrifices made in going to the mission field, the sacrifice I asked my other family members to make outweighs any I have personally encountered. Putting my allegiance to my family lower than my allegiance to the mission field, then, is something I have chosen to do. But to hate myself, well, that is a bit closer to home.

A couple of years ago I had lunch with a good friend, and I admitted to him something I had not told anyone else. I felt at times that I was languishing in Namibia and watching all my dreams pass me by. (How many of you had even heard of Namibia before reading this book?) Even as I write this book—and this chapter—I am hoping that with it I will become well known and make a fairly sizable amount of money. In the words of Martin Luther, I am a "stinking sinner." Even as I work on a project I think can be used by God to help others, I am selfishly thinking about myself.

Once in a private conversation with a pastor for whom I hold the utmost respect, he confided in me that sometimes while he is preaching, he will become arrogant. Even in the middle of the message, while he is standing there with hundreds of people watching him and listening intently to every word that flows from his mouth, a thought would pop into his mind: *Isn't it nice to have all these people waiting upon every word you speak? Doesn't it feel nice to have all their eyes concentrating on you and nothing else?*

Can you hear the lisping lips of the Serpent? Or is that just me talking to myself? A chill runs down my spine as I realize that sometimes I cannot tell the difference.

So here I am, in a corner of the world few people have heard about, working in a small seminary with students who might amount to nothing. Couldn't I be more useful in a large Christian college or university, back in mainstream America, making a name for myself and selling tons more books? And can I not justify all this egotistical rationalization by talking about how much more work I could do for God's kingdom if placed in such a situation?

The more I dwell on these things, the more I hate myself for such selfish thoughts. And miraculously the more Christlike I become. The more Christlike I think I am becoming by this self-loathing, the more arrogant I become, thinking that I have now arrived at true Christlikeness. Will this vicious cycle never end?

Many people thought Martin Luther was crazy. All his talk about sin and self-loathing made many of his enemies, and even some of his friends, think he might be demon-possessed. Throwing an inkwell at demons supposedly meandering in the corner of his office did not help matters much.[7]

Luther drove his superiors nuts in his early years in the monastery. Whereas most monks would spend several minutes in daily confessions, Luther sometimes spent several hours. Faced with the prospect of a holy God who demanded perfection, Luther scoured his conscience, thoughts, and actions for sin. Believing a sin was not properly covered by Christ's atonement until it was confessed, he often returned to the confessional later the same day to confess other grievances he had recently recalled.

Did Luther go overboard? Was his behavior borderline insane?

# TEN THINGS I WISH JESUS NEVER SAID

When compared with a holy God and living in a system that taught that one's good works were necessary to be justified, I do not think so. Luther was taking things to their logical conclusion. Only a perfect being can have eternal communion with another perfect being. Falling short of this perfection, Luther was rightly terrified.

Many people today are cavalier in their relationships with God. They either categorize most of their sins as "venial" or negligible or reconfigure their image of God as feeble and frail. All God is interested in is sincerity and that we genuinely try our best. He is more than willing to overlook minor infractions. I often wonder, given such attitudes, where eating a piece of forbidden fruit would fall on the spectrum. My guess is it would come just under "little white lies" and the occasional piracy of computer software. That it would be enough to banish our first parents from Eden and cause spiritual and physical death is often thrown in the trash heap of allegory by people with such perspectives.

> All those who do not in all their works or sufferings, life and death, trust in God's favor, grace and good-will, but rather seek His favor in other things or in themselves, do not keep the [First] Commandment, and practice real idolatry, even if they were to do the works of all the other Commandments, and in addition had all the prayers, fasting, obedience, patience, chastity, and innocence of all the saints combined.
>
> Martin Luther (1483-1546), *Treatise Concerning Good Works*

"The fear of the Lord is the beginning of wisdom" (Ps. 111:10). Luther was no madman. In fact, he was probably one of the sanest men of his generation. Those who do not have a healthy fear of God are the ones who should be considered lunatics. Likewise, those who do not have a healthy self-loathing cannot truly follow God.

## EMULATING THE TAX COLLECTOR

Perhaps the quintessential statement from Jesus concerning this problem of confidence in self is found in the parable of the Pharisee and tax collector (Luke 18:9-14). Luke begins this parable by providing the reason Jesus gave it: "To some who were confident of their own righteousness and looked down on everybody else, Jesus told this parable" (v. 9). It is easy for us in the twenty-first century to miss the shock or sting of this teaching.

Jesus juxtaposes two men in the story, a Pharisee and a tax collector. In the eyes of most Jews in that day, a Pharisee was the epitome of holiness and righteousness, whereas the tax collector was the opposite. Normally a tax collector was a fellow Jew who worked for the oppressor, the Roman Empire, and extorted money from his own people. In most instances, he gained a large amount of personal wealth from the collecting of taxes. Capitulating to the oppressor, while making personal gain from the oppression of their own people, tax collectors were greatly hated by the Jews.

No doubt for this reason Jesus chose these two figures for his story. The people would expect the Pharisee to appear righteous in the story, while the tax collector would earn scathing disapproval. As is typical in Jesus's teaching, the opposite happened. The Pharisee proclaimed his own worthiness before God. He touted personal acts of righteousness by commending his almsgiving and fasting. In fact, we note that the Pharisee was in the temple praying, yet another laudable activity by him. However, he was really there to exalt himself.

On the other hand, the tax collector displayed true humility. While the Pharisee stood up and declared his own righteousness, the tax collector would not even raise his eyes upward, too ashamed of his sin. He beat his breast, a sign of humility and self-loathing. His plea was twofold: He declared he was a sinner, and he asked for mercy.

So much of our teaching today—both secular and sacred—tells us such acts of self-loathing are bad for our self-image and self-esteem. However, only when we recognize the extent of our sinfulness in the eyes of a holy God can we begin to experience God's grace and mercy, from which come renewal and rebirth.

The shock of Jesus's first-century hearers must have been incredible. Should we not applaud the Pharisee for the great things he has done? Does he not pray, fast, and give as he should? Note that the

Pharisee's "plea" is twofold as well: he declares his own righteous deeds while condemning others around him.

Perhaps the sting of this parable will become more apparent once we dwell on the attitude of the Pharisee. One of the classic evangelism questions asked today, popularized by the Evangelism Explosion course, is, "What would you say if you died today, and God asked you why he should let you into heaven?" I have heard that question asked numerous times, and in the majority of instances, people begin to list the good things they have done and the bad things they have not done. And I am struck at how similar that answer is to the one the Pharisee gives in this parable.

We can call this tendency "comparative obedience." So many of us find great comfort when we compare ourselves to others. Fact is, we can always find someone who appears to be more of a sinner than we are. And in finding comfort in the sins we do not commit, we ignore the ones we do commit. Many people answer that Evangelism Explosion question by saying, "I haven't murdered or stolen or committed adultery," and claim that for these reasons, they should be allowed to enter heaven. But what of pride, or self-indulgence, or other sins of the heart? Are they free of these too?

The Pharisee looked at the good things he had done and, coupled with a comparative obedience that made him appear better than the tax collector, declared himself justified before God. Not so, Jesus tells his first-century listeners, and he tells us that today as well. This attitude is similarly reported by Luke after the parable of the shrewd manager (16:1ff.). Jesus claims that the Pharisees "justify [themselves] in the eyes of men" (v. 15). He then notes, "What is highly valued among men is detestable in God's sight." Jesus loathed this type of self-justification and self-righteousness.

Have you ever seen a person who is sick or terminally ill acting as if nothing is wrong? The situation is pathetic. The dying person is told to take medication but refuses to do so, pretending he has no ailment or condition that warrants undergoing the treatment. The Pharisee praying in the temple does much the same thing. He acts as if nothing is wrong. It is like going to the doctor and declaring yourself completely healthy when you have a disease that will soon take your life. Failing to recognize your sickness, you also fail to recognize the needed cure. The Pharisee stands before the physician of the soul and tells him he is perfectly healthy.

"I am glad I am not like that Pharisee." How often have you said this or heard someone else say it? Even after reading this parable, many of us have a tendency to make this declaration and in so doing, we have unwittingly made the error the Pharisee did. So many of us are self-deceived by our supposed self-righteousness. We look around us and see the evil acts of others, and because we do not do those things, we pat ourselves on the back and declare ourselves righteous, all the while ignoring the numerous other sins in our lives.

The problem is that we are comparing ourselves to the wrong person. Instead of comparing ourselves to other sinners, we should be comparing ourselves to the sinless Son of God. Once we make this comparison, no matter who we are, we should realize how short we fall. It is the universal experience of truly godly people that the closer they walk to the Lord, the more they realize how sinful they are. The closer you move an object to a penetrating light, the more the defects of that object become obvious. The same is true with believers. The longer we are exposed to the penetrating light of the Son of God, the more our weaknesses and sinfulness become apparent, and the more readily we recognize our need for the mercy and forgiveness of God. Too many people act like the Pharisee. The longer they are Christians, the more self-righteous they become, and the more arrogantly they treat other Christians less holy than themselves.

The parable ends with these words: "For everyone who exalts himself will be humbled, and he who humbles himself will be exalted" (v. 11). Many people walk the earth today expecting their exaltation as a sure thing and will only find themselves humbled in the final analysis.

He that humbleth himself, whatever be he: if, instead of fasting twice in the week, he has been drunk twice in the week; if, instead of giving tithes of all that he possesses, he has cheated the minister of his tithes, and the king of his taxes; notwithstanding he be unjust, an extortioner, an adulterer, nay, notwithstanding the sins of all mankind center and unite in him; yet, if through grace, like the Publican, he is enabled to humble himself, he shall be exalted.

George Whitefield (1714-1770), *The Sermons of George Whitefield*

## THE BALANCING ACT

Am I saying we should care for nothing else, period? Am I saying Christians should abandon all other obligations in their quest for Christ?

The quest for Christ comes with other obligations that must also be properly balanced. There are many Christian workers, especially pastors, whose work has become their idol, a "ministry workaholism." Consider the great evangelist whose own children are not believers or the many people who have grown up despising the Christian faith because their pastor-father was never around to care for their needs. Is Christ saying we must ignore our families so we can get on to the real business of following him? Does this mean that as a minister I must always make my family come second? In other words, must I neglect the needs of my wife and children in the name of working for Christ?

Some might think I have painted myself into a corner and must answer them with the blunt reply, "All other obligations must take a backseat to our obligation to follow Jesus." However, I do not think formulating the answer in that way is necessarily the best.

God has placed us on planet earth. He does not ask us for a commitment to him that is produced in a vacuum. It is a commitment that comes in the environment of the real world. Pastors who have families have a godly obligation to care for them, and this obligation can be seen as part of their obligation to follow Christ. Too often those in the ministry play their commitment to family against their commitment to Christ, but this is a false dichotomy.

When my wife and I decided to go to the mission field, a potential difficulty was foremost on my mind, that of educating our children. Rightly or wrongly, I thought an education in Africa might not be as good as one in the States. My wife, who grew up on the mission field and from the age of six attended a boarding school, did not have as much difficulty with this decision.

Some would say that if I had enough faith, I would not worry about such things. If God called me to Africa (and discerning the "calling" is not as easy as some flippantly make it out to be), I should have enough faith to know he will provide for the education of my children. On the other side of my shoulder was the little demon telling me I should look at reality and all the children who were raised on the mission field who came to despise their parents and God for it. Should I not be concerned with the education of my children?

Consider the greater concerns. By moving to Africa I placed my family at greater risk of contracting tuberculosis or malaria, the two biggest killers on the African continent. And what about the increased political unrest or the potential for violent crimes such as rape or abduction?[8] How many missionaries have had family members die of exotic diseases they never would have had to worry about had they stayed home? Of course, if I moved from the western suburbs of Chicago to the inner city, would I not also have similar safety concerns? Thus the arguments swirled around in my mind.

As it turned out, my children are getting a better education than I did in the small, rural school I attended in America. God has provided in wonderful ways in this regard. Were my original concerns unfounded? Of course not. God has given us earthly obligations that must be balanced with our spiritual duties. In fact, I would say earthly obligations *are* spiritual duties, as everything we do should be done to the glory of God.

This being said, at what point does a pastor determine how many funerals, prayer meetings, and church-related functions are taking him away too often from his family responsibilities? This I believe must be left to the individual person and his conscience, with a keen eye to prevent ministry for the Lord from damaging his responsibilities in other areas. Christ's command of familial hatred should be understood in the context of family members who oppose our commitment to Christ. It should not be used as an excuse to neglect those family members God has placed under our care.

## THE PATH TO SELF-LOATHING

For the remainder of this chapter, I would like to suggest four areas where we can avoid the idolatry of self and inculcate a proper self-loathing.

### Put God Before Yourself

On the surface, this may seem like a self-evident truth for Christians, but too many of us have simply forgotten it. As A. W. Tozer wrote, "The essence of idolatry is the entertainment of thoughts about God that are unworthy of Him."[9] We possess too many low and mean views of God, either by envisioning him as a cosmic Santa Claus or as our buddy and pal whom we slap on the back while we share a crude joke. For other Christians, God is a grandfatherly figure sitting in heaven wringing his hands, hoping humans will buy into his plan of salvation but not sure if they will.

If we do not properly understand that we exist for the sole purpose of bringing God glory and serving him, we will never attain the level of spiritual maturity Christ wants in his disciples. We have a propensity for creating God in our image and then claiming to be following him, when all we are following is a false image. A person only rises to the level of his or her image of God. If it is a low image, we can expect the person's life to similarly reflect this low image.

> Our God is in heaven;
> he does whatever pleases him.
> But their idols are silver and gold,
> made by the hands of men.
> They have mouths, but cannot speak,
> eyes but they cannot see;
> they have ears, but cannot hear,
> noses, but they cannot smell;
> they have hands, but cannot feel,

*feet, but they cannot walk;*
*nor can they utter a sound with their throats.*
*Those who make them will be like them,*
*and so will all who trust in them. (Ps. 115:3-8)*

Each time we sin, we allow the idolatry of self to flourish. We must daily submit our will to God's. The expectation is complete surrender of the self. If Jesus asks me to sell everything I possess and give the proceeds to the poor, I must do it if I intend to be his disciple. If he commands me to move my family overseas, despite the difficulties I must do it. If he tells me to preach the gospel in a hostile environment where I might lose my life, I must obey him completely. The military adage is apt here: "Ours is not to question why. Ours is but to do or die." Paul, quoting Isaiah, says something similar: "We are like sheep led to the slaughter."

If you attempt to explain to people of the world this seemingly mindless obedience, they will consider you the greatest fool. Precisely. Jesus is opposed to the world and its order, and he expects his disciples to conform to his will, not that of the cosmos. As we saw in chapter 5, persecution is to be expected, not avoided. If the world thought Jesus was a fool, it will think the same of us.

Christian singer Michael Card recognizes this. In his song "God's Own Fool," Card calls us to become fools in the eyes of the world just as Jesus did:

*We in our foolishness thought we were wise,*
*He played the fool, and he opened our eyes.*

God delights in using foolish material to shame the world. In fact, he delights in commanding us to do seemingly foolish things to display his power and might.

Few of us are familiar with apprenticeships and what it means to be under the discipleship of another. A film that popularized this notion in the 1980s was *The Karate Kid*. A young boy seeks the help of a karate master to fend off bullies in his life, but he does not get what he expected. The whole time the karate kid is told to do seemingly menial tasks at the command of his mentor, Mr. Miagi, he is learning important karate moves.

Perhaps the best-known instance is the "wax on, wax off" scene in the film. Miagi has the youth wax his car in the noonday heat, using clockwise circular motions to put the wax on and counterclockwise motions to take it off. At one point the boy runs off in a huff, thinking Miagi is taking advantage of him. Only later does he learn that Miagi has been training him for the ultimate test and that the circular waxing motions emulate karate blocks.

God does similar things in the Old Testament. Three examples stand out. The Exodus from Egyptian slavery was a study in the inability of the Israelites and the wondrous provision of God, from the ten plagues to the parting of the Red Sea. Even in the desert God miraculously provided them water from a rock, manna and quail from the sky, and never allowed their clothing to wear out for forty years. The Jews were hardly in a position to claim self-reliance in the face of these events.

Similarly, God preserved Hezekiah and Judah from the advancing army of Sennacherib, in one night killing 185,000 men in the Assyrian army (Isa. 37:36). The Israelites, clearly outnumbered and outclassed by the advancing Assyrians, could never have won the battle in any natural way.

Again in the account of Gideon's victory over the Midianites (Judg. 7), God stacked the odds heavily in the favor of the enemy. Using only 300 men armed with trumpets and empty jars filled with torches, the Jews defeated the superior Midianite army. God made it clear why he stacked the odds in this fashion: "In order that Israel may not boast against me that her own strength has saved her" (Judg. 7:2).

Time and time again God put his chosen people in situations where they could not save themselves so that his power and might would be displayed. In fact, whenever the Jews became arrogant and self-reliant, they were soundly punished by God, usually in the form of military defeat at the hands of their enemies.

Nay, even the holiest of men, however well aware that they stand not in their own strength, but by the grace of God, would feel too secure in their own fortitude and constancy, were they not brought to a more thorough knowledge of themselves by the trial of the cross.

John Calvin (1509-1564), *On the Christian Life*

In each instance, the reason God commanded the Israelites to do seemingly foolish things was so they could never claim they had succeeded in their own strength. Is God not doing the same thing with us? Does he put us in ministries that seem destined for failure, yet that miraculously succeed? Does he ask us to share a message that appears foolish to a perishing world? Yet he brings life from it.

God hates self-reliance in his children, whereas we praise such a quality in our earthly children. The moment we think we are self-reliant, we have become branches that claim to no longer need the vine for sustenance and, as such, are suitable for burning. Independent-minded people need not apply for the discipleship training of Jesus. He wants dependent people who are willing to conform to his yoke, not think they can coerce Jesus to their own will.

God is a jealous God. He wants nothing else to stand in the way of our complete, unswerving devotion to him. We must not think idolatry is limited to fashioned pieces of wood or precious metals. Anything that takes us from our absolute, focused commitment to God can serve as an idol.

God wants to break us away from all things that impede our relationship with him. It is a dangerous thing to fall into the hands of a God fully committed to seeing us grow more intimate with him. We must be prepared to lose everything dear to us. Those things we deem of greater value to us than our fellowship with God will be purged by him—family, possessions, employment, money, anything.

God has not ceased being jealous. When we profess our commitment to him, we must expect the commitment will be reciprocated by him. Therefore, we must always be mindful that everything we do must be done with his glory in mind lest he burn it away like chaff.

To purify me the more from the mixture I might make of His gifts with my own self-love, He gave me interior probations, which were very heavy.

*Autobiography of Madame Guyon* (1647-1717)

## Put Others Before Yourself

One important way to crucify the egotistical self is to begin to cultivate an others-focused mentality. When Paul writes, "consider others better than yourselves" (Phil. 2:3), this is not a command to manufacture false humility. This is genuine humility, displayed by our willingness to forgo our rights for the sake of others. Paul's supreme example is Jesus Christ, who did not greedily hold on to his equality with the Father, but who humbled himself and "made himself nothing" so he could save us.

We are so used to personal rights and inalienable privileges that we lose sight of the radical nature of Christlike humility. We have forgotten that genuine disciples of Jesus put the needs of others first, even if it hurts. I have seen Christians arrogantly flaunt their freedom to drink alcohol by swilling a beer in front of believers they know are offended by it. Paul tells us elsewhere (Rom. 14) that such attitudes are unacceptable for Christians.

I was struck by this attitude of selfishness when talking with a person whose sister is an unwed mother with a small child. The young lady hardly finds time for herself, constantly with the toddler on her shoulder wherever she goes. One evening I asked her older sister why she did not take care of the child so that her younger sibling could go out to watch a basketball game with young people from the church. Her reply was, "I work all day during the week. This is *my* time, and I am not going to compromise it."

So often we harbor the same damaging attitudes. "It is my right to speak up, and no one is going to tell me differently, even if it hurts others." "My conscience is clear when it comes to this behavior. It's your problem if you are offended by it." "No one has the right to tell me what to do, and I'll take you to court if you impede my right." Many churches have been split by these selfish attitudes.

In Namibia beggars are a consistent problem. Fact is, if you help them once, you can never shake them again. One such man constantly comes to our home asking for money. I must admit, at times I hate the fact that he shows up and wish he would never come again. This is my hard-earned money that he is asking me to give him.

Then I realize that if every Christian had the same attitude, I could never be a missionary in Africa, as I benefit solely from the charitable giving of believers willing to give what is clearly theirs so I can have a living as a missionary. These believers are willing to crucify their egotistical selves to provide for me. Can I now stingily hold on to what has already freely been given to me?

> How difficult it is to perform the duty of seeking the good of our neighbour! Unless you leave off all thought of yourself and in a manner cease to be yourself, you will never accomplish it. How can you exhibit those works of charity which Paul describes unless you renounce yourself, and become wholly devoted to others?
>
> John Calvin (1509-1564), *On the Christian Life*

## View the Church as a Place for Giving of Oneself

George Barna recently reported that he sees a major shift in the church and its focus in America. This he considers a "revolution," which is the title of his book that catalogues this megashift in Christian thinking about what constitutes church.[10] What I found disconcerting about this revelation is not that people are rethinking better ways to serve God; that is Barna's positive take on the change. Rather it is the fact that Christians still approach church with the what's-in-it-for-me mentality.

"Church hopping" has become a common practice with many believers. For some this practice is as sinister as finding the best church to pick up single women, their sole motivation for attending. However, I am talking about something far tamer and yet equally damaging—the attitude that only has self as the sole factor in one's selection of a place of worship. "How does the worship make me feel? Do I get motivated by the speaker? Are there people here who make me feel accepted and loved?" Me, me, me.

Clearly, one aspect of church is how it affects my life, but this can hardly be the only factor to consider. Thousands, if not millions, of Christians (dare I say the majority of believers?) only show up at church to get fed but do little feeding of others. They wander up to the trough each week, gorge themselves until they are satisfied, and then do not show up again until they feel more hunger pangs. If the slightest thing goes wrong or something occurs that they do not like, they move to the next shop in the ecclesiastical mall. They never become members; they never get involved in anything that helps the church, but when things go bad, they are the first to object.

The idolatry of self has produced Christians who have an anemic view of church, what I like to call freelance Christians, the ones who bounce from church to church. Church is all about what they can get out of it, and there is no understanding that the body of believers can only mature when we all actively work to edify it. Many foolishly believe they can be better Christians (something Barna reports) if they are *not* active participants in a local body of believers.

I think that fact bears repeating. There are Christians who think they have a better, stronger relationship with God so long as they avoid sustained interaction with God's people.[11] Their mentality is that a believer can be fed via the Internet or television and need not become a member of any local church. Is it no wonder that many churches today struggle with keeping church and outreach ministries alive when there are tons of believers who are not exercising their spiritual gifts in their congregations? The old adage that 10 percent of the people do 100 percent of the work is apt here. Is it any wonder that many pastors experience burnout and leave their ministries? How many churches have a Moses as their pastor with no elders or judges to help him with the never-ending work?

Barna thinks this revolution may be the most influential movement to happen in the church in the past century, good or bad. If he is right, I tend to believe it is the latter effect, not the former. It can only be unhealthy both for the church and for individual believers if large numbers of Christians sit at home getting "fed" and not actively participating in their local church body.

Can you imagine all your fingers and toes saying they will no longer accompany the rest of your body when you go out? How many of our churches today are absent eyes and ears, hands and feet? When Jesus proclaims, "It is more blessed to give than to receive," do we honestly believe this?

Let me suggest that we take a proverbial statement from a former president of America and apply it when it comes to church participation: "Ask not what your church can do for you; ask what you can do for your church." Identify your spiritual gifts or natural talents and actively pursue ways to use them in your local church. We must not view church as existing only to benefit ourselves. Rather we must view ourselves as existing to benefit the church. If we do not see ourselves in this selfless manner, we can expect Christianity to have an increasingly diminishing effect on our society and the world.

## Cultivate a Selfless Prayer Life

When my oldest daughter was young and we would pray together, her prayers were normally characterized by the following: "Dear Jesus, give me this, give me that." I told her she must also pray for others, not just keep asking for things for herself. So then she would begin, "Thank you, God, for my family. Please give me this, please give me that."

Too often our prayers are selfish, characterized by a barrage of personal requests, needs, and desires. Clearly we are supposed to present our requests before God, but if our prayers become dominated by requests for ourselves, with little focus on others, we have an imbalanced prayer life.

I find it instructive that in Christ's "high priestly prayer" in John 17, he begins by praying for himself. He then prays for the disciples and lastly for Christians who believe their message. I do not want to make this a formula we must now follow, but it is interesting that the bulk of the prayer is for others, not for Jesus himself. Even in the Lord's Prayer, there is no element of prayers for self, only for "us" as envisioned as the entire community of disciples. Of course, this prayer can be spoken by the individual ("lead me not into temptation, deliver me from evil"), but I hope you see my wider point. We need to avoid selfish, self-centered prayers and have a more body-corporate prayer life.

I also find it instructive that the Lord's Prayer begins with God and his glory: "hallowed be thy name." As we already noted, we must put God before self, lest we make self an idol. We exist for one thing and one thing only, to bring glory to God. If we are not doing that, we have ceased to exist for the reason we have been created. God did not create us solely to give us what we want, to pamper and coddle us, but rather to serve him. The psalmist says, "Not to us, O LORD, not to us but to your name be the glory" (115:1). Our prayers should be characterized by this jealousy for God's glorification, not our satisfaction.

When I pray, I often employ a useful acronym in directing my prayers. Again, I do not intend to create a formula that *must* be followed, but it is a helpful guideline so that I do not fall into the error of imbalanced or selfish prayers. The acronym is ACTS, and it stands for adoration, confession, thanksgiving, and supplication. I cannot recall where I learned this acronym, but it is not something I created, and I am certain some readers will have seen it before.

ACTS guards me against making prayers that are only and always about me and my needs. It helps me focus first on God and who he is, a characteristic of prayer too often ignored. We have come to view prayer as a time to present our cosmic wish list to God, but we have forgotten that prayer must also be a time where we are transformed. It is not that we are bending God's will to our own in prayer, but the opposite must happen. Our will is bent to his.

So much of prayer today, especially in the prosperity movement, is an exercise in arm-bending. We have adopted an immature view of prayer that pictures us twisting God's arm until he gives in to our demands. Such a pathetic image of God is nothing more than the idolatry of self. We have made our limited, temporal will the determinative factor in our relationship with the infinite, eternal Lord of glory.

ACTS also helps me to admit I am a sinner. I do not come to God with demands, calling him to task when he does not respond in the way I have predetermined. Instead, I come recognizing I am a beggar in need of mercy, grace, and guidance. When I make my confession before God, I admit my spiritual destitution and poverty. Without such an attitude, we can hardly expect God to answer our arrogant prayers. We must profess our dependence upon him. Only then is his ear attentive to our petitions and requests.

Even further, ACTS guards us from forgetting the great things God has done for us. Paul tells us, "Do not be anxious about anything, but in everything, by prayer and petition, with thanksgiving, present your requests to God" (Phil. 4:6). Some people keep a prayer journal to track their requests and God's answers. This seems like a good idea to me because we have such a tendency to forget the promises of God and how he fulfills them. By bringing to mind all the things he has already done for us, we can guard ourselves against selfish prayers devoted solely to our personal desires and perceived needs. A thankful heart also keeps us from repetitious prayers, as the pagans pray (Matt. 6:7), thinking that if we inundate God with a specific request, he must ultimately see things our way.

There are times when a special problem presents itself, such as a sudden illness or accident, and we come to God solely with that pressing need on our mind. Heaven forbid that my readers think I am saying one must go through the formula of ACTS for God to hear our prayers. There are times when we come to God with only this or that request because it is an urgent need. There is nothing wrong with this. For that matter, we can come to God only in confession, or only in thanksgiving or adoration, and we need not always present requests. What I am concerned with is our habitual prayers, that they not be dominated by self-centered considerations.

## "MY GOD, MY GOD, WHY HAVE YOU *NOT* FORSAKEN ME?"

This is my cry to God. I am amazed that he has not abandoned me although I so often fail him in thought, word, and deed. If my salvation depended upon my will, I would surely be lost. Despite all his benefits, despite all the loving kindness he has shown me, I still actively rebel against him. I am an ungrateful, obstinate believer. I loathe who I am; yet I eagerly await the day when I am set free from this struggle with myself and am made perfect in the image of God's Son.

Jesus says we must sacrifice familial relationships if need be to follow him. But he also tells us that if we do so, the rewards of such sacrifice are an actual increase in our family. "Everyone who has left houses or brothers or sisters or father or mother or children or fields for my sake will receive a hundred times as much and will inherit eternal life" (Matt. 19:29). Often spiritual relationships between believers can be stronger than blood ties.

By following Jesus, we become members of a family that is stronger and longer lasting than temporal family ties. The bond is eternal. Jesus identified his true family, his mother and brothers, as those who do the Father's will (Mark 3:33-35). Similarly, even if our faith in Jesus causes a sword to slice between us and our earthly familial bonds, a greater family awaits us in the children of God.

> We are not conformed to the fear of God and do not learn the rudiments of piety, unless we are violently slain by the sword of the Spirit and brought to naught.
>
> John Calvin (1509-1564), *Institutes*[12]

# THE ART OF
# SPIRITUAL DISCERNMENT

*Do not judge, or you too will be judged.*
JESUS CHRIST, MATTHEW 7:1

*If in my praise I am moved with the good of my neighbour,*
*why am I less moved if another be unjustly dispraised than if*
*it be myself? Why am I more stung by reproach cast upon*
*myself, than at that cast upon another, with the same injus-*
*tice, before me?*
AUGUSTINE (354-430), *CONFESSIONS*

*Often we are not aware that we are so blind in heart.*
THOMAS À KEMPIS (1380-1471),
*THE IMITATION OF CHRIST*

She was in the church for over thirty years, and no one was immune
to her critical eye. She criticized the way people dressed; she criticized
the way people walked; she criticized the way people talked. If she
thought you were too fat, you would hear about it. If she thought you
were too thin, she would gossip that perhaps you had a secret illness.
She complained about the pastor's sermon when it was too long, and
she complained when she thought it was too short. If it was too long,
he was longwinded. If it was too short, he had not prepared enough to
feed the sheep. She even criticized the way the pastor's wife dressed. She
was the most critical person most parishioners ever knew.

In this chapter we are going to see that Jesus has strong words for people who have a critical spirit, who are always finding fault, who are quick to point out others' deficiencies and shortcomings.

We will also find that few passages in Scripture have been more misused and misapplied than this one. This passage is often quoted, especially by unbelievers, at Christians who speak out against certain activities, seemingly breaking this command. But even worse, many Christians have misunderstood it and have fallen into grave error, putting aside all reasonable determinations on questionable behavior, making it their own and hence falling into sin.

I have seen non-Christians chastise believers for judging homosexuality, or abortion, or numerous other sinful activities because, as Jesus has clearly commanded us, we should *never* judge anybody or anything. I have been told, "Jesus says you should never judge," in response to my determination that this or that activity or practice was wrong or sinful.

We will attempt to determine the difference between good and bad judgment and if Christians are ever meant to judge other people. We will find that Christians are not meant to have a critical or judgmental attitude toward others, but we *are* meant to be discerning people who are commanded to judge between right and wrong.

This will not be an easy chapter as there is a fine line between being judgmental and being discerning, between condemning sin in the lives of others and subtly condoning it. Before we look at how we should understand this command of Jesus, it may be helpful to examine the two extremes taken with respect to this directive.

## BOUNCING BETWEEN THE POLES

There are two equal yet opposite problems when it comes to Christians and the issue of judgment. I label these two poles Pharisaical legalism or fundamentalism and postmodern relativism or liberalism. To use political terminology, it is as simple as those on the far right versus the far left. Biblically, it is an imbalance produced when we do not properly "speak the truth in love." Let me begin with the problem of legalism.

## Judgmental on a Corporate Level

Christianity has fallen on hard times lately, and part of it is our own fault. Certainly the world is watching us, but they are doing a selective job of it. Consider the caricatures of Christians in Hollywood portrayals. You can count on one hand the number of films that have fairly depicted evangelical Christians in the last ten years. Almost always we are portrayed as loud-mouthed, bigoted hate-mongers.

But part of it is our fault. How many squabbles and quarrels do we have to entertain between fellow believers before we realize the world selectively records such incidences? It is a sad fact of church history that Christians simply cannot get along. Thousands of churches have split because fellow believers could not work together. Then we expect the world to be attracted to the message of salvation in Jesus Christ.

Gossiping about other members is rampant in our churches. Slandering fellow believers, talking about them behind their backs, and bad-mouthing them to others is standard practice. Jealousy and envy fuel bitter rivalries; the desires for fame and power cause many of our leaders to split churches so they can have things their way and answer to no one else. Sad to say, I know of two churches in America that split, one over which color to paint the church, the other over which side of the church should house the organ.

Much of the last four hundred years of the history of Christianity has been characterized by Christians killing other Christians or one church persecuting the members of another church. Where is the body of Christ? How do we imagine with any reasonable expectation that people will want to come to our church when we cannot even get along in it ourselves?

Jesus told his disciples in John 13:34-35: "A new command I give you: Love one another. As I have loved you, so you must love one another. By this all men will know that you are my disciples, if you love one another." Unfortunately, when the world looks at many churches, it gets the real sense that Christians are contentious, disagreeable people who cannot even get along with one another. Our churches are filled with members who do not like each other, but instead of living with an attitude of humility, we fight one another. Our churches will never be strong in the faith when, instead of contending for the gospel, we contend among ourselves.

Before I entered the mission field, I worked as a sales engineer for a metallurgy company. I covered a large portion of the Midwest spanning several states, with the opportunity to meet a variety of interesting people. During a sales call on a manufacturer in Wisconsin, I had a healthy discussion over lunch with an engineer about religion. Both of us had Baptist backgrounds, so you would think we had much in common. At the time, though, I was a member of a large nondenominational, evangelical church in the Chicago suburbs.

As we talked, we shared details of our respective churches. Mine had roughly 2,000 people in attendance each Sunday, his about forty. I had no problem with his church being small, especially since I was raised in a Baptist church about twice the size of his. However, he had a difficult time believing my church was a true church following Jesus Christ. I can still recall his words: "How can you have a true church with that many people in it? They can't possibly all be believers." And then came the crucial point in his reasoning: "When is the last time you publicly disciplined one of them?"

I honestly answered that I could not recall the last time that had happened, and at that point I lost all credibility in his eyes. For him, a true church should constantly be busy disciplining its members, and right then I realized why his church was so small.

However, let me ask a hard question of my own church: Were we so big because we made it easy for people to attend, become members, and not have their sins exposed? In all honesty, I would have to say no. The Word of God was preached weekly from the pulpit. There was no compromise when it came to the gospel and its call on our lives. My church had (and still has) a rigorous missions program and a healthy outreach to the local community. No, we were not big because we had watered down the message to get people into the pews.

So why did this sales acquaintance think that to be the case? My guess is because he suffered from a healthy dose of truth without the proper balance of love and grace. I do not blame him, and if I had my druthers, I would probably opt for a church heavy on truth and light on love than the opposite—heavy on love and devoid of truth. Both have their problems, of course, and I am well aware that I open myself up to argument by saying one error may not be as bad as the other. Still, love without truth will get you nowhere, but truth without love may still have some legs.

Regardless, my Baptist friend came from a church Hollywood most likes to pick on and with good reason. The bad press Christianity often receives is because we do not have the proper balance. We are too judgmental at times, and one Christian holding a "God hates gays" sign at the funeral of a homosexual is going to counterbalance one hundred acts of kindness by dozens of other believers. So goes the general rule, unfortunate as it may be. One harsh act easily counteracts several compassionate ones. How many times can you tell someone, "I love you," only to have the relationship shipwrecked over one careless utterance?

## A Religion of Tolerance

On the other hand, where do we draw the line when it appears that many Christians mistake tolerance for unity? Are the critiques laid at the feet of "seeker-sensitive megachurches" always that off base? Have many not, in the desire to appear more user-friendly in our modern age, watered down the gospel? Can we not strike a balance somewhere between the thirty-thousand-member churches and the thirty-member ones? Put another way, where is the proper balance between churches that appear to water down the gospel and those that seem too narrow-minded and judgmental?

Paul speaks of sharing the truth in love, and I see this as the ideal to aim for. Too many churches today, in the name of defending the truth, have become so unwelcoming as to be embarrassing. On the other hand, in the name of love do we not have many churches that have lost any saltiness to their faith because they have opted to trade in the sodium chloride for a glucose-enriched gospel? Where do we draw the line between love and truth, tolerance and discernment?

# TEN THINGS I WISH JESUS NEVER SAID

Speaking the truth in love is not easy. Many Christians today, seeing how difficult it is to stand for the truth, have opted to excise much of it from their Christian portfolio. What they have unwittingly done, though, is conform not to Christ's but to the world's understanding of love. That understanding equates love with tolerance.

On the other hand, many believers have opted to scream the truth through a megaphone of harshness. Truth by its nature is intolerant; that makes the matter all the more abrasive. When Jesus says he is the way, the truth, and the life, and that no one can come to the Father except through him, that is about as intolerant as you can get. In a world that is extra sensitive to "my way is the only way" messages, no amount of love is going to mollify the sting of intolerance found in Jesus's bold proclamation. If we want a tolerant gospel, we will not find it in the message of Jesus Christ. Yet it seems some Christians are bending over backwards to make the message even more difficult to swallow.

We can be so petty concerning the man-made traditions we have developed, considering them to be the will of God. Much like the Pharisees, we create superfluous rules and regulations and raise them to the level of God's law. How many churches judge the veracity of the faith of others based on whether or not they play with "face cards," or wear blue jeans to the worship service, or have a glass of wine with their dinner? Some are uncomfortable when people in the church lift up hands while singing, while in other churches, if you do not do it, you must be suffering from an impassionate faith.

> Christ said to the adulteress: "Neither do I condemn thee, go, and sin no more." To the murderer, he said: "This day shalt thou be with me in Paradise." But to the Scribes and Pharisees, who set themselves against the righteousness of the gospel, Christ said: "Woe be unto you."
>
> Martin Luther (1483-1546), *Table Talk*

One of my seminary students in Namibia recounted an incident in his church, one that even has the word *evangelical* in its name. They had a guest speaker who preached a biblically solid message with a clear presentation of the gospel. After he was done preaching, one of the elders from the church stood and publicly chastised the guest speaker for not wearing a suit jacket while preaching. Now in Namibia it is rare that a pastor wears a suit jacket given the heat. This church, though, saw it as a sign of genuine commitment. I cannot imagine how the guest speaker felt, but I am certain the elder believed himself to be justified in the eyes of God because he wore a suit jacket.

As I sit criticizing the elder for his judgmental behavior, I must ask myself if I have ever been similarly judgmental. Unfortunately, the answer is yes.

## JUDGMENTAL ON AN INDIVIDUAL LEVEL

So much of my present job is judgmental. For example, I teach two courses on preaching. There I appraise the sermons of every student, from the broad issues of content and outline to the more mundane, such as hand movement and eye contact. In some instances, I critique how students dress or how often they drink from their glass of water. My job is to make them better speakers, so my analysis is meant to produce positive fruit in their future ministries.

On the negative side, I cannot sit through *any* sermon—whether at the seminary or in a church on Sunday morning—without thinking critically about it. At times I do not enjoy a worship service simply because I cannot turn off my critiquing and just listen.

To compound matters, I also teach several systematic theology courses. In these courses you need to critically analyze various options and points of view, with an eye for illogical arguments and faulty conclusions. Again few theological statements go past me without my mind going through rigorous gymnastics designed to produce the best doctrinal product.

Is this too judgmental, or is it necessary discernment? At times the line is fine. Clearly, we need people in our churches who are not only able but willing to make hard judgments. However, such people are rarely the most popular members of their churches. More often someone becomes offended when his theology is corrected, no matter how gently.

No matter how hard I might try to be appeasing and tender in my comments, at times what I say can offend someone. Rarely does a person separate his views from himself. If you say his views are faulty, such a conclusion can rub off on his person.

How often have I pushed someone away with the truth? While I was working in the secular world, I attempted to share the gospel in a non-offensive way with those with whom I came into contact. At one point our office lost a secretary, and we had a temp working with us. She was a woman in her early forties, talkative and friendly.

At some point we were alone in the office; so I decided to attempt to broach the topic of religion as we were discussing a James Bond movie she had recently seen. I told her my favorite Bond movie was *Live and Let Die*, one she had also seen.

In that movie, a woman named Solitaire reads Tarot cards. It soon came out that my temp thought highly of fortune-telling, noting that her personal fortune-teller was accurate "85 percent of the time." I asked where she thought her fortune-teller got the ability to do this. My temp replied, "God gives gifts to everybody." I then asked, "If the gift is from God, why isn't she 100 percent accurate?"

Immediately her demeanor changed. She looked at me with a scowl and barked, "God's not perfect. He made you, didn't he?" She then stormed out of my office.

I was shocked. What I thought was an innocent conversation instantaneously became hostile. Unfortunately, this quick temper was not only revealed to me but to others in the office, and this secretary was only with us for a few more days. I was never able to address the matter again, but I am not sure how I would have done so, given the opportunity.

Was I too judgmental? I am confident that if you asked the temp, she would say I was. Clearly something major was boiling under the surface with her; so an innocent question was viewed as antagonistic. Still I felt guilty about the situation.

Even as I write this book, I wonder if I am being too judgmental in my tone. Am I? Is my approach in this book more encouraging than off-putting? Do I appear to be another of those judgmental believers in his ivory tower looking down upon sinners he would rather not associate with? I hope not. That is not my intention.

## LOOKING THE WRONG DIRECTION

At times it seems to me Jesus can be unfair. First, he makes me give up some of the things I most enjoy. Then he demands I revoke my rights and privileges. He wants absolute, unquestioning obedience, and he does not allow me to retaliate against those who want to harm or destroy me. Rather he demands that I love them.

The last vestige of retribution I could maintain is in my ability to judge others. Is it not a favorite pastime of many Christians, looking down on others and condemning them for their doctrines, personal habits, or political affiliations? This was often the attitude of the Old Testament Israelites. The prophet Amos was sent to the northern tribes of Israel to deliver God's message of judgment. He began with six nations around Israel and then moved to the southern kingdom of Judah. With each oracle of judgment, I am sure the Israelites expressed glee at the condemnation of their hostile neighbors.

However, Amos had an eighth oracle, and that was directed at Israel herself. The shock must have been incredible. Normally judgment speeches concerning the nations around Israel were salvation messages for the Jews. This time, though, even God's chosen people received an oracle of judgment.

Consider this modern example. Suppose someone comes into your church claiming to be a prophet of God. He begins to preach a message from God about the sins of the people in the pubs and bars, the women who hang out in the dark corners of town, and those who waste their life savings in gambling houses and casinos. I can imagine that with each oracle, the people in church would be saying, "Yes, God, give it to them. Those nasty sinners deserve it."

Then the prophet begins to speak about the churches in your city.

With each successive oracle, the people cheer more loudly. "That's right, God. Those people claim to know you, but they teach heresy. Let your judgment rain down upon them."

However, the prophet's last speech is directed at your church. A deafening silence falls upon the congregation. "Is he talking about us?"

We love to hear judgment when it is directed at someone else, particularly if those people oppose us. But when judgment speaks directly to us, we want nothing of it. It is this attitude that Jesus warns us against in his classic statement about the beam and sawdust, which we will look at shortly.

> There is hardly any person who is not tickled with the desire of inquiring into other people's faults.
>
> John Calvin (1509-1564), *Harmony of the Gospels*

Too many Christians suffer from an unholy sense of superiority. We are quick to judge because we have no fear of the judgment falling on us. But once we embrace the understanding that judgment *begins* with us, we should think twice before wantonly condemning others. If we deign to judge others, we must exercise extreme caution.

Fostering a judgmental attitude negates any opportunities we do have for rightly condemning certain behavior. When we scream heresy at every little thing, we lose the ability to call heresy, heresy. It is the cry-wolf syndrome. We lose credibility when we waste our time complaining about nonessentials such as hairstyles and dress codes. "For it is time for judgment to begin with the family of God; and if it begins with us, what will the outcome be for those who do not obey the gospel of God?" (1 Pet. 4:17).

## CULTURALLY CONDITIONED CHRISTIANITY

I am familiar with all the arguments that call for the contextualization of the gospel. If the gospel does not make sense within the context of a certain people, they will not embrace it as truth. Therefore, we must be sensitive to the cultural context, attempting to offer the gospel in a culturally understandable way.

In principle, I see nothing wrong with this argument. My problem comes when we *change* the gospel to fit the culture. I am a firm believer in the notion that the gospel judges each culture, not the other way around. With each culture, be it American or Namibian, Eskimo or Herero, the gospel exposes and judges those values and norms that must be radically altered if one is to embrace the Good News.

Unfortunately, we often look at things the opposite way. This is nothing new as each generation has had its share of people who watered down or altered the gospel so it would become more palatable to their culture and its values.

Some people have noted that in the previous generation, the most quoted verse in the Bible was John 3:16. Now, however, it is "do not judge." I am not sure how one goes about measuring the veracity of such a claim, but on the surface it appears believable. So why has this verse become so popular today? With this section I want to examine the opposite end of the pole, what I call postmodern relativism.

Much of modern Christianity is gun-shy. Our culture has preconditioned us so much *against* being judgmental that too often we do not speak up when we should. Nobody likes to be unpopular, and one of the quickest ways to getting there in our world is to be labeled intolerant. Therefore, many believers produce a knee-jerk reaction—let's never judge anyone or anything. Then we will not have to bear the brunt of the world's condemnation of us as closed-minded and intolerant.

The pressure for tolerance and dialogue is so great today that, incredibly, in the name of religious tolerance we have Christian theologians and scholars calling for a Christianity not centered on Christ. I am certain others would find the notion of a Christianity not centered on Christ as odd as I would. It would be akin to having a Muslim scholar suggest that Islam should no longer be based on the teachings of Mohammed, or a Buddhist theologian calling for a Buddhism that is not centered on the teachings of the Buddha. Or to put it in everyday terms, it is tantamount to calling for refrigerators to not be based on the science of refrigeration, or for suggesting that lawn mowers not have as their essential characteristic the task of cutting grass.

Many evangelicals are calling the inerrancy of God's Word into question with increasing frequency. They are teaching that God is limited in his knowledge of future events, changes in his nature, and can make mistakes. Others are calling for the abandonment of the notion that Jesus Christ atoned for our sins as a substitute for us. I cannot help but wonder if these radical changes to evangelical theology are not due to the pressure our culture creates on a gospel that appears to be harsh and intolerant.

Often the rebuttal is that we should be asking questions of our faith and looking for ways to correct wrongs. But again I must ask the same question: Is this penchant for questioning the ways of the past a product of our current cultural norms and specifically postmodernism? Our times are nothing new. Modernism was into asking questions, no matter how difficult they might be. A quest for truth was the hallmark of the Enlightenment, and that quest poured into the twentieth century with vigor.

Now we sit in postmodernism. The quest for truth is still there, and the questions being asked are the same basic questions. The difference lies in the answers provided. Where modernism had a rigid sense of objective truth and only certain answers were deemed acceptable, postmodernism is different in that all answers are tolerated, no matter how contradictory or convoluted.

There is nothing wrong with asking hard questions; they just need to be good questions. The postmodern badge of courage is an inquisitive nature, to probe authority figures and structures, to look for ways to tear them down. Martin Luther did something similar, and we applaud his effort. But asking questions for the sake of asking questions is a waste of time. This is particularly true when it comes to the cardinal doctrines of Christianity, ones that have served us well for 2,000 years. Questions like, "Are we too judgmental today?" are nice to ask, but ones like, "Shouldn't we question the whole notion of the Trinity?" are unnecessary and dangerous.

Then there are the Christians who parrot postmodern mantras:

"Christianity is meant to be relational, not propositional." The latter is normally characterized as cold and bigoted, while the former welcoming and all-embracing. This is coupled with the fuzzy thinking that allows for differences of opinion, as opposed to rigid thinking that appears to be too dogmatic. In short, it is the overemphasis of love at the expense of truth.

Let's forget for the moment that even the statement, "Christianity is relational, not propositional" is itself a propositional statement. The real problem is that it is creating a false dichotomy between love and truth.

I have already quoted John 13:35: "By this all men will know that you are my disciples, if you love one another," and I used it in one of my arguments above. But let me point out how I think this passage too has been misused by many Christians. Many label it as *the* apologetic for Christianity, seemingly at the exclusion of all others, and that would be true if it were the only thing Jesus ever said, or if we did not have another twenty-three books in the New Testament outside of the Gospels. This statement is often coupled with "thou shalt not judge" to make it appear that the Christian faith is only about love and never about judgment. At times it seems these Christians believe that because "God is love," the reverse must also be true, namely, "love is God." Whereas their goal is often noble, the Christian faith can hardly be boiled down to something this simplistic.

Granted, the historical penchant of Christianity has leaned toward the side of judgment rather than to the side of tolerance and love, and this tendency needs a corrective but not one that is skewed too strongly to the other side.

Why is this brand of postmodern Christianity becoming so popular? Some would say it is because it speaks to the present generation and as such should be welcomed. I am not convinced. A generation that embraces relativism and "truth is what is true to me" must be corrected, not placated. Screaming at them that they are going to hell is not the solution, although some discussion concerning hell is warranted if we take Jesus seriously. Yet I cannot help but see parallels between today and the time of the Judges of Israel where "everyone did as he saw fit" (17:6; 21:25).

## TEN THINGS I WISH JESUS NEVER SAID

I am more inclined to believe postmodern Christianity is more appealing to our present generation because of what this generation does *not* like, not what it does find attractive. Ours is an exculpatory society, one steeped in pluralism and relativism. "Judge not" is a wonderful phrase in such a society. I have heard it labeled "the great American open-mindedness mantra," the favorite phrase of those who have come to equate love with tolerance.

It is also a product of our culture's love affair with positive self-esteem. The best way to damage the self-esteem of someone else is to negatively judge that person's beliefs or behavior.

> Judging has been in bad odor for quite some time in American culture. It is equated with being punitive, or with insensitivity, or with various "phobias" and "isms." It is the mark of antiquated ways of thinking, feeling, and willing. Better, no doubt, to be something called "open-minded," a trait thought to be characteristic of sensitive and supportive persons.
>
> Why is judging . . . at a nadir among us? Surely much of the explanation lies in the triumph of the ideology of victimization coupled with self-esteem mania.[1]

So where is the proper balance between these two poles? One side accuses the other of being legalistic and loveless while the other is called liberal and wishy-washy. Jesus wants us to walk a fine line between discernment and condemnation, between holiness and hypocrisy. Legalists are not relational, worrying too much about truth and not enough about love, while those who argue for a relational Christianity do so at the expense of a solid stance on the truth. Trying to find the proper balance can be tricky. After we look at two historical examples, we will examine more closely the context of Jesus's command to judge not.

### LESSONS FROM HISTORY

Few spots on the history of Christianity are as black as what occurred in the eleventh century when Christendom split in two. Historians call this the Great Schism. Because Christians could not get along, the church split into a Western half that became Roman Catholicism and an Eastern half that became Eastern Orthodoxy. The split remains to this day, although in recent years some reconciliation has occurred between the two.

Still this recent reconciliation cannot correct the damage done for many centuries by the animosity between Catholicism and Orthodoxy. For example, consider this description of the situation nearly a century ago by the great American church historian Philip Schaff:

> No two churches in the world are at this day so much alike, and yet so averse to each other as the Oriental or Greek, and the Occidental or Roman. . . . The very affinity breeds jealousy and friction. . . . They are equally exclusive. . . . The one is proud of her creed, the other of her dominion. . . . Where the two churches meet in closest proximity, over the traditional spots of the birth and tomb of our Saviour, at Bethlehem and Jerusalem, they hate each other most bitterly, and their ignorant and bigoted monks have to be kept from violent collision by Mohammedan soldiers.[2]

The hatred between these two Christian groups was at such a level that it required non-Christians, in this case Muslims, to keep the two apart and maintain the peace. I wonder how attractive this made the gospel in the Middle East.

I do not mean to minimize the differences between the East and West when in 1054 they found it impossible to coexist. There were major theological and doctrinal issues that necessitated disagreement, and the two halves had drifted apart for centuries before due to disparate language and cultural divergence. Still one cannot help but wonder if a little less pride and judgmentalism and a little more love and tolerance might have prevented the schism.

Two stubborn and conceited men, the bishop of Rome and the bishop of Constantinople, clashed heads and with their conflict effectively tore apart the "one, holy, universal, apostolic" church. Schaff characterized it as "politico-ecclesiastical rivalry," and we can only mourn when church leaders are more interested in building their own fiefdoms and spheres of influence than in the spiritual growth and vitality of the members under their care.

The bitterness between the two halves was at such a level that one of the Crusades from the West, normally targeting the Holy Lands and the Muslim occupiers, was turned against the Orthodox church in Constantinople in 1204, most certainly weakening that Christian kingdom in its stand against the increasing onslaught of the Turks.

At the time of the schism, Pope Leo IX butted heads with the bishop of Constantinople, Michael Cerularius. Some of the pickier points of contention included the West using unleavened bread in the Eucharist, fasting on Saturday during Lent, and not singing the hallelujah during the fast. For their part, the West was unhappy because the East did not baptize their infants before the eighth day, and they allowed their priests to marry. Fighting over who could control the most ecclesiastical property should not be overlooked as another factor. In the end, Christianity was shamed by a split that should have been avoided and that certainly contributed to the deterioration of Orthodoxy's influence in Asia Minor in the coming centuries.

On the other hand, consider the example of St. Francis of Assisi (1182-1226), founder of the Franciscan order of begging monks.[3] Brother Angelo had become the guardian of the Convent of Monte Casale at a time when three famous robbers wreaked havoc in that part of the Italian countryside. One day the robbers came to the convent and asked Brother Angelo for something to eat. Angelo chastised them for their evil ways and refused them food. "You are not worthy of the earth which bears you, for you neither respect man nor the Lord who made you. Go about your business, and do not appear here again."

Shortly after, St. Francis arrived at the convent with a sack of bread and a little vessel of wine, and Angelo related to him how he had sent away the robbers. Francis reproved him sharply, saying Angelo himself had behaved cruelly, for sinners are brought back to God more easily by kindness than by harsh words. Francis commanded Angelo to go look for the men and give them the food that had been donated to

Francis. While Angelo did this, Francis prayed that God would touch the hearts of the robbers and bring them to repentance.

The men were cut to the quick by the kindness shown them, to the point that they returned to the convent and submitted themselves to Francis. All three became members of the Order, serving until their deaths.

The example of St. Francis serves as a wake-up call for many Christians who are quick to judge and meager in dispensing mercy. It certainly serves as a relevant example for me. I fear that had I played a part in both of these accounts, I would have acted more like Brother Angelo and Michael Cerularius than Francis of Assisi. And yet, "A gentle answer turns away wrath, but a harsh word stirs up anger" (Prov. 15:1).

## ANOTHER BALANCING ACT

How often have you heard the complaint that a verse was "ripped out of context"? We hear it so often because it is too often true. If the three cardinal rules of real estate are "location, location, location," then the three rules of biblical interpretation should be "context, context, context." The reason "judge not" has been so misapplied is because its context has been ignored.

Jesus provides three reasons why we should not judge, and it is only in the context of those reasons that we can properly understand this command.

1) *Do not judge because . . . you will be judged by the same measure.* We may often find ourselves hoping bad judgment would fall upon our enemies. Jesus warns us, though, that if we are concentrating on the evil that would befall others, we will have the same level of evil befall us.

This teaching is similar to the earlier one given by Jesus concerning forgiveness: "Forgive us our debts, as we forgive our debtors." In other words, God, only forgives us so long as we ourselves are forgiving people. Similarly, then, he judges us with the same measure with which we expect others to be judged.

# TEN THINGS I WISH JESUS NEVER SAID

If we are hypercritical of others, this is the way we will be judged by God. If we attempt to find fault in the littlest of things, this is the way God will treat us. If we have the habit of scraping over the lives of others with a fine-toothed comb, be forewarned. Jesus says our treatment of others will be used as a benchmark for how we are treated.

Only the most self-righteous will think themselves worthy to stand under such scrutiny. I know that if every little imperfection and sin in my life were exposed and treated with the condemnation it deserves, I could not stand. This being the case, I had better be willing to grant others mercy.

Unfortunately, though, many believers think they could withstand such scrutiny. All I can say to them is, watch out. Keep in mind that the final analysis will not be an assessment between you and your neighbor. It will be a comparison between you and the perfect Son of God. If such knowledge does not work to banish all pride and self-righteousness in us, Lord, help us.

Although we may not find fault too often with people we like, this matter especially regards those people we consider our enemies. We might find ourselves hoping bad to befall those who oppose us. In some instances, I have heard Christians say how they hoped so-and-so would get hit by a car or come down with a horrible disease, or they wished a curse on his or her family. We should know as believers that every time we speak such horrible judgments, Jesus tells us that with the same measure that we judge others, it will be meted out to us.

Our hope should be that our enemies have their attitudes changed toward us so they begin to favor us and not continue to oppose us. It should not be the hope that they come to ruin. As believers, we should be people who consistently seek reconciliation and hope for positive resolution, not those who yearn for judgment. Those who want judgment will themselves be judged.

> Though Christ gives this, firstly, as a rule by which we should judge of others, yet in the words that next follow he plainly shows, that he intends it also as a rule by which we would judge ourselves.
>
> Jonathan Edwards (1703-1758), *Religious Affections*

2) *Do not judge because . . . you often have the same or worse problems.* "Why do you look at the speck of sawdust in your brother's eye and pay no attention to the plank in your own eye?" (Matt. 7:3).

Jesus uses an example that would have been well known to him. As the son of a carpenter who most likely followed in his father's footsteps before his ministry years, he was familiar with the tools and paraphernalia of the woodworking shop with its planks and sawdust. Pictured is a person with a piece of wood stuck in his eye the size of something that would have been used to make rafters in a roof. And this person is attempting to remove a speck of sawdust from his brother's eye. Of course, a speck of sawdust is infinitesimal and virtually impossible to see.

The example is clear. It is easy for us to point out the faults in others and difficult for us to recognize them in ourselves, even when they are the same type of fault. Paul says this to his Jewish brothers:

> *You, therefore, have no excuse, you who pass judgment on someone else, for at whatever point you judge the other, you are condemning yourself, because you who pass judgment do the same things. Now we know that God's judgment against those who do such things is based on truth. So when you, a mere man, pass judgment on them and yet do the same things, do you think you will escape God's judgment? (Rom. 2:1-3)*

It is this attitude by the Jews that Paul says has made the Gentiles hate God. Jesus is commanding his disciples to not behave similarly. Before being fixated on the sawdust in our brother's eye, perhaps we should first soberly judge ourselves and our own faults and shortcomings.

Is this not the problem we have when it comes to the debate on homosexual marriage? For decades our churches have decided to ignore the ill of wanton divorce in our congregations. Now when it comes time for us to defend family values and the institution of marriage, we look like hypocrites. Why wasn't the institution of marriage important to us when it came to the plague of divorce in our churches? Perhaps some

TEN THINGS I WISH JESUS NEVER SAID

of our critics are correct: We have done more to damage the institution of marriage than any homosexuals will do.

Please do not misread me. I am not condoning homosexual marriage, nor am I saying we must not speak against it because we are hypocrites. If that were the case, we could never speak against any wrongs. But because we were not willing to deal with sin in our own lives, we have lost the ability to condemn it rightly in wider society.

However, one could counter that because we are *all* hypocrites, we should never condemn any sins in the lives of others. I once attended a missions conference where the speaker made this point. He said Christians are not the protectors and guardians of social morality, that we are not supposed to be the spiritual police of the world, and that we should not attempt to legislate morality. He quoted 1 Corinthians 5:12-13a as his justification: "What business is it of mine to judge those outside the church? Are you not to judge those inside? God will judge those outside."

He then used the example of Janet Jackson and her exposed breast during the Super Bowl 2004 halftime show. He noted that the night before, a news show had run a program on adolescent prostitution in an Asian country. Something like 35,000 young boys and girls were annually exploited through this perverse practice. The next day there was little press about the topic.

Once the Janet Jackson incident occurred, though, religious leaders all over America complained nonstop. The complaints did not come only from religious figures, but the speaker's point was that we were wasting our time on a little problem when a greater one was entirely ignored.

There is some value to his critique, but I do not think his conclusions were helpful or necessary. I saw the Super Bowl show, and I thought the exposed breast was a fitting ending to the twenty minutes of grinding and gyrating that preceded it. The entire show was unworthy of our time, not just the last five seconds. We should have been complaining about the whole show, not just its indecent finale.

But that's not my complaint about the conference speaker's perspective. When it came time for questions, I asked what he thought we as Christians should do concerning Asian prostitution. Had he not just undercut our ability to judge *any* sinful activity? If we are not called or allowed to judge "those outside the church," how could we have stopped slavery in the Western world? Unfortunately, the speaker had painted himself into a corner. In the hope of creating an atmosphere of love and tolerance, he had eliminated any ability or right for Christians to judge the sins of the world and look to correct them.

Even further, if Christians are *not* the spiritual police of the world, who is? Should we allow the morality and ethics of our societies to be determined by atheists? How about the State? Should we leave it to the politicians and bureaucrats? And what if some of them are Christians?

Jesus has not commanded us never to judge in the sense of exercising good and proper discernment. If that were the case, there would be no hope of ridding ourselves of sinful ways. What Jesus wants to eliminate in his disciples is *hypocritical* judgment. How many pastors chastise their congregants for greed and stinginess in not contributing more to the church, while these same pastors embezzle church funds? It is this kind of judgment Jesus wants us to eradicate.

> We want them to be perfect, yet we do not correct our own faults. We wish them to be severely corrected, yet we will not correct ourselves. Their great liberty displeases us, yet we would not be denied what we ask. We would have them bound by laws, yet we will allow ourselves to be restrained in nothing. Hence, it is clear how seldom we think of others as we do of ourselves.
>
> We take others to task for small mistakes, and overlook greater ones in ourselves. We are quick enough to feel and brood over the things we suffer from others, but we think nothing of how much others suffer from us. If a man would weigh his own deeds fully and rightly, he would find little cause to pass severe judgment on others.
>
> Thomas à Kempis (1380-1471),
> *The Imitation of Christ*

3) *Do not judge because . . . that is God's job.* Implied in all these statements from Jesus is that God is the only righteous judge. His activ-

ity is implied in the first command in the opening verse. If we are judgmental, we will be treated in the same manner. By whom? By God.

God and God alone can make perfect judgments because only God knows all the facts. How do we know if in the future someone will repent of evil done against us, seek our forgiveness, and desire to be reconciled to us? We do not know, but God does. We do not have all the information necessary to make a final judgment.

I once heard of a man who lived in a house in disrepair. If we automatically judge the owner as lazy, we are violating this command. We may come to learn later that the man does not have the money to fix his home or that he is physically incapable of doing so. That is why the consistent theme in both the Old and New Testament concerning judgment is that we leave things to God. Certainly we are called to be discerning people as we will see, but we are not meant to be judgmental, hypercritical people. Believers characterized by a critical spirit are not pleasing to God and may suffer his judgment and discipline as a result.

"You, then, why do you judge your brother? Or why do you look down on your brother? For we will all stand before God's judgment seat" (Rom. 14:10). So often Christians are quick to judge, forgetting that it is not their business to condemn others.

## HOW SHOULD CHRISTIANS JUDGE?

We have examined the ways in which this command is not to be understood. How, then, should we understand it? Are Christians ever allowed to judge? Our passage certainly does allow for it, as does the rest of the New Testament. John writes, "Dear friends, do not believe every spirit, but test the spirits to see whether they are from God, because many false prophets have gone out into the world" (1 John 4:1). It is impossible to test the spirits without judging between them. Similarly, Paul says in 1 Thessalonians 5:21 that Christians are to "test everything." Clearly this too involves judging.

The Greek word normally translated *judge* literally means to divide or sift, much as one would sift flour to remove impurities. What is pictured here is a person who makes certain determinations, removing the bad and retaining the good. The verb *to judge* can possess a positive or negative connotation, and this is the key to understanding why Christians are sometimes told not to judge and at other times called to exercise judgment, both commands utilizing the same Greek word. The word not only has a connotation of condemnation but also one of discernment.

There is also the matter of discipline in the church, something we touched upon in the previous chapter. In Matthew's Gospel Jesus gives us direction in how to deal with a sinning brother (see Matt. 18). In 1 Corinthians 5 we learn that the church in Corinth did not judge a brother in their congregation living in open sin; so Paul condemned them for it. In the area of church discipline, then, clearly we need to judge others.

To take this command as a blanket prohibition against all forms of judgment would be to rip it out of its context, making its conclusion entirely contrary to Christian morality, a point not lost on the great Orthodox pastor John Chrysostom (350-407):

> And besides, if this were to obtain, all would be lost alike, whether in churches, or in states, or in houses. For except the master judge the servant, and the mistress the maid, and the father the son, and friends one another, there will be an increase of all wickedness.[4]

Christians should be the most discerning people in the world. Later in the Sermon on the Mount Jesus will tell his followers they should be able to judge people based on their fruit; they should judge if a person is a false prophet, and they should even determine if people are "dogs" or "pigs." Clearly all this involves some form of judgment. We desperately need this type of judgment today, particularly in a postmodern Christian world dominated by Pentecostalism.

Extreme relativism is fostered by both postmodernism and Pentecostalism. With each speaker who declares he has a "word from the Lord," or who is bold enough to claim he has received a special visitation from God, our spiritual antennae should go up. If these special dispensations are accompanied by miraculous signs and wonders, speaking against them becomes a greater risk. Who can argue with a blind man who now can see, or a man previously confined to a wheelchair who now can walk?

Do you believe every miracle claimed today is a bona fide miracle from God? If you answer yes, I would like to sell you some land I own on the moon. If you answer no, then you must agree that we need discernment to delineate between false ones and real ones. As we will see in the next chapter, many who have no relationship with Jesus will perform miracles in his name.

The frequent warnings in the New Testament against false prophets, teachers, apostles, and even christs should create in us a desire for godly discernment. Rather than excluding all ability for believers to judge, we should see judgment as a necessary gift from God's Spirit meant to direct the body into greater spiritual maturity.

Back to the example of the speck and plank in Matthew 7:5, Jesus allows us to judge properly, but only after we have examined ourselves: "You hypocrite, first take the plank out of your own eye, and then you will see clearly to remove the speck from your brother's eye." Removing a speck of sawdust from someone's eye involves careful work. The eye is one of the most sensitive parts of the body. If you are blinded by the large piece of wood in your own eye, how can you help remove a speck of dust from your brother's eye? You cannot, without doing great damage to your brother.

Note that Jesus does not give us a command that negates all forms of judgment. The fact is, the example of the speck and beam *allows* for judgment rather than excludes it: "then you will see clearly to remove . . ." But it does exclude the type of judgment that constantly sees faults in others while ignoring one's own faults. Jesus is not saying Christians should not speak out against sin. Jesus's concern is that we not be hypercritical or hypocritical people, but he expects his followers to be discerning people who can sift between various options and distinguish the good from the bad.[5]

In these commands Jesus is as much interested in heart attitude as in actions. Not many of us are in positions where we can enact judgment upon those who harm us, but we *are* in the position of harboring ill feelings and desires toward those people. Our passage warns us to not hold grudges or wish ill upon others.

## THE NEED FOR GODLY DISCERNMENT

The two errant poles must be avoided. When we are consistently sifting other people with our words and actions, we are not being pleasing to God. When we are constantly looking at others with a critical or condemnatory eye, we are not being the disciples Jesus wants.

However, we should not make the opposite error, namely, to put aside all judgment. Unfortunately, this passage has been misused by so many people for so long that its misinterpretation and misapplication is thought by many to be correct. We live in a day when godly discernment is desperately needed. Yet many believers fear that any exercise of discernment is an automatic violation of the command not to judge. This leaves many Christians and churches adrift in a sea of heresy and false teaching, fearful that to speak against it would make them appear intolerant.

Christians are expected to judge between right and wrong. How can we expect to be holy people if we do not judge between good and evil? Christians should be people of discernment, able to judge between a good tree and a bad tree, a real prophet and a false one, a dog and a pig.

Lastly, we should be *self-critical* people. Instead of constantly worrying about the sins of others, we should be concerned with our own failings. A powerful antidote to the sickness of a critical spirit is to be self-critical. A self-critical form of judgment is something I will address in the next chapter.

> "What then!" say you: "if one commit fornication, may I not say that fornication is a bad thing, nor at all correct him that is playing the wanton?" Nay, correct him, but not as a foe, nor as an adversary exacting a penalty, but as a physician providing medicines.
>
> John Chrysostom (350-407), *Homilies*

# 10

# THE ART OF
# SPIRITUAL SELF-ASSESSMENT

*Not everyone who says to me, "Lord, Lord," will enter the kingdom of heaven.*

JESUS CHRIST, MATTHEW 7:21A

*O perplexed discomposition, O riddling distemper, O miserable condition of man!*

JOHN DONNE (1572-1631),
*DEVOTIONS UPON EMERGENT OCCASIONS*

*Turn your attention upon yourself and beware of judging the deeds of other men, for in judging others a man labors vainly, often makes mistakes, and easily sins; whereas, in judging and taking stock of himself he does something that is always profitable.*

THOMAS À KEMPIS (1380-1471),
*THE IMITATION OF CHRIST*

Much of what we have said so far relies on how honestly we evaluate ourselves. If we tend to minimize our sinful desires, for example, we might not believe we need to amputate an appendage. Some may consider themselves truly committed to Christ because they attend church regularly and tithe their cumin and spices, but their lives are otherwise devoid of Christian commitment. Those who think themselves spiritually okay may need to heed the old adage: "Those who think themselves humble are probably not."

## TEN THINGS I WISH JESUS NEVER SAID

My uncle told me of a woman who stood up in her church during Sunday evening testimony time and said, "I want to thank the Lord that I have not sinned in the past seven years." This was a product of the particular theology her church had, but the statement is shocking nonetheless. It became one of the reasons my uncle and his family left that church.

If we look at ourselves through rose-colored glasses, we will conclude that everything about us is, well, rosy. Of course, the less dire we determine our situation to be, the less drastic will be its solution. For example, if I believe myself to be standing in a three-inch gully, I will hardly take seriously the offer of a ladder. But if I realize I am eight feet in the ground, my reaction to such assistance will be to welcome it heartily.

Sinners have an obscene propensity for lying to themselves, and Satan uses this greatly to his advantage. It is one of the ploys Wormwood teaches Screwtape in the classic by C. S. Lewis, *The Screwtape Letters*. Wormwood, the senior demon, tells his apprentice Screwtape to work with the human tendency toward self-deception, explaining that the best way to tempt human beings is to work with their innate predisposition to think highly of themselves.

As we come to the tenth thing in the teaching of Jesus that I wish he had never uttered, we find perhaps the most difficult aspect of them all, the ability to judge ourselves properly. As sinners, we rarely do an adequate job of it although we love judging others, as we saw in the previous chapter. Yet if we are truly disciples of Christ, we must judge ourselves. Every wart and imperfection must be admitted and addressed. Otherwise, we run the risk of fooling ourselves into believing we are genuine followers of Jesus.

This chapter will be slightly different from the others. It does not have a "Lessons from History" section. Since this teaching of Jesus deals with future events and especially the end times, I can hardly produce historical examples to support it. Also this teaching does not speak directly to how we should live our lives now. However, because how we live now determines our fate in the future judgment, we can draw practical conclusions about this teaching, although not to the extent that we have done in previous chapters.

I will take two broad approaches. First, I want to investigate the picture of Jesus as Judge, something that must be addressed if we are to understand how Jesus could reject people at the end of the age. Then I will look at how, in the light of this knowledge of Christ and his person, we should evaluate ourselves.

## JESUS OFTEN SCARES ME

We have a tendency to turn away from the passages in the Bible—especially when they come from the mouth of the Savior—that speak about wrath and judgment. Is it no wonder that with any New Testament you find in the bookstore, the book of Psalms is also included? Why do Christians so enjoy the Psalms more than any other portion of the Old Testament? The Psalms are soothing and encouraging and lift us up when we are down. No one gets any lift when reading about the total destruction of Jericho or Ai. Can you imagine a New Testament that tacks on the text describing the obliteration of Sodom and Gomorrah and other favorite judgment passages from the Old Testament? Hardly. I certainly would not want such a volume.

We do not like judgment, except perhaps when it happens to our enemies. And when it falls from the lips of our Lord and Savior, the loving Son of God, we find it particularly troublesome. Yet in avoiding the edgy teachings of Jesus, aren't believers putting themselves at risk of being among the "Lord, Lord" class?

> Understanding of the preaching and person of Jesus depends absolutely on understanding of His concept of judgment. If there is no judgment of God as Jesus bears witness, then Jesus and His preaching can have only a constantly diminishing historical significance.[1]

We must embrace the picture of Jesus as awesome Judge if we are going to properly understand this "Lord, Lord" teaching. How often is the picture of Jesus as Judge taught in our churches today? The "meek and mild" Jesus is much preferred, the "What a Friend We Have in Jesus" image. We like the Lamb of God who lays down his life but not the Lion of Judah who judges our deeds. When we think of him as the Great Shepherd, we picture him caring for his sheep, not separating the sheep from the goats for judgment.

The common medieval portrait of Jesus was that of Judge, coming with his angels to exact wrath and justice upon sinful humans. That image is appalling to most sensitive consciences today. In reaction to such depictions of Jesus, we have tended to emphasize his lovingkindness, his mercy and forgiveness, as if a dichotomy exists between a shepherd who cares for his sheep and one who separates sheep from goats; between a harvester who grows wheat and one who destroys the weeds in the process; or within a fisherman who picks through the fish and keeps the good ones, necessarily discarding the ones he finds unacceptable.

But there need be no dichotomy, no playing of one portrait against the other. This is, after all, what good shepherds, farmers, and fishermen do; they discern between the good and the bad of their produce and make judgments of separation. What needs to be taught in our churches is not the medieval portrait of Jesus as righteous and angry Judge to the exclusion of the Good Shepherd who loves and cares for his flock, nor is it the modern picture of Jesus as a meek and mild teacher who never harmed a fly to the exclusion of the Son of Man who will come on the clouds and judge the nations. We need *both* portraits because both are given in Scripture, particularly from the teaching of Jesus about himself. If we do not portray Jesus as both a loving, caring shepherd and as a judge of the unrighteous, we have failed to teach our people properly. We have done a great disservice to the teaching of Jesus, whom we call Master and Lord.

A tweedy poetaster who spent his time spinning out parables and Japanese Koans, a literary aesthete who toyed with first-century deconstructionism, or a bland Jesus who simply told people to look at the lilies of the field—such a Jesus would threaten no one.[2]

There are real, eternal consequences to sin. That is the lesson Jesus is teaching us. The consequences are so drastic and dramatic that it would be better for you to cut off a hand or gouge out an eye if in so doing you were able to escape such consequences. Jesus is no fluffy preacher filled with feel-good messages. He was no "power of positive thinking" prophet or self-actualization sage. His message was stark and severe. Like a meteorologist who warns of an impending hurricane or monsoon, Jesus stands before us and warns of disaster to come for those who do not repent of their sins and follow him.

If we do not like the meteorologist because he constantly tells us bad news, we may be tempted to turn off the television or switch channels to another meteorologist who gives us warm, sunny weather reports. But once the storms come, we may grow to appreciate a weather man who tells us the truth so we can prepare for the coming disaster.

## WE MUST EMBRACE ALL OF JESUS OR NONE OF HIM

Right after his teaching on this matter, Jesus speaks of a wise builder and a foolish one. We know the parable well. The wise builder constructs his home on solid rock while the foolish one builds his house on sand. The wise man took the time to dig deep, beyond the sand and into the ground, until he found solid rock on which to plant the foundation of his home. The foolish man was too lazy to do that.

Jesus uses this example to characterize two types of people. The wise builder builds on all the teaching of Jesus, not just a select portion he has found acceptable, while chucking the rest. The foolish person decides to ignore or excise portions of the teaching of Jesus that he finds undesirable. In so doing, he places himself at great personal risk. A time will come when a storm will hit him so hard that he will be unable to recover from it. Is this not precisely what will happen to the "Lord, Lord" people?

Part of the problem with these people is that they have decided to follow only *part* of Jesus's teaching. In the specific case provided by Christ, they have errantly thought following him was embodied only in miraculous deeds such as exorcisms, prophesying, and performing miracles. They concentrated on the flashy aspects and missed the relationship. Understood this way, does this not characterize a large portion of global Christianity today?

## TEN THINGS I WISH JESUS NEVER SAID

A few years ago, Trinity Broadcasting Network began to transmit into Namibia. The channel is on around the clock, and Namibians can watch any number of TBN preachers twenty-four hours a day. Much on TBN is good, but some of it is less than adequate and can be misleading.

You must understand the context of Namibia to understand how TBN could be so influential. We only have one television station in Namibia, after which if you want more, you must pay for satellite stations. The majority of Namibians who cannot afford to pay extra have only two channels, the one run by the Namibian government and TBN. Because there is little good to watch on the former station, they flock to the latter.

So much TBN is being watched by Namibians that many churches have expressed difficulty when it comes to their worship services. If there are no signs and wonders in your worship services, many Namibians now believe you cannot have a genuine church. Unless your church has miraculous healings, frequent words of wisdom or knowledge, or people falling down while "slain by the Spirit," you will be viewed as less than spiritual.

It is not a matter of just being a boring church that does not have the hoopla many churches on TBN possess. It is a matter of being judged as spiritually destitute if you do not have the excitement of healings and speaking in tongues or the constant barrage of "hallelujahs" and "amens." At bare minimum, the speaker must dance around and entertain, or people will go elsewhere.

I find it striking that the three deeds Jesus mentions in his "Lord, Lord" teaching are often viewed in a similar way. It is frequently assumed that churches with miracles and prophecy are the more spiritual churches, and those who lack these characteristics are inferior. Paul dealt with this idea in first-century Corinth, and we are experiencing the same problem twenty centuries later. So often we judge others based on their spiritual gifts, placing certain gifts at a higher value than others. Which gifts are deemed more important and spiritually significant? Usually the ones *we* possess.

I also find it informative that in the scope of the Sermon on the

Mount, there is not one hint that genuine followers of Jesus must perform miraculous deeds. In fact, the only mention of such deeds is in the negative, namely, those who fooled themselves into believing that because they performed these deeds, they must be Christ's disciples. Rather to be a disciple of Jesus Christ involves forgiving one's enemies, possessing a spirit of poverty, not critically or hypocritically judging other people, and all the things we have discussed in the previous chapters.

We have a tendency to excise the portions of the teaching of Jesus we find offensive, too cumbersome, or beneath us. Once we do this, we risk being included in the "Lord, Lord" camp. It is only when we embrace *all* the teaching of Jesus that we can truly be considered his disciples.

Let's put the "Lord, Lord" words of Jesus in their full context in the Sermon.

> *Not everyone who says to me, "Lord, Lord," will enter the kingdom of heaven, but only he who does the will of my Father who is in heaven. Many will say to me on that day, "Lord, Lord, did we not prophesy in your name, and in your name drive out demons and perform many miracles?" Then I will tell them plainly, "I never knew you. Away from me, you evildoers!" (Matt. 7:21-23)*

Few statements from the mouth of our Savior rival this one in sheer terror. The shock of this proclamation is found not so much in the fact that judgment exists but to whom the judgment will come. Had Jesus said, "At that time many atheists and perverts and people of horrible practices," we would not be surprised. But these people refer to him as "Lord." They not only know *of* him, but they claim to know him in an intimate way. This is not only signified by the title they use to address him, but it is also signified in how they lived their lives. Their lives were marked by miraculous signs supposedly performed in his name.

Superficial Christianity is marked by the constant need for a spiritual fix, as if the converts cannot exist unless their beliefs are repeatedly reaffirmed, mainly through experiential events. Stale, old promises found in a book written 2,000 years ago are not enough. We must live by sight, not by faith. Why should we believe things spoken to others long ago in a culture and time different from our own? We want God to speak to us today, right now.

Such is the state of much of modern Christendom. At times the miraculous signs and wonders are deemed more important than an actual relationship with Christ. This is precisely the problem with those condemned in Jesus's sermon. They believed that because they exhibited or performed miraculous wonders, they must have a *de facto* relationship with Jesus; but this simply is not the case.

A somewhat related account is found in Acts 19, where the "seven sons of Sceva" attempted to invoke the name of Jesus in casting out evil spirits. Luke records that these Ephesian residents fell on hard times in so doing: "One day the evil spirit answered them, 'Jesus I know, and I know about Paul, but who are you?' Then the man who had the evil spirit jumped on them and overpowered them all. He gave them such a beating that they ran out of the house naked and bleeding" (Acts 19:15-16).

Although Luke does not say it as such, we can assume that the sons of Sceva were not Christians. Luke refers to them as Jews, and from the conclusion of this brief account, it is evident that what they attempted to do failed because they believed that in simply evoking the name of Jesus, devoid of relationship with him, they could control the evil spirits. Interestingly, once this incident occurred, Luke records that many residents of Ephesus were struck with fear and renounced their sorcery.

This is a troubling account, but it does not rival the portentous words of Jesus concerning a similar matter. With the Jewish sons of Sceva, they had simply seen what Paul was doing in the name of Jesus, assumed Paul was invoking this name as a magical formula, and believed they could incorporate it into their own sorcery practices. But with the Sermon warning of Jesus, the people he turns away look for all accounts to be Christians, followers of Christ. In other words, the whole time they believed themselves to be in a right relationship with Jesus, they were lost evildoers. They too were invoking the name of Jesus as if it were a magical formula, but they did not have a relationship with him.

He orders those persons to go out from his presence, who had stolen, under a false title, an unjust and temporary possession of his house.

John Calvin (1509-1564), *Harmony of the Gospels*

## THE NEED FOR HONEST SELF-EVALUATION

This self-deception is frightening, but it is something we must face. The Pharisees were equally self-deceived. The entire time they believed themselves to be the quintessence of holiness and the epitome of godliness, they were hypocritical vipers, but they did not know it. Although there seems to be an underlying current in the Gospels that, perhaps, the Pharisees and religious leaders purposefully and willfully deceived, the overall picture points to the fact that they considered themselves blameless of any wrongdoing. However, in John's account of a blind man healed by Jesus, John took the opportunity to record words of Jesus speaking of a spiritual blindness that mirrored the physical:

> Jesus said, "For judgment I have come into this world, so that the blind will see and those who see will become blind." Some Pharisees who were with him heard him say this and asked, "What? Are we blind too?" Jesus said, "If you were blind, you would not be guilty of sin; but now that you claim you can see, your guilt remains." (John 9:39-41)

John goes on to record the "Good Shepherd" sayings of Jesus in the next chapter where Jesus equates the religious leaders with thieves, robbers, and wolves.

These accounts clearly portray the religious leaders as willfully deceptive, all the while believing themselves (or at least claiming) to be innocent. Jesus implies that, had they not known they were guilty of sin, they would not be guilty. The simple fact is, the Pharisees were not blind. They had the Scriptures but preferred their man-made laws. As such, they were subject to judgment. They were self-deceived but on a subtler level.

It is one thing for a man to be born blind. No one would condemn him for his blindness. It is another thing for a man with good eyes to walk around with them shut. He is blind in the sense that he cannot see, but his problem of sightlessness is of his own making.

If we wish to have fellowship with the Son of God, then it is part of our wisdom to know ourselves.

John Owen (1616-1683),
Puritan pastor and theologian, *Communion with God*

Many Christians in our age are similarly self-deceived. The Scriptures are there for them to read and obey, but they choose to follow their own devices. To live by faith is difficult; so they choose to live by sight. Signs and wonders are constantly sought, and the gospel message needs regular reconfirmation for them. They say, "Lord, Lord," but they are faithless.

I venture that only the most self-righteous people would not find this passage alarming. Those who are comfortable in their security and who have no doubts about their eternal destiny will find little difficulty with this saying from Jesus. I wish I could count myself among that happy group, but my Christian walk is occasionally plagued with doubts and worries. I know some will think I do not understand the gospel or the fact that the Bible teaches "once saved, always saved," but that would be too simplistic a conclusion. I well understand how the doctrines of election and perseverance bring together what we frequently call "assurance of salvation" or "eternal security." I know God never fails in his promises, but my problem is not with God. My problem is with myself.

I am not saying I struggle with *constant* doubts about my eternal fate. If that were the case, then the above concerns about poor theology would have justification. No, I am saying that every so often, in private moments when I contemplate who I am as a sinner, a little fear creeps in. "How can God truly save a person like me?" I know what a rotten sinner I am, and each time I compare myself to Christ, I find myself wanting. I think had I been in the Garden, I would have stripped bare the tree of forbidden fruit. In the final analysis, I wonder if I am not just fooling myself into believing I will gain entrance into heaven.

Do any of my readers have similar misgivings? May I make the bold statement that if you do not occasionally have these feelings of doubt, perhaps you should be worried? I know how strange that sounds, that those who do worry should not be concerned, but that those who do not really should.

This passage in God's Word ranks at the top of my list of the most ominous portions of Scripture. Accounts such as the Great Flood or the burning of Sodom and Gomorrah do not scare me nearly so much. The reason is simple. The people at the time of Noah or living in Sodom did not think themselves to have a lifesaving relationship with the one, true God. But I do.

I believe that when I die, I will live an eternal life with my Creator because I have a relationship with Jesus Christ. So when Jesus says there will be people who die, thinking they had a relationship with him but who are in fact eternally lost, I take great notice.

I suppose if the opposite were true, that upon reading this passage I had no fear within me whatsoever, such an attitude would be cause for concern. After all, Jesus says these things to warn us. For all those people who play church or have lives filled with religious ritual, or who even perform miraculous deeds but who do not have a living, vibrant relationship with the Son of God, Jesus says these things as a warning. Do not be self-deceived. Do not think your life—even if it is characterized by works that normally are ascribed to God's power—has any true value if it is not intimately linked to all the teaching of the Master. We should not strive to be religious. We should strive to be Christlike.

> A religion which costs us nothing, and consists in nothing but hearing sermons, will always prove at last to be a useless thing.
> J. C. Ryle (1816-1900), Anglican minister, *Matthew*

People in the "Lord, Lord" crowd have all the external signs of religiosity, but they do not have a personal relationship with Jesus. They are like the Pharisees, whitewashed tombs that appear clean on the outside but inside contain the bones of dead men, or like the Israelites at the time of the prophet Amos, who came with tithes and offerings to the temple, but who only did so to boast about themselves (Amos 4:4-5). This was the denunciation of the northern tribes of Israel just before they were wiped out by the Assyrian forces, something Amos prophesied about earlier: "Even while these people were worshipping the LORD, they were serving their idols" (2 Kings 17:41a). What a horrible indictment. We can go through all the right religious maneuvers, say all the theologically correct statements, and even claim to be following the Lord, and yet be eternally lost. If this does not send a shiver down your spine, I don't know what will.

The "Lord, Lord" people want the flashy Christianity but are unwilling to slog through the sloppy stages of being Christ's disciples. They want the fancy suits and fine automobiles, and they look down upon those believers who do not possess such accoutrements that come with following Jesus. They fall on the floor slain by God's Spirit and yet are unwilling to love their enemy or suffer for Christ's sake.

> The benefit of Christ's sufferings depends almost entirely upon man coming to a true knowledge of himself, and becoming terror-stricken and slain before himself. And where man does not come to this point, the sufferings of Christ have become of no true benefit to him.[3]

## REAL MIRACLES DO NOT NECESSARILY MEAN REAL ACTS OF GOD

There is another form of deception also at work in this Sermon warning of Jesus, and it is more insidious. These people actually performed the miracles to which they appealed. There is nothing in this Matthew 7 passage to make us think otherwise. Their appeal was an honest one, pointing to actual experiences in their lives. They were not foolish enough to stand before Christ and claim to have done things they had not done. Rather these evildoers had actually performed miracles; they had actually cast out demons; they had actually prophesied.

We are left with few options at this point. If these miraculous events had occurred, their ability to perform them could only have come from one of two sources, God or Satan. As these are ultimately reckoned as worthless deeds, we conclude they did not come from God. Therefore, these works done in the name of Jesus have come from the devil.

This should not surprise us. Jesus tells us Satan is the father of lies (John 8:44). His ability to deceive is incredible. From the Garden of Eden to the temptation of the Son of Man in the wilderness, Satan has been adept at twisting the words of God to suit his own purposes. He is a counterfeiter and deceiver: "For Satan himself masquerades as an angel of light" (2 Cor. 11:14). As A. Scott Moreau writes,

> Satan has his own trinity—the dragon, the beast and the false prophet (Rev. 16:13). He has his own church, a "synagogue of Satan" (Rev. 2:9). He has his own servants who, "masquerade as servants of righteousness " (2 Cor. 11:14-15). He has formulated his own system of theology, "doctrines of devils" (1 Tim. 4:1, KJV). He has established his own sacrificial system, "the Gentiles . . . sacrifice to devils" (1 Cor. 10:20, KJV). He has his own communion service, "the cup of demons . . . and the table of demons" (1 Cor. 10:21). His ministers proclaim his own gospel(s), "a gospel contrary to the one we have preached to you" (Gal. 1:7-8, ESV). He has his own throne (Rev. 13:2) and his own worshipers (Rev. 13:4).[4]

In the "Lord, Lord" warning, we see that Satan is willing to suffer a temporary loss for a greater, long-term gain. He is willing to provide some temporary healing or to cast out one of his servant demons, if only to deceive a person into believing he is actually doing the work of Christ.

This reminds me of an account given by a Namibian student during a course I taught on African traditional religions. The student recounted a story of a witchdoctor who later came to Christ and who told of his past. When someone would come for healing, say, of a headache, he would remove the headache and put it into the person's stomach. Later the pain would develop in the stomach, and the person, remembering that his headache was healed earlier by the witchdoctor, would come to have his stomach healed as well. The witchdoctor would then remove the stomach pain and put it in his foot, and so on. In this way, the witchdoctor deceived the person into believing he was actually being healed. The witchdoctor was willing to provide temporary relief to gain long-term enslavement.

The people in Jesus's warning lived their lives thinking they were doing the work of the Lord, only later to be found evildoers, banished from his presence. "I never knew you" signifies an absence of relationship between Jesus and the persons in question.

A related saying of Jesus warns of a similar consequence: "Whoever acknowledges me before men, I will also acknowledge him before my Father in heaven. But whoever disowns me before men, I will disown him before my Father in heaven" (Matt. 10:32-33). Our immediate reaction when reading these words of Jesus is an uncomfortable surprise, a squirming in our seats. Do these words really fall from the lips of the one we normally picture standing with open arms, ready to accept each one of us? How can Jesus speak of actually disowning people before the Father in heaven?

The message of the Son of Man was not one that would unite all of humanity into a global group hug. Rather it would divide people, even within households as we saw in chapter 8. The message of Christ brings with it crucial finality and a need to make a decision. It is an either/or message. To attempt to ignore it is to choose condemnation. Each person not only must make such a decision, but each individual already has made one.

There is no neutrality in the message of Christ. Each human being stands at a fork in the road at the intersection of which is Jesus, and he is pointing to the way of life. Judgment falls not only upon those who choose the wrong path, but it even falls upon those who attempt to stand in one place and not choose. The verdict of acceptance or rejection rises and falls with the person of Jesus Christ and what we make of that person. He who has an intimate relationship with the Father is entrusted with such a judgment, to either recommend or oppose the travelers on the two roads.

The judgment of God rests upon his person. Heaven and hell lie in the balance, and the ultimate destiny of each individual is to be determined by his acknowledgment or rejection of the person of Jesus. This is more than many Christians are willing to admit when it comes to Jesus. Many envision him only as a wise sage or a miracle worker but are unwilling to acknowledge that in Christ all truth is embodied.

To embrace him personally one must embrace his teaching; to embrace his teaching one must embrace him personally. You cannot do one to the exclusion of the other; nor can you ignore one and assume the other is valid. Jesus does not say, "if you acknowledge my teaching," but "if you acknowledge *me*." An acceptance of his personal claims about himself lies at the heart of his recommendation to the Father of particular individuals.

Too many Christians look for the easy road of discipleship. For them, the Christian life is all about ostentatious wonders and showy signs. The daily grind is beneath them. It is to these people that Jesus says, "I never knew you."

> He satisfies himself with listening and approving, but he goes no further. He flatters himself, perhaps, that all is right with his soul because he has feelings, convictions and desires of a spiritual kind. In these he rests. He never really breaks off from sin and casts aside the spirit of the world; he never really holds on to Christ; he never really takes up the cross. He is a hearer of truth, but nothing more.
>
> J. C. Ryle (1816-1900), Anglican minister, *Matthew*

## THE RIGHT PLACE OF WORKS

If I as a sinner can be so adept at deceiving myself, how can I know for sure that I am one of Christ's genuine disciples? Are there no external measures that I can consult to help me guard against being among the "Lord, Lord" people? If we cannot appeal to miraculous working as a fruit of genuine faith, what can we appeal to?

I believe there is a sense in the teaching of Jesus that if we do not strictly adhere to his teaching, we have the real possibility of self-deception. In other words, if we do not obey the commands of Jesus we covered in the first nine chapters of this book, the warning of self-deception found in this chapter becomes a viable option. One measure, then, is to ask ourselves: Do we see positive fruit in our life?

However, such a question brings us into a theological dispute often seen among evangelicals. Where do works fit in? Evangelicals have a tendency to downplay good works in light of our firm conviction concerning justification by faith. Because we know our salvation is not dependent upon what we do, many of us shy away from the idea that good works can be a sign or measure of genuine faith.

There are two competing views within mainstream evangelicalism today, and they fall generally along the lines of the roles of Jesus as Savior and Lord. The one is to say that simple belief is all that is required to be saved, emphasizing Jesus as Savior. The other says works must play a part in the salvation process, what is often called Lordship salvation.

To most Christians, it is probably surprising to see that such arguments exist. It seems self-evident to us that Jesus is both Lord and Savior—so why the disagreement? Simply put, the issue involves the crucial role that works play in one's salvation. Let me be clear. I do not espouse a salvation process that involves a cooperation between God and myself, a "God helps those who help themselves" mentality. In such a system, salvation is by faith but not by faith alone. Works play an instrumental part in the process. As I become more righteous, God does his part, and I do mine. For those more theologically inclined, it is a semi-Pelagian system where salvation is a cooperative effort between man and God.

Evangelicals, though, profess justification by faith alone. We do not believe our salvation is a reward for doing good works, which seems to be the case with the above notion. We believe salvation is entirely by grace through faith (Eph. 2:8-9).

This biblical view, however, has caused problems within evangelical circles. Because we are saying works are not necessary for salvation, some of us have subtly slipped to the position that works are no longer necessary, period. Let me try to explain the difference by comparing two statements, one from a major council of Roman Catholicism, the other from a major Protestant reformer:

• The Council of Trent: "Justification is by faith, but not by faith alone."

• John Calvin: "Justification is by faith, but not by a faith which is alone."

In theology, unfortunately, semantics is often king, and this is the case here. There is a subtle difference between the meaning of the two statements, but the difference is of great magnitude when it comes to our understanding of salvation.

How do we know if a person is saved? We might say simple profession of faith in Jesus is enough, and we would not be wrong. The thief on the cross had no chance to perform good works or get baptized; yet Jesus told him he would be in paradise with him. But what about the person who professes faith in Jesus and yet has little fruit to show for it over a long period of time?

My late grandfather was an itinerant evangelist who preached the gospel for several decades throughout the United States. He was a positive evangelist who always made an altar call at the end of each message. If fifty people raised their hands or came up front to accept Christ, my grandfather believed fifty people were saved that day. I have often wondered if that was true godly faith or simple naïveté. The latter word certainly could not be used to describe my grandfather, and yet what about false professions of faith? Did he not allow for such a category of people?

I think we must. I would like to check back in five years and see how many of those fifty people are still walking with Christ. This would be no empty exercise, by the way. Some statistics in Africa claim that twenty to fifty thousand Africans become Christians each day. Yet how many fall away shortly thereafter? How many are the type of soil that becomes choked by daily worries or material lusts? This situation is one reason I am teaching in a seminary in Africa. The need for solid discipleship in the churches is dramatic, with so many people pouring into the churches and so few biblically trained leaders there to help them grow spiritually.

In our first two years in Namibia, we lived in the small town of Grootfontein. Along with other missionaries, we shared the gospel with many people in that area. One young woman in her early twenties showed keen interest for several months and with the guidance of a missionary colleague professed faith in Jesus. Within two weeks, she became involved with a cult in town, one that had a self-professed prophet who claimed one must follow him to be saved. Despite our pleas, this young woman would not leave the group.

Assuming for the moment that she will never leave this cult, can we say her initial profession of faith in Jesus has saved her? Many evangelists say we can know today, right now, that when we die we will go to heaven. Often televangelists will have their viewers pray a short prayer and then promise them that they are saved. Of course, this promise is given with no clue as to what the viewer will do afterward with his or her life. Five years from now, if an individual who prayed that prayer is off blaspheming God and cursing Christ, are we seriously going to entertain the notion that his brief profession in front of his television was good enough for his salvation?

> All true Christians say, "Lord, Lord." But not all who say "Lord, Lord" are true Christians![5]

Whenever a discussion of the importance of works crops up, especially as it relates to testing one's faith, some evangelicals fear we are treading on heretical ground. They worry that by saying good works *must* be a product of genuine faith, we are inadvertently making good works necessary for salvation. Some of these Christians will go so far as to say that the act of repentance is not necessary because it constitutes a good work.

I strongly disagree. If a person is truly a new creation and is being transformed into the image of God's Son, we would expect positive fruit from such a transformation. This does not mean the fruit is a prerequisite of conversion, but it is a necessary byproduct of it.

Consistently Jesus uses fruit as an image of the productivity of a believer. For example, Jesus employs the imagery of productive soil to speak of genuine believers. Other types of soil, ones that are not productive, are used to represent those who fall away or those whose faith is choked and unproductive. Consider the image of unfruitful branches that are cut off and burned, or trees that are uprooted and destroyed because they do not bear produce. Jesus consistently uses such images as a test and sign of a person's profession. Why we would now object to good works being a measure of the vitality of one's faith is beyond me.

Yet evangelicals often do object, and that is one reason there are many who speak against "easy believism." Some Christians are saying good works need not be present at all, and yet a person can be genuinely saved. It seems self-evident from the teaching of Jesus that a tree that does not produce good fruit is not a good tree.

Consider the parable of the two sons (Matt. 21:28-32). There Jesus tells us it is not the son who says he will do his father's work but does not, who will be commended, but the son who does his father's work even though initially he refused to do so. Professions of faith not backed by real actions are empty.

Simple believism appears to be interested in making converts, but that is not the heart of the Great Commission. We are called to make disciples, not converts. Disciples by definition follow the commands of their master and are formed through a process that normally involves a passage of time.

This is not to say our salvation is by works. Rather what I am saying is that if we voluntarily choose to ignore some of the teaching of Jesus, that may be a sign that we are not actually his sheep. The true disciples of Jesus obey all his teaching. To willfully ignore portions of it may be an indication that one's faith is not genuine. Who can claim to follow a "lord" without making that lord's commands his desire? Calling someone "lord" whom we choose not to follow entirely is just playing word games, the kind that may fool others around us but will not fool Christ in the end.

Jesus uses the imagery of fruit to warn us about false prophets and also about *false believers*: "Not everyone who says to me, 'Lord, Lord,' will enter the kingdom of heaven, but only he who does the will of my Father who is in heaven." Some evangelicals will go on to define "the will of my Father" as simple belief in Jesus, and whereas it certainly includes this, it cannot possibly be limited only to it.

I took this doctrinal digression because in the passage from the Sermon on the Mount, we have some people who think they are saved, but they are not. This is no theological speculation with which seminary professors busy themselves. This is actual fact, a real-life situation Jesus warns us about. In light of this revelation, I want to be certain I do not become one of these people.

## WHOSE PERSPECTIVE IS IT?

What about eternal security? Am I not minimizing my assurance of salvation by worrying about this passage? In a sense, yes, I am. And yet I am not so sure "eternal security" as we have commonly envisioned it is truly biblical. There are so many warnings in Scripture, too many calls for us to make certain of our salvation and walk with Christ that it would appear that "once saved, always saved" is a dangerous statement to make without providing clear qualifications for it.

When Paul commands the Philippian believers to "work out your salvation with fear and trembling" (2:12b), I think he is speaking directly to this issue. *The NIV Study Bible* provides an insightful commentary on this passage:

> Work it out to the finish; not a reference to the attempt to earn one's salvation by works, but to the expression of one's salvation in spiritual growth and development. Salvation is not merely a gift received once for all; it expresses itself in an ongoing process in which the believer is strenuously involved—the process of perseverance, spiritual growth, and maturation.[6]

Part of the problem is that often we muddy the difference between God's perspective and man's. From God's perspective, genuine faith is always saving faith. God is not fooled by false confessions or external displays of religious gymnastics. He knows perfectly who has genuine faith and who does not.

However, from man's perspective, our knowledge even of ourselves is less than perfect, and we have the potential for both self-deception and deceiving others. In light of this truth, even the confession, "I have saving faith in Jesus Christ," can be wrong. This is what the "Lord, Lord" people have done. They have fooled themselves into believing they have genuine faith in Christ when they do not.

Salvation is never by works. An imperfect sinner can never do what the Law requires; nor can he improve on the atoning work of the perfect Son of God. Sinners are only justified through faith in what Christ has done for them. Only then can salvation truly be said to be by grace and not by meritorious acts of righteousness. However, from man's perspective, how can we be certain we have salvation when even a profession of faith can be deceptive? Again eternal security is all well and good from God's perspective, but from the perspective of a self-deceptive sinner, what does it mean to me?

I think we have given people false hope of salvation. We tell them that by saying a few words, they can be eternally secure, but this is doing an injustice in light of the fact that there are people who not only say a few words but even have signs and wonders to accompany them and yet are not saved. Committing apostasy is a real possibility in Scripture, and the reality of self-deception is also present. A person can indeed be saved the moment he or she says the "sinner's prayer" and professes genuine faith in Christ, but only God can truly know at that moment if such a profession is true or false. A sinner, unfortunately, cannot. It will only be proved over time.

With the remainder of this chapter I will highlight several ways sinners such as I can have assurance that we are not just fooling ourselves into believing we are genuine disciples of Christ. If afterward we want to continue to use phrases such as "once saved, always saved," I am all for it. But only after we fully understand what that means.

## DISCERNING DECEPTION

Before we look at these general tests, please understand that I am not suggesting we go around and evaluate others and their fruit. There is a place for that, especially when it comes to false prophets (e.g., Matt. 7:16), but in the following suggestions for how to evaluate one's faith, I am worried about *myself* here, not Joe in the pew next to me. That is why this chapter's title is "The Art of Spiritual *Self*-Assessment." Am I deceiving myself into believing I am a genuine believer? If you begin with that question and use these measures as a way to evaluate others, you have lost the intent of this chapter.

1) *Have I really professed faith in Jesus Christ?* This may seem ridiculously obvious, but we must state it nonetheless. Occasionally I will run into a Christian who says he never made a profession of faith but was always a believer. He was raised in a Christian home, his parents and siblings were all believers, and he has been in church since he was an infant. Christianity has been a natural part of his life as long as he can remember.

What a magnificent experience for a person to have. Whereas we normally admire those testimonies from people who came from the filth of the world's ways into the purity of faith in Christ, I love to hear of those people who from childhood have been kept unpolluted from such things. What a wonderful testimony to have.

And yet we all must make Christ our own. As great as it is to always know about Jesus, we must make the conscious decision to trust in him fully, to turn from ourselves and the world and to follow him.

This is no small point to make. There are tons of people who have attended church their entire lives and who do not know Jesus as their personal Savior and Lord. They may not claim in the end times to have performed miracles or cast out demons, but many may say something similar to this: "But didn't we attend church, get baptized, and regularly tithe?"

There must be an assent to the gospel, embracing the good news and making it our own. No one is naturally born into the family of God. All of us must enter it spiritually through faith (John 1:12-13).

Such a confession involves genuine poverty of spirit. If we claim to have faith in Christ and yet claim ourselves to be more than nothing, we do not understand genuine faith, and we deceive ourselves.

For if anyone reads this life with attention, he will see on God's part, nothing but goodness, mercy, and love; on my part, nothing but weakness, sin and infidelity. I have nothing to glory in but my infirmities and my unworthiness, since, in that everlasting marriage-union thou hast made with me, I brought with me nothing but weakness, sin and misery.

*Autobiography of Madame Guyon* (1647-1717)

2) *What is your doctrine like?* Paul wrote this to young Timothy: "Watch your life and doctrine closely. Persevere in them, because if you do, you will save both yourself and your hearers" (1 Tim. 4:16).

How often have you heard someone say, "I love Jesus. It doesn't matter what I believe so long as I am a loving person." The history of Christianity, especially the past three hundred years, has been littered with thoughts that one's doctrine is unimportant, and all that matters is how one lives his or her life. This is clearly a false dichotomy, though, between belief and practice, what technically is called orthodoxy and orthopraxy.

What we believe intimately affects how we live our lives, and conversely how we live our lives is determined by what we believe. Paul tells Timothy to watch his life *and* doctrine closely. One isn't more important than the other. Both are equally vital to a Christian's walk.[7]

Too many believers are shamefully ignorant when it comes to Christian doctrine and theology. They have bought the lie that doctrine is reserved for academics and eggheads, but this is hardly the case. Because I touched upon this matter in chapter 3 in the section on commitment of mind, I will not dwell on it further here.

3) *Is there evidence my life is changing for the better, evidence that regeneration has genuinely taken place?* We have already noted the part works should play in the life of a believer, but I want to repeat that my concern in this chapter is how to evaluate myself, not others, so that I do not deceive myself into thinking I am a disciple of Christ when I am not. Looking for fruit in my life is one way to discern this.

Although it is difficult to determine what "good works" or "fruit" must be, it seems clear that those who believe them to consist only in the miraculous or supernatural are mistaken. Paul argues in 1 Corinthians 13 that speaking in the tongues of angels, possessing a mountain-moving faith, and even giving one's life in martyrdom will all amount to nothing if they are not motivated by love. The Old Testament Israelites along with the Pharisees during Jesus's time were consistently condemned for believing that religious rituals and rites were all that were needed to be pleasing to God, but sacrifices without justice and tithes without mercy were deemed worthless by God.

James speaks of worthless religion and says: "Religion that God our Father accepts as pure and faultless is this: to look after orphans and widows in their distress and to keep oneself from being polluted by the world" (1:27). He also says those who merely listen to the Word but do not become doers are like people who look into a mirror and immediately afterward forget what they look like (1:22-25). Speaking empty words, even if the words are, "I believe in Jesus Christ," without having palpable fruit of genuine faith, may fool other people but will not fool God. In fact, these words may even fool ourselves, which is precisely the problem.

Is there the possibility of someone having saving faith and not producing one good work? Although I cannot know if such a hypothetical situation could take place, let me say I would have to cast my vote against such a notion. Saving faith *always* produces good works unless it is immediately followed by the death of the convert, like the thief on the cross. If in the passage of time no evidence of fruit is present, then it would not be wrong to question the validity of the original profession of faith.

Works are like the smoke that comes out of the exhaust pipe of an automobile. When you see the smoke, you know the car's engine is running. It isn't the smoke that makes the engine run. Rather the smoke is a sign that the engine is working. Similarly, a faith not accompanied by works is a dead faith. But what kind of works? Didn't the "Lord, Lord" people have works, and miraculous ones at that?

Consistently Jesus encourages his disciples to be different from those in the world. Pagans love people who love them back; so the disciples of Jesus must even love people who hate them. Persecution is not something normally to be desired from the world's point of view, but the disciples of Jesus must rejoice when it happens to them. Things that are typically considered religiously satisfying are often viewed by Jesus as impediments to a genuine relationship with him.

Sacrifices, tithes, and offerings were important to God, but only if they were accompanied by the deeper works of mercy, humility, and justice (Mic. 6:8). Jesus chastised the Pharisees for their outward show of religion while they secretly ignored the weightier matters of the law (Matt. 23:23). The weightier matters involve the things that separate the disciples of Christ from all other religious people, such as loving our enemies, carrying our cross, joyfully enduring persecution for Christ's name, and so on.

> It is the mature fruit which comes afterwards, and not the beautiful colors and smell of the blossoms, that we must judge by.
>
> Jonathan Edwards (1703-1758),
>
> *Religious Affections*

After what is for many evangelicals the quintessential statement on salvation, Ephesians 2:8-9, Paul says, "For we are God's workmanship, created in Christ Jesus to do good works, which God prepared in advance for us to do" (v. 10). If this is what we were created for, it stands to reason that good deeds will follow from our saving faith. This is why we exist as believers. Note that the good works come after salvation is secured. Good works are a byproduct of saving faith, not a prerequisite. The bottom line is, good works are a litmus test of genuine faith.

4) *Do you see long-term growth in your Christian life?* I would view this both from a positive and a negative point of view. Positively, how are you in those aspects of the Christian walk that are meant to cause you to grow in closer fellowship with God? Is your life a spiritual wasteland devoid of prayer and study of God's Word? Are you an infrequent church attendee who lacks involvement in a local body of

believers? Or is your life positively characterized by the opposite of these, a walk that is generally growing in life and vibrancy?

Negatively, is there known sin in your life that you fail to or refuse to confess? Has there been a long-term trend of such sin? Have you allowed it to become such a part of your life that you no longer feel God's Spirit convicting you of it? A seared conscience may be a warning sign of a false profession of faith (1 Tim. 4:2).

Let me briefly explain two important theological terms, *justification* and *sanctification*. Justification is the term used to describe our right standing before God. It is something that happens one time in our life, at the moment of conversion when we profess genuine, saving faith in the atoning work of Jesus on our behalf. There is nothing we can do to earn it or improve upon it.

Sanctification describes the process believers go through after they are justified. They grow more and more into the image and likeness of Christ. In the above discussion, we have in essence been asking the question, "Can my sanctification be used as a measure of whether or not I am genuinely justified?" In other words, is my profession of faith real or sham, and can I look at how I live my life as a factor in determining that? We have been saying yes to both questions.

If a person is justified, that person will become sanctified as well. Of course, there is no sanctification without justification, but let us not make the mistake that we can have genuine justification without a hint of sanctification.[8]

If a person became a believer at the age of twenty, at fifty he should be able to look back on his life and see growth in his walk with Christ. Certainly there will be ups and downs in that process, but the general trend should be upward. As he becomes more aware of the teaching of Christ, he should have a greater willingness to embrace it. If he does not, then perhaps he does not have genuine faith.

Because Scripture makes it clear that there will be some people who say the words but are not saved, it would be naïve at best and misleading at the worst to tell people all they need to do is say the words to be saved. Continuing in the faith is a sign of genuine disciples, and we can only know that we are continuing in the faith if indeed we are continuing in it. "We have come to share in Christ if we hold firmly till the end the confidence we had at first" (Heb. 3:14).

When people ask me when I became a believer, I tell them at the age of eight I professed faith in Jesus Christ. At that time I believe I moved from the kingdom of darkness and Satan to God's kingdom of light found in his Son.

But did I truly understand what I was getting myself into when I put my trust in Jesus? Could I have explained entirely what it meant to be dead in sin or for Jesus to come back from the dead never to die again? No, I could not, but my childlike trust in Jesus was all that was needed for my complete justification.

What about my life afterward though? I can say that I have shown signs of genuine conversion and faith, and I continue to do so. Do I occasionally have doubts? Yes, as I have said earlier. When I contemplate my sinful state, doubts do creep in; yet I know in whom I believe, and I know he is able to deliver me despite myself.

Am I now, thirty-three years after my conversion, more justified than I was then? Definitely not. The same perfect, atoning blood of Jesus covers me now as it did then, and I can never add to that or make it better. But am I more sanctified now than I was at the age of eight? Yes. And that process is continuing.

However, if there were no signs of spiritual fruit in my life since the time of my profession of faith, it would be reasonable for me to question that original profession.

5) *Be honest with yourself.* Lastly, and perhaps most importantly, we personally need to admit the possibility of self-deception. Few things are more difficult than honestly evaluating ourselves. More often than not, we lie to ourselves because we want to think more highly than we ought. We want to believe that we are on the road to salvation and that we exhibit all the signs of a genuinely born again believer.

Often out of ignorance or arrogance many Christians will not admit the possibility of self-deception, which makes them easier targets for Satan. Because Jesus recognizes the reality of self-deception, we should do the same. As usual Jesus is telling us something awful about ourselves, not to discourage us, but to free us.

"The heart is deceitful above all things" (Jer. 17:9a). This being the case, we would be foolish to just assume that saying a few words should provide us with absolute assurance of our salvation. If in time there is no fruit to accompany those words, we have every reason to doubt the genuineness of our conversion.

Are we saved by grace? Absolutely, 100 percent. We cannot save ourselves, and our good works do not in any way contribute to our salvation. However, even though good works are not a prerequisite of our salvation, they are a necessary product of it. In honestly evaluating ourselves, if we cannot find good works and fruit that comes from genuine faith, we have reason to be greatly concerned about our future fate.

We cannot offer God anything more pleasing than to say: Take us, Lord, we give thee our entire will.

Saint Alphonsus de Ligouri (1696-1787),
*Uniformity with God's Will*

# 11

# THE ART OF
# SPIRITUAL SURRENDER

*Come to me, all you who are weary and burdened, and I will give you rest. Take my yoke upon you and learn from me, for I am gentle and humble in heart, and you will find rest for your souls. For my yoke is easy and my burden is light.*

JESUS CHRIST, MATTHEW 11:28-30

*And Thou knowest how far Thou hast already changed me . . . who didst curb my pride with Thy fear, and tame my neck to Thy yoke.*

SAINT AUGUSTINE (345-430), *CONFESSIONS*

*In that day those who set not their hearts aright will feel, too late, how easy is Christ's yoke, to which they would not bend their necks and how light His burden, in comparison with the pains they must then endure.*

SAINT BERNARD OF CLAIRVAUX (1090-1153),
*ON LOVING GOD*

After all we have seen so far—the need for the disciples of Jesus to be forgiving to the nth degree, to endure persecution without retaliation or defense to the point of loving their enemies and praying for their well-being, and being absolutely committed to the call of Christ even if that means forsaking all love of family and self—how on earth can Jesus say his yoke is easy and his burden light? If ever there were a time to attribute irony or sarcasm to the words of Jesus, surely this must be it, right?

John Chrysostom (350-407) seemed to have had a similar feeling when looking at the increasing weight of the teachings of Jesus when he wrote: "For He was not contented with His former sayings, many and great as they were, but He adds others also, more and more alarming."[1]

Had we not seen any of the previous teaching of Jesus as found in our earlier chapters, perhaps we could accept the notion that the burden of Jesus is light. Fact is, many Christians today come to Jesus with just such a notion. They come looking for a Savior but not a Lord.

The idea of a Savior is appealing to many people. Even unbelievers who reject Christianity can confess Jesus was a good man who taught self-sacrifice and love of others. It is when we come to the idea that he expects us to submit our lives entirely to him that we find the rub. Everyone loves a Savior, but nobody wants a Lord.

This chapter will serve as a conclusion to our previous ten. In those chapters I enumerated the ten things I find most disconcerting about Jesus and his teaching. Now we will try to understand how Jesus could possibly say the burden he places upon us is light and the yoke easy.

## TREADING THE MILL

As we noted earlier, agricultural images often lose their power in an industrial civilization. Consider the agricultural society of Ethiopia: In a land without sophisticated farming equipment and mechanized horse-power, ox-power and donkey-power are the order of the day. Donkeys are ubiquitous, and few Ethiopians are unfamiliar with the strength of an ox and the pitch of a plow. The imagery of a yoke is recognizable for such people, while most of us will miss the vividness of the metaphor.

Yet there is an even greater difficulty to surmount. Once we *do* understand the imagery, we may be all the more ready to balk at it. Today the idea of submission is a foul concept. It smacks of sub-servience, inferiority, and even slavery. We prefer an autonomy of will, especially if we are talking about our own will. To explain to people with such an attitude that what Jesus means to tell us is that we should be strapped up to a yoke—a big, wooden frame positioned across our hunkering shoulders—is not a picture people like to see. Add to that the almost laughable comment that such a yoke is really easy, and, well, you see why sinners do not enjoy such teaching.

When I think of a yoke, I envision a dumb beast treading a mill, walking round and round and round, no will of his own, no mind to do anything else lest he feel the sharp whip on his back. Is this what Jesus intends for me to find easy and light? I would like to suggest briefly three reasons why Jesus said what he did.

## DO OUR NECKS HAVE THE RIGHT FIT?

Like all of our Lord's teaching, there is a profound truth here that is only uncovered through diligence. The reason the yoke is easy and the burden light is that this is what we were created for. Our necks were originally fitted for such a task. Mankind was created to glorify God and to serve him. This is the first reason Jesus can say his calling is easy and light.

The reason the yoke appears to be so difficult for me is that I am a sinner. I fight and groan each time I wear it. I reject the discipline that comes with it and much prefer, like a dumb mule, to go my own merry way. If you have ever driven through Botswana, you will know what I am talking about. It does not matter if you are speeding down the highway at seventy miles per hour in a big Land Rover, if a donkey or mule is crossing the road, *your* life is the one in danger if you do not slow down. Heaven forbid the dim-witted creature get out of the way. Stupidly it will wander into oncoming traffic. It just does not know any better.

As demeaning as that may sound, the illustration does a fairly accurate job of characterizing sinners like I am. How often have I foolishly wandered right into traffic, off the path of God's design, and flat out on my own trail? Donkeys that are not occasionally whipped or oxen that are not yoked are of little use for constructive work.

## TEN THINGS I WISH JESUS NEVER SAID

The always-insightful Eugene Peterson has this to say about the Christian life:

> There is a general assumption prevalent in the world that it is extremely difficult to be a Christian. While it is true that many don't completely disqualify themselves, they do modify their claims: *ordinary* Christian they call themselves. They respect the church, worship fairly regularly, try to live decently. But they also give themselves somewhat generous margins to allow for the temptations and pressures put upon them by the world. To *really* be on the way of faith, take with absolute *seriousness* all that the Bible says—well, that requires a predisposition to saintliness, nameless austerities that they are quite sure they cannot manage.
>
> But this is as far from the truth as the east is from the west. The easiest thing in the world is to be a Christian. What is hard is to be a sinner. Being a Christian is what we were created for. The life of faith has the support of an entire creation and the resources of a magnificent redemption. The structure of this world was created by God so we could live in it easily and happily as his children. The history we walk in has been repeatedly entered by God, most notably in Jesus Christ, first to show us and then to help us live full of faith and exuberant with purpose. In the course of Christian discipleship we discover that without Christ we were doing it the hard way and that with Christ we are doing it the easy way. It is not Christians who have it hard, but non-Christians.[2]

The first time I read this passage by Peterson, I thought he was way off base. *Peterson must be one of those Christians who expects the Christian life to be easy,* I thought, much like our modern-day health-and-wealth, prosperity preachers. But the more I contemplated his words, the more they made sense to me. I have been created for precisely this task.[3] I should gladly be yoked with Christ, if not for my selfish and sinful ways. What should be natural and pleasing to me becomes burdensome because my sinfulness causes me to fight against it.

Paul echoes a similar sentiment: "It is for freedom that Christ has set us free. Stand firm, then, and do not let yourselves be burdened again by a yoke of slavery" (Gal. 5:1). What a powerful phrase, "yoke of slavery." It immediately conjures up images in our mind, but instead of the taskmaster commonly portrayed in popular films and television programs, picture the taskmaster of sin. There it is, desiring to master you, "crouching at your door" (Gen. 4:7) like a lion savoring the prey.

How easily we are duped. The serpent promised godhood to Adam and Eve. Since that time fallen humanity has consistently struggled to attain it, subject only to the greatest frustration and discontentment. Vainly we attempt to usurp God's authority. Like the builders at Babel, we want to create a structure that reaches the heavens where we think we can boot God off his throne. But one generation comes and another goes, and still God remains.

The yoke with which Jesus would have us fitted is easy in comparison to the tribulation that ensues if we do not accept it. The world cries out for peace but rejects the Prince of Peace. It bemoans war and strife and disease; yet it rejects the cure for all the ills of mankind.

> *O shame to men! Devil with devil damned*
> *Firm concord holds; men only disagree*
> *Of creatures rational, though under hope*
> *Of heavenly Grace: and God proclaiming peace,*
> *Yet live in hatred, enmity, and strife*
> *Among themselves, and levy cruel wars,*
> *Wasting the Earth, each other to destroy:*
> *As if (which might induce us to accord)*
> *Man had not hellish foes enow besides,*
> *That day and night for his destruction wait!*
> John Milton (1608-1674), *Paradise Lost*

The first reason, then, that the yoke is easy and the burden light is because both the yoke and burden are conforming us to something we have been created for. The reason we so often perceive them to be difficult and heavy is because we are sinners. Our will is being conformed to the yoke's will, but we kick and claw against it, always to our own detriment.

> Hence we may know, that the rebellion of our Will is the chief occasion of our disquiet; and that because we will not submit to the sweet yoke of the Divine Will, we suffer so many streights and perturbations.
>
> Miguel de Molinos (1628-1696),
> Spanish mystic, *The Spiritual Guide Which Disentangles the Soul*

## WHOSE YOKE IS IT, ANYWAY?

The second reason Jesus can say it is easy and light is that it is *his* yoke. Jesus says, "Take *my* yoke." Jesus is yoked with us. Consider a small, scrawny ox yoked side by side with a massive, muscular one. Who is going to be pulling most of the weight?

Because it is the yoke of Christ, pictured here is not a person treading the grain mill alone or solitarily laboring to pull the plow through the field. That would be a heavy and tiresome yoke to bear, and that is the point Jesus wants to make. Jesus is yoked with us; it is *his* yoke he calls us to accept. Therefore, we do not tread the mill alone. Jesus is yoked with us; together we carry the yoke.

But Jesus goes even further. "Take my yoke upon you and *learn from me.*" When we are coupled with Jesus, not only do we participate in his life and power, but we also learn from him. We see how the Master bore the burden, we observe how he carried the yoke upon his shoulders, and we learn to do likewise. He does not command us to carry a cross he himself was not willing to bear. He does not demand us to place our hand upon a plow—and not turn back—that he himself was not willing to do. He does not call us to forsake anything he himself was not also willing to forsake.

Listen to the words of the great Danish philosopher Søren Kierkegaard (1813-1855), from *Preparation for a Christian Life*:

> There is, indeed, an unbridgeable gulf fixed between God and man. It therefore became plain to those contemporary with Christ that the process of becoming a Christian (that is, being changed

into the likeness of God) is, in a human sense, a greater torment and wretchedness and pain than the greatest conceivable human suffering, and moreover a crime in the eyes of one's contemporaries. And thus will it always be; that is, if becoming a Christian in reality means becoming contemporaneous with Christ. And if becoming a Christian does not have that meaning, then all your chatter about becoming a Christian is a vanity, a delusion and a snare, and likewise a blasphemy and a sin against the Holy Ghost.[4]

This call would not make sense if Jesus were not himself accustomed to burdens and heavy loads; nor would it be possible if Jesus were not willing to yoke himself with us.[5]

The Old Testament law forbade the yoking of an ox with a donkey (Deut. 22:10) because it would unfairly disadvantage the ox. Donkeys are lazy and dumb while oxen are hardworking and smarter. The stupid donkey would inhibit the ox's ability to get the work done. Incredibly, Jesus (more like an ox) is willing to yoke himself voluntarily with sinners like me (more like a donkey).

The imagery of a yoke is similar in purpose to another image Jesus used, that of the vine and branches (John 15). There Jesus tells us plainly, "apart from me you can do nothing" (v. 5b). If we combine the point of the two images, what Jesus is telling us to envision is a yoke where only we are strapped to it. Can you imagine a bony, emaciated ox attached to a massive yoke? How far will such an ox be able to push before failing in strength?

Living in the desert country of Namibia, I have become fascinated with succulents. Cacti are strewn all over my yard, and I cannot seem to get enough of them. So many shapes and sizes, many with beautiful flowers, each a different design on prickly pleasure and pain. Cacti are the perfect plant to weather, well, little weather at all. They can go for years without water and incredibly bloom seemingly from the dead once the rains arrive.

If you cut a piece of a cactus off and stick it in the ground, it retains enough water that it can develop a new root and grow into a mature plant. However, if you cut off a piece and do not place it in the soil, no matter how hardy and full of moisture the plant was originally, in time it will wither and die. When it is cut off from its life source, it soon perishes.

While potentially mixing metaphors, I want us to consider the cactus cutting and the ox. Neither has a purposeful existence without something giving it life or direction. This is exactly the case with sinful humans. Left to our own design, we will wander around purposelessly like the unyoked ox, or we will shrivel up and die like the cactus pruning.

> *Without the Way, there is no going.*
> *Without the Truth, there is no knowing.*
> *Without the Life, there is no growing.*[6]

The yoke is easy and the burden light because Christ bears it with us.

## THE HEAVY BURDEN OF SELF

When we compare the yoke of Christ to the yoke of self, we learn the third reason Jesus's yoke is easy. It is light and easy in comparison to what I would otherwise be carrying. Jesus promises that his yoke will bring "rest for your souls." What a wonderfully comforting thing to hear, especially to a sinner like me. Like the protagonist in Bunyan's *Pilgrim's Progress*, I sludge around with a heavy pack on my back. My knees buckle, my legs grow fatigued, and, shamefully, I endeavor to grab hold of the pack and not let it go. Why do I covet this blasted burden on my back?

God wants so much more for me, and so often I become angry with him for it. I want to become a beautiful tree, but I object whenever God prunes me. I want happiness and contentment in my life, but I protest when God wants to give me a peace that comes from holiness. I am such a lazy, disagreeable servant who aspires to have the things of the Master without taking the Master's path. What a wretched soul I am.

St. Bernard of Clairvaux (1090-1153) made this insightful observation nearly a millennium ago: "The eternal law of righteousness ordains that he who will not submit to God's sweet rule shall suffer the bitter tyranny of self: but he who wears the easy yoke and light burden of love will escape the intolerable weight of his own self-will." I must endeavor to crucify my will. All the selfish, egotistical ways to which I have become accustomed must be eliminated if I am to be conformed to the image of Christ.

In the Garden of Eden, the first Adam was not willing to submit his will to God's. Because of his stubbornness, he brought misery to us all. The second Adam, while also in a garden, did what the first Adam was unwilling to do. Jesus experienced a crucifixion of his will in Gethsemane. He plainly expressed his own will concerning the cup he was about to drink, but our sinless Savior did not back down. Rather he continued to submit his will to the will of the Father. Even while sweating drops of blood, he submitted. Oh, that I would have such commitment.

As believers in Jesus Christ, we have this same likeness in us, by faith through his Spirit. We have become joint heirs with the Son of God, with the same indwelling Spirit that raised Jesus from the dead (Rom. 8:11). If we would but submit to him and his will, we would feel the load being lifted.

To all those who are weary and burdened, Jesus offers rest for our souls. "Burdened with what?" we might ask. It is not simply the cares of this world or too much work and not enough leisure that Jesus is referring to. Jesus offers rest for our souls, not our backs. It is rest from the burden of selfishness. It is peace from sorrow and sin, remorse and guilt. It is respite from the crouching monster at our door and in our depraved nature. Fallen. Hopeless. Sinful self. Jesus wants to free us from our own bondage. With the sacrifice of self, Jesus offers us something much greater: knowing his Father.

## HAPPILY PLACING YOUR NECK IN THE YOKE

Thus we have come full circle. The burden is sin, and only the poor in spirit recognize it. Those who do not recognize it will find no relief from it. There will be no entrance into the kingdom of heaven without a consciousness of sin. Until we confess in humble submission our poverty of spirit, we remain with the heavy burden upon us.

Much of modern Christianity has a love affair with "Jesus-lite." The rigorous demands of Christ are washed away in a sea of prosperity and privilege. Suffering for Jesus is to be avoided at all costs and is in fact a sign that one does not have proper faith. We sing with arms reaching to heaven, "Bless me, Lord," but we are unwilling to lift a finger to truly serve our Master.

This tendency should not surprise us. As sinners, we have always been busy trimming down the exacting elements of the gospel. Anything we determine too offensive, beneath us, or intolerant by modern standards we simply throw out. Consider this analysis by a theologian in the middle of the last century: "A God without wrath brought people without sin into a kingdom without judgment through the ministrations of a Christ without a cross."[7]

We always have had a tendency to excise in the teaching of Jesus what we find uncomfortable. However, we must not fool ourselves into believing that the lightened load we have created for ourselves will get us to our intended destination. Ironically, the more we look to remove from the burden of Christ, the more we have unwittingly placed on our own backs.

## PARTING WORDS

I hope as you have read to the end of this book that you have come to appreciate my struggle in the Christian walk. As God prunes this old tree, the clipping and cutting hurt. I like my right eye and right hand. I do not find persecution appealing; nor do I enjoy blessing my enemy or giving up my grudges. Pushing a plow and carrying a cross are often difficult for me to stomach. And the self-evaluation and self-criticism I am called to perform, well, they do not always yield the heady accolades I would like to receive about myself. I do not find the art of spiritual surrender easy.

Martin Luther's favorite biblical character was Jacob because he wrestled with God. I often feel like Jacob because of my struggles with him too. Jesus calls me to turn from my own selfishness, and at times I find myself turning from Jesus instead. May God grant me grace and mercy because without them I have no hope.

> He, therefore, is the devout man, who lives no longer to his own will, or the way and spirit of the world, but to the sole will of God, who considers God in everything, who serves God in everything, who makes all the parts of his common life parts of piety, by doing everything in the Name of God, and under such rules as are conformable to His glory.
>
> William Law (1686-1761),
> *A Serious Call to a Devout and Holy Life*

# NOTES

PREFACE

1. Dorothy L. Sayers, *Creed or Chaos?* (Manchester, N.H.: Sophia Institute Press, 1974), 6.

## CHAPTER 1: THE ART OF SPIRITUAL POVERTY

1. *Blessed* actually involves more than simple happiness. Biblical blessedness is normally indicative of how God views a person; in this sense it also has the connotation of God's approval.

2. Jesus's teachings often relied on what Leland Ryken calls "delayed action insight" (*The Word of God in English*, Wheaton, Ill.: Crossway Books, 2002). "Those who ponder Jesus' sayings will come to an understanding of them, whereas people who are unwilling to penetrate beneath the surface will not" (68; also 239, 285).

3. *Vine's Expository Dictionary of Biblical Words* (Nashville: Thomas Nelson, 1985), 56, 476.

4. Erasmus of Rotterdam, *In Praise of Folly*, in Christian Classics Ethereal Library, compiled by Calvin College, *www.ccel.org/*. All references from this source are in the public domain.

5. Some Christians do not believe *any* of the Sermon on the Mount is applicable to us today. They believe it was a) only for the Jewish disciples of Jesus during his ministry years and up to his crucifixion, or b) only for those people living in the future millennial reign of Jesus on earth. In either case, it does not apply now to believers who live between the two advents of Christ. In this way several uncomfortable teachings of Jesus are eliminated, including "judge not or you too will be judged," "love your enemies," and "if your right eye causes you to sin, pluck it out." This dispensational view of the Sermon on the Mount is wholly unsatisfactory as it also eliminates the Lord's Prayer, the Beatitudes, the commands from Jesus concerning divorce and adultery, and a whole list of other important teachings for those who would choose to follow Christ. It also leaves one wondering what else in the teaching of Jesus does not apply to Christians today.

6. I recognize that a main argument used by those who say we need not fast today is the fact that outside of the Gospels and Acts, we see little on fasting. Whereas prayer and charitable giving are commanded in the New Testament epistles, no such command is found concerning fasting. In fact, the only dis-

cussion loosely associated with fasting comes from Paul's condemnation of false teachers who taught that believers must abstain from certain foods (1 Tim. 4:3). This "argument from silence" is perhaps the most powerful argument for those who say fasting is no longer necessary. However, I find little comfort in the argument that because only Jesus expected his disciples to fast—with no clear repetition of this from the later New Testament authors— his disciples need not do it today. Interestingly, we find no command of baptism in the epistles either; yet it is the universal practice of the church to baptize based on the command of Jesus. In the Book of Acts, which is a record of the first thirty years of the history of the early church, we find both baptism and fasting regularly practiced. Jesus expected his disciples to fast, and this should be good enough for us today.

7. My favorite book on fasting is *God's Chosen Fast* by Arthur Wallis (Fort Washington, Pa.: Christian Literature Crusade, 1968). This book is not a thorough, theological treatment of the topic but a more practical one dealing with the do's and don'ts of fasting.

8. Ibid., 73.

9. Dietrich Bonhoeffer, *The Cost of Discipleship*. Excerpts found in *Spiritual Witness* (Wheaton, Ill.: Crossway Books, 1991), 115-130.

10. *Vine's Expository Dictionary*, 187. The King James Version rightly translated this word with the stronger "dung."

11. Robert Farrar Capon, *The Parables of Grace* (Grand Rapids, Mich.: William B. Eerdmans, 1988), 9.

12. Perhaps the most disturbing aspect of the prosperity gospel is that it is not even overtly Christian. "God loves you and wants you to succeed in life" could be said by any number of people, including a New Ager, pluralist, Scientologist, humanist, or Oprah Winfrey.

13. As quoted in *The Wisdom of Saint Augustine*, comp. David Winter (Grand Rapids, Mich.: Eerdmans, 1997), 41.

14. To avoid potential confusion, let me make it clear that I am *not* saying that rich people are automatically outside of the favor of God, or cannot be poor in spirit because they are materially well-off. There are many godly, generous, wealthy individuals in the world who are proper stewards of the money God has given them. My concern is with those believers who make material success a necessary goal of the Christian life or a sure sign of the favor of God.

15. Thomas à Kempis, *The Imitation of Christ*, "Thoughts Helpful in the Life of the Soul," Book 1, chapter 21.

16. I recognize that this point is debatable, and often the counterpoint is to state that because humans are created in the image of God, they have intrinsic value. This is frequently coupled with Psalm 8:4b-5: "What is man that you are

mindful of him, the son of man that you care for him? Yet you have made him a little lower than the angels and crowned him with glory and honor." These verses are then used to support the notion that as humans, we should possess high self-esteem. Although thoroughly debating that point is not the intention of this book, I think it worth noting that another understanding of this passage is equally possible. Rather than an ode to man, these verses could be saying the exact opposite. The psalmist's astonishment makes better sense in the context of man's lowliness, not his exaltation. If man *is* of great value and worth, then the consternation the psalmist expresses would make little sense. David is shocked that God cares for man because, in comparison to God, man is not worth caring for. Reading these verses from the perspective of a "poverty of spirit" makes more sense.

17. John Wesley, as quoted in R. Kent Hughes, *The Sermon on the Mount* (Wheaton, Ill.: Crossway Books, 2001), 19.

## CHAPTER 2: THE ART OF SPIRITUAL SELF-MUTILATION

1. "This view [penal substitution] of the atonement is sometimes called the theory of vicarious atonement. A 'vicar' is someone who stands in the place of another or who represents another. Christ's death was therefore 'vicarious' because he stood in our place and represented us. As our representative, he took the penalty that we deserve" (Wayne Grudem, *Systematic Theology* [Grand Rapids, Mich.: Zondervan, 1994], 579).

2. Remember Hebrews 2:10, which says that Jesus was "made perfect through suffering" (compare Heb. 5:8). We will look at this in chapter 5.

3. A full-blown theological defense of this point is not within the scope of this book, but for those wondering, the reality of the temptations of Jesus is not my only reason for believing he was capable of sinning. In the fifth century, Eutyches proposed that the human nature of Jesus was swallowed up by his divine nature, much like a drop of vinegar would be absorbed by the ocean. The Fourth Ecumenical Council at Chalcedon condemned Eutyches's view. The position that says Jesus could not have sinned because he possessed a divine nature appears to me to be making the same mistake as Eutyches.

4. Two examples include the contrast between the lines of Seth and Cain, and the attitude of the builders at Babel versus that of Abram. In the first contrast, Cain's line is consistently shown to become more and more depraved; seventh from Cain is the despicable Lamech, a violent man who is the first polygamist recorded in Scripture. The seventh in the line of Seth is Enoch, a man who "walked with God" and was preserved from natural death. The other contrast involves the arrogance of the Tower of Babel builders ("let us make a name for ourselves") and the account of Abram, where it is God who promises to make Abram's name great.

5. Although Abram's name does not change for several chapters, I am going to use "Abraham" throughout this account for clarity.

6. I could have chosen someone more familiar to us, like King David or King Solomon, but although Lot makes an excellent example, we rarely study his story.

7. Another example of this is when the inspired author of Hebrews recounts the thoughts of Abraham concerning the sacrifice of his son Isaac. Although the Genesis account does not tell us that Abraham reasoned that God could bring back his son of promise from the dead, Hebrews tells us that he did (11:19).

8. *Hard Sayings of the Bible* (Downers Grove, Ill.: InterVarsity Press, 1996), 361. This book is a compilation of four previous "hard sayings" works.

9. John Woodbridge, *Great Leaders of the Christian Church* (Chicago: Moody Press, 1988), 55-58. Over fifty years later, Origen was arrested, imprisoned, and severely tortured under the Decian persecution and died three years later.

10. John Calvin, *Institutes of the Christian Religion*, ed. John T. McNeill (Philadelphia: Westminster Press, 1960) , 2.1.2. Later Calvin states, "Why do we presume so much on ability of human nature? It is wounded, battered, troubled, lost. What we need is true confession, not false defense" (2.2.11).

11. Quoted in *Institutes*, 2.1.3, n. 3.

12. *NIV Study Bible* (Grand Rapids, Mich.: Zondervan Publishing House, 1985), footnote on Mark 9:43.

## CHAPTER 3: THE ART OF SPIRITUAL COMMITMENT

1. These items come from the main headings of a section in Andrew Murray's *The School of Obedience*, Christian Classics Ethereal Library, *www.ccel.org/ccel/murray/obedience.iv.html*.

2. My main source for the histories of these three men is Gideon David Hagstotz and Hilda Boettscher Hagstotz, *Heroes of the Reformation* (Rapidan, Va.: Hartland Publications, 1951). Consult the following sections: Jerome of Prague (225-229), John Laski (232-240), and Francisco de Enzinas (261-265).

3. Ibid., 28-29.

4. Ibid., 263.

5. Eva B. Lloyd, "Come, All Christians, Be Committed," copyright 1966 by Broadman Press (SESAC).

6. J. C. Ryle, *Expository Thoughts on Luke* (Carlisle, Pa.: The Banner of Truth Trust, 1986), 342.

7. Timothy George, *Faithful Witness: The Life and Mission of William Carey* (Christian History Institute, 1998), E48.

8. Leon Morris, *Luke* (Leicester, England: InterVarsity Press, 1988), 197.

9. In the parable of the sower (Matt. 13:1-23), Jesus describes two kinds of soil

that echo this idea of faulty commitment. One soil represents someone who immediately receives the word "with joy, but since he has no root, he lasts only a short time. When trouble or persecution comes because of the word, he quickly falls away" (vv. 20-21). The other soil also becomes unfruitful because it is choked by the thorns of worldly wealth and worries (v. 22).

10. Jesus speaks to this issue in the Sermon on the Mount in his "Lord, Lord" comments, and we will devote an entire chapter to it later.

11. A. Roberts and J. Donaldson, eds., *The Ante-Nicene Fathers*, Vol. 3 (American reprint of the Edinburgh edition, 1975), 686.

## CHAPTER 4: THE ART OF SPIRITUAL SELF-CRUCIFIXION

1. To avoid confusion, let me explain. It isn't that I am saved from my sins as much as I am saved from the *effect* of my sins. To be precise, it is from the wrath of God that I am saved. Similarly, I do not really ask Jesus into my heart, no matter how helpful this image is, especially for children. In fact, there is nowhere in the Scriptures where we are told to ask Jesus into our hearts. These phrases, while helpful in their simplicity, can yield confusion because they are inadequate and imprecise.

2. F. F. Bruce makes this point, but does it more eloquently. "As commonly applied, the expression is used of some bodily disability, some unwelcome experience, some uncongenial companion or relative that one is stuck with: 'This is the cross I have to bear,' people say. It can be used in this watered-down way because its literal sense is remote from our experience" (*The Hard Sayings of Jesus* [Downers Grove, Ill.: InterVarsity Press, 1983], 150).

3. In our next chapter, when we look more specifically at persecution, I will argue that at times it is right to run from persecution when all options are weighed. Not only will I use examples from the history of the church, but I will use biblical examples as well. In short, there is a proper time to make your stand even unto death, and there is a proper time to take your leave and face it better another day.

4. John Piper, *Don't Waste Your Life* (Wheaton, Ill.: Crossway Books, 2003), 59.

## CHAPTER 5: THE ART OF SPIRITUAL MARTYRDOM

1. A third type of suffering could be delineated as suffering for doing something wrong. A person who suffers in prison for housebreaking could be said to be getting what he or she deserves. However, the suffering I am dealing with in this chapter is either a result of natural, human frailty (which has no moral determinant attached to it) or for following Christ (which is undeserved suffering).

2. Philip Yancey, *Where Is God When It Hurts?* (Grand Rapids, Mich.: Zondervan, 1990), 9.

3. David Dryer, SIM speaker, Namibia Field Conference, August 2001.

4. It is uncertain who wrote this letter, although it is commonly attributed to the fourth bishop of Rome, Clement, who died around A.D. 96. The exact date of the letter, therefore, is unknown. My source for the quotation comes from Michael W. Holmes, ed., *The Apostolic Fathers* (Grand Rapids, Mich.: Baker Book House, 1989), 78.

5. Ibid.

6. This is another reason I believe Jesus could have sinned when tempted, something I initially addressed in chapter 2.

7. Oswald Chambers, *So Send I You* (London: Simpkin Marshall, Ltd., 1934), 19.

8. Augustine, *The City of God*, ed., Vernon J. Bourke (New York: Image Books, Doubleday, 1958), 46.

9. acacia.pair.com/Acacia.John.Bunyan/Sermons.Allegories/Pilgrim.s.Progress/Pilgrim.Text/Part.Two/21.html.

10. Dick Anderson, *We Felt Like Grasshoppers* (Nottingham, England: Crossway Books, 1994), 318-319. The quotation comes from Paul Stough's unpublished biographical notes. Paul Stough, who is now with the Lord, was my wife's grandfather.

11. The reader is referred to the following passages as examples: Matthew 5:11-12; Acts 5:41; 16:25; Romans 5:3; 8:29; Philippians 1:10, 29; James 1:2; 1 Peter 1:6; 4:14; Hebrews 10:32-34.

12. David McCasland, *Oswald Chambers: Abandoned to God* (Grand Rapids, Mich.: Discovery House, 1993), 232.

13. For passages that speak of Jesus's time to die not yet upon him, see John 2:4; 7:6, 8, 30; 8:20. For passages that recount those instances where people wanted to kill Jesus but he escaped their grasp, see Luke 4:28-30; John 8:59; 10:39.

14. Dallas Willard, *The Divine Conspiracy* (San Francisco: HarperCollins, 1998), 214. Willard cites two *Christianity Today* articles, July and August 1996, as his source for this statistic.

15. Ethiopia, for example, has had the Christian faith for nearly 2,000 years, as it is traditionally believed that the Ethiopian eunuch of Acts 8 (who was the treasurer of the queen of Ethiopia) introduced it to that country.

16. Mark Shaw, *The Kingdom of God in Africa: A Short History of African Christianity* (Grand Rapids, Mich.: Baker Books, 1996), 182.

## CHAPTER 6: THE ART OF SPIRITUAL LOVE

1. The divorce rate among American Christians is relatively equal to that of non-Christians, so says Christian researcher George Barna. For 2001 stats, see: *www.barna.org/FlexPage.aspx?Page=BarnaUpdate&BarnaUpdateID=95*. *www.barna.org/FlexPage.aspx?Page=BarnaUpdate&BarnaUpdateID=170*

shows the stats for 2004. For a wealth of information on the data for divorce in America, go to: *www.divorcereform.org/rates.html.*

2. R. Kent Hughes, *The Sermon on the Mount* (Wheaton, Ill.: Crossway Books, 2001), 141.

3. Which is similar to the parallel passage of Luke 6:26-27.

4. Recorded in *The Life of Benedict* by Pope Gregory the Great (590-604).

5. John Calvin, *Institutes of the Christian Religion* (Philadelphia: Westminster Press, 1960), 2.8.56-57.

6. Martin Luther, *Table Talk*, trans. William Hazlitt (Philadelphia: The Lutheran Publication Society, no date), chapters 661—682.

7. Matthew 3:7; 12:34; 23:33; 16:23.

8. Luther, *Table Talk*, chapter 733.

9. Luther is worth quoting again: "If a robber on the highway should fall upon me, truly I would be judge and prince myself, and would use my sword, because nobody was with me able to defend me; and I should think I had accomplished a good work; but if one fell upon me as a preacher for the gospel's sake, then with folded hands I would lift up mine eyes to heaven, and say: 'My Lord Christ! here I am; I have confessed and preached thee; is now my time expired? so I commit my spirit into thy hands,' and in that way would I die" (Ibid., 784).

10. Alfred Plummer, as quoted in Hughes, *The Sermon on the Mount,* 141.

11. J. C. Ryle, *Matthew* (Wheaton, Ill.: Crossway Books, 1993), 34.

## Chapter 7: The Art of Spiritual Forgiveness

1. I recognize that there is a subtle difference between "grace" and "mercy," but I am using the terms interchangeably here. For my purposes, the main issue is that both are undeserved.

2. The talent was the largest unit of currency, and 10,000 the largest Greek numeral. The servant owed 10,000 talents. If a talent was equivalent to about a month's wages, this man was in debt to the king for over 800 years.

3. Editorial comments in the Preface of the *Journal*, www.ccel.org/ccel/wesley/journal.ii.html

4. *Journal*, October 24, 1751.

5. John Woodbridge, *Great Leaders of the Christian Church* (Chicago: Moody Press, 1988), 287.

6. Christian Classics Ethereal Library, *The Lord's Prayer, www.ccel.org/ccel/watson/prayer.titlepage.html.*

7. Philip Schaff, ed., *Nicene and Post-Nicene Fathers of the Christian Church*, vol. 9 (New York: Christian Literature Publishing, 1886), 475. *www.ccel.org/fathers2/NPNF1-09/npnf1-09-70.htm*

8. Ibid., 472.

CHAPTER 8: THE ART OF SPIRITUAL SELF-LOATHING

1. Charles Krauthammer, as quoted in *Christianity Today*, March 6, 1995, 41.
2. John Calvin, *Institutes of the Christian Religion* (Philadelphia: Westminster Press, 1960), (1.1.1).
3. Compare Calvin's comments with the comments of a well-known American televangelist who said, "I don't think anything has been done in the name of Christ and under the banner of Christianity that has proven more destructive to human personality, and hence counterproductive to the evangelistic enterprise, than the unchristian, uncouth strategy of attempting to make people aware of their lost and sinful condition. . . . Classical Reformed theology has erred in its insistence that theology be God-centered, not man-centered."
4. As quoted in R. Kent Hughes, *James* (Wheaton, Ill: Crossway Books, 1991), 183.
5. Bruce Shelley, *Church History in Plain Language* (Nashville, Tenn.: Thomas Nelson Inc., 1982), 330.
6. Dallas Willard, *The Divine Conspiracy* (HarperSanFrancisco, 1998), 214.
7. Even today when going through Luther's home in Wittenberg, a tour guide will point out the ink stain still on the wall.
8. There is always the problem of HIV/AIDS in southern Africa, the worst hit region in the world. Despite irrational fears concerning the disease and how my children might inadvertently catch it, it is still disconcerting that we serve in a country that according to the United Nations recently ranked third worst in the world in terms of infection rate.
9. A.W. Tozer, *The Knowledge of the Holy* (San Francisco: Harper & Row, 1961), 3. Also, "Wrong ideas about God are not only the fountain from which the polluted waters of idolatry flow; they are themselves idolatrous" (4).
10. George Barna, *Revolution* (Carol Stream, Ill.: Tyndale House, 2005).
11. Perhaps this was the mentality addressed in Hebrews 10:25.
12. Calvin, *Institutes*, 3.3.8

CHAPTER 9: THE ART OF SPIRITUAL DISCERNMENT

1. Jean Bethke Elshtain, "Judge Not?" *First Things: The Journal of Religion, Culture & Public Life*, www.firstthings.com/ftissues/ft9410/elshtain.html.
2. Philip Schaff, *History of the Christian Church* (Grand Rapids, Mich.: Eerdmans, 1994; originally published by Charles Scribner's Sons, 1910), 306.
3. This account is taken from *The Little Flowers of St. Francis of Assisi*, by Brother Ugolino, in the public domain.
4. Philip Schaff, ed., *Nicene and Post-Nicene Fathers of the Christian Church*, vol. 10 (New York: Christian Literature Publishing, 1886), 154.

5. Another test for knowing if these statements from Jesus mean that we can never judge is to ask a related question: Does this mean that if we do not judge, we will not be judged either? Obviously not. As the Bible states, everyone will stand in judgment before God. But it seems we have a say in the tenor and tone of that coming judgment, based on how we have treated others. This command, then, is not against all forms of judgment, but only against hypocritical ones.

## Chapter 10: The Art of Spiritual Self-Assessment

1. Gerhard Kittel (ed.), *Theological Dictionary of the New Testament* (Grand Rapids, Mich.: Eerdmans, 1965), 938.

2. John P. Meier, *A Marginal Jew: Rethinking the Historical Jesus*, vol. 1 (New York: Doubleday, 1991), 177.

3. Martin Luther, *The Sermons of Martin Luther*, vol. 2 (Grand Rapids, Mich.: Baker Book House), 186-187.

4. A. Scott Moreau, *The World of the Spirits—A Biblical Study in the African Context* (Nairobi, Kenya: Evangel Publishing House, 1990), 83.

5. R. Kent Hughes, *The Sermon on the Mount* (Wheaton, Ill.: Crossway Books, 2001), 255.

6. *The NIV Study Bible* (Grand Rapids, Mich.: Zondervan Publishing House, 1985), 1806.

7. "Those who begin to deny major doctrines of the faith give serious negative indications concerning their salvation" (Wayne Grudem, *Systematic Theology* [Grand Rapids, Mich.: Zondervan, 1994], 804).

8. There is a vast difference between saying there are some unbelievers who have certain external signs of saving faith, yet are not saved, and believers who do not look like believers at all. The latter is popular today. "She spoke like a sailor and drank like a wino, but she was one of the most godly people I knew." Incredibly, I have heard and read such statements. I am certain that genuine believers struggle with sin, but at what point are we willing to conclude that people who are incredibly worldly in their way of life are truly saved? Fortunately, God will be the one to make the final, and perfect, determination in such matters.

## Chapter 11: The Art of Spiritual Surrender

1. Philip Schaff, ed., *Nicene and Post-Nicene Fathers of the Christian Church*, vol. 10 (New York: Christian Literature Publishing, 1886), 143.

2. Eugene Peterson, *A Long Obedience in the Same Direction: Discipleship in an Instant Society* (Downers Grove, Ill.: InterVarsity Press, 1980), 111, emphasis in original.

3. J. C. Ryle makes this wonderful analogy: "His yoke is no more a burden than

the feathers are to a bird," quoted in *Matthew,* The Crossway Books Classic Commentaries (Wheaton, Ill.: Crossway Books, 1993), 89.

4. Christian Classics Ethereal Library, *www.ccel.org/k/kierkegaard/selections/preparation.htm.*

5. There is even a biblical sense in which we are yoked with fellow believers, thus making our burden lighter (see Phil. 4:3, NIV "yokefellow").

6. I have taken a short saying by Thomas à Kempis's *The Imitation of Christ* and have adapted it here.

7. H. Richard Niebuhr, *The Kingdom of God in America* (New York: Harper Torchbook, 1959), 193.

# AUTHOR INDEX

Albertus Magnus (1193-1280) 14, 18, 119

Alphonsus de Ligouri (1696-1787) 120, 125, 272

Athanasius (296-377) 75, 128-129

Augustine (354-430) 14, 31, 52, 53, 97, 112, 116, 119, 123, 194, 219, 273, 286, 290

Barna, George 67, 213-214, 290, 292

Baxter, Richard (1615-1691) 15, 184

Benedict of Nursia (480-547) 145, 291

Bernard of Clairvaux (1090-1153) 14, 85, 193, 273, 281

Bonhoeffer, Dietrich (1906-1945) 27-28, 286

Bracciolini, Poggio 64

Bruce, F. F. (1910-1990) 89, 289, 292

Bucer, Martin (1491-1551) 65

Bullinger, Johann (1504-1575) 65

Bunyan, John (1628-1688) 11, 14, 112, 120, 280, 290

Calvin, John (1509-1564) 24, 53, 55, 59, 65, 95, 96, 97, 145, 181, 185, 191, 193, 211, 213, 218, 228, 253, 261, 288, 291, 292

Card, Michael 209

Carey, William (1761-1834) 71, 105, 288

Cassian, John (360-435) 55, 92

Catherine of Siena (1347-1380) 193

Cerularius, Michael 234-235

Chambers, Oswald (1874-1917) 116, 122-123, 190

Chrysostom, John (350-407) 180, 182, 241, 243, 274

Clement of Rome (c. 96) 113-114, 131, 290

Constantine the Great (275-337) 131

Cowper, William (1731-1800) 133

Cranmer, Thomas (1489-1556) 65

Cyprian (200-258) 131, 181

Donne, John (1572-1631) 245

Edwards, Jonathan (1703-1758) 70, 98, 236, 269

Erasmus of Rotterdam (1469-1536) 20, 65, 99-100, 113, 146, 285

Forsyth, P. T. (1848-1921) 181

Francis of Assisi (1181-1228) 20, 234-235, 292

Francisco de Enzinas (1520?-1550) 66, 288

Green, Keith 36, 71

Gregory the Great (540-604) 291

Hughes, R. Kent 287, 291, 292, 293

Hus, Jan (1369-1415) 64

Ignatius of Antioch (35-107) 131, 169

Ignatius of Loyola (1491-1556) 97

Irenaeus of Lyons (115-190) 131

Jeremias, Joachim (1900-1979) 109

Jerome of Prague (1365?-1416) 64-65, 288

John of Avila (1499-1569) 128

Justin Martyr (100-165) 131

Kant, Immanuel (1724-1804) 191

King, Martin Luther, Jr. 154

Kierkegaard, Søren (1813-1855) 46, 278, 294

Laski, John (1499-1560) 65-66, 288

Law, William (1686-1761) 61, 73, 283

Leo IX (Pope, 1048-1054) 234

Lewis, C. S. (1898-1963) 103, 123, 246

Lloyd, Eva B. 67, 288

Luther, Martin (1483-1546) 13, 15, 17, 24, 66, 67, 85, 112, 115, 145-148, 171, 189, 192, 193, 200-202, 224, 230, 282, 291, 292, 293

Lutzer, Erwin 55

Lyte, Henry F. (1793-1847) 100

MacDonald, George (1824-1905) 134

Madame Guyon (1647-1717) 43, 123, 212, 267

Mahatma Gandhi 154

Mandela, Nelson 154

Melanchthon, Philip (1497-1560) 65, 145

Meier, John 293

Meister Eckhart (1260-1327) 109

Milton, John (1608-1674) 37, 277

Molinos, Miguel de (1628-1696) 278

Moreau, A. Scott 257, 293

Morris, Leon 288

Murray, Andrew (1828-1917) 64, 111, 183, 288

Neale, John Mason 54

Niebuhr, Richard H. 294

Origen (185-254) 52, 128, 288

Owen, John (1616-1683) 254

Peterson, Eugene 276, 293

Piper, John 105-106, 289

Plummer, Alfred 291

Polycarp (69-155) 131

Rembrandt 86

Rolle, Richard (1295-1349) 51

Ryken, Leland 285

Ryle, J. C. (1816-1900) 61, 70, 157, 159, 255, 259, 288, 293

Sayers, Dorothy 12, 285

Schaff, Philip (1819-1913) 233, 291, 292, 293

Shaw, Mark 132, 290

Simons, Menno (1496-1561) 65

Stough, Paul 290

Tertullian (150-212) 84, 122, 177

Thomas à Kempis (1380-1471) 17,

# Index

34, 41, 76, 135, 185, 189, 219, 239, 245, 286, 294
Thomas Aquinas (1225-1274) 18, 145
Tozer, A. W. 208, 292
Tyndale, William (1490-1536) 52
von Schlegel, Katharina 133
Watson, Thomas (1620-1686) 159, 178, 179, 291
Watts, Isaac (1674-1748) 43

Wesley, John (1703-1791) 14, 24, 32, 172-173, 287, 291
Whitefield, George (1714-1770) 206
Willard, Dallas 129, 197, 290, 292
Yancey, Philip 112, 289
Zwingli, Ulrich (1484-1531) 65, 146